Praise for *Sell More with Science*

"In *Sell More with Science*, David Hoffeld reveals science-backed insights that will help you thrive in today's hypercompetitive environment. If you're serious about improving your career, this book is a must-read."

—**Dave Kerpen,** *New York Times* bestselling author of *The Art of People*

"David Hoffeld gives his readers incredible insights into why we buy and how to leverage that knowledge to sell more. Like his last book, *The Science of Selling*, David uses proven science to support his strategies and techniques. Unlike most sales trainers and speakers who rely on unique anecdotes and personal experiences, David makes his scientific approach much more applicable and relatable to a wide range of situations. He empowers salespeople by turning science into practice. If you want to harness the power of science to sell more, this book is a must."

—**Terry Wu,** PhD, neuroscientist and neuromarketing consultant and speaker

"After reading David Hoffeld's *Sell More with Science*, I got rid of over seventy-five books and courses on selling, because it had rendered them all obsolete. The book is packed with actionable, evidence-based strategies, formulas, exercises, and assessments that demystify sales success. In a hypercompetitive market, you need to adjust your sales strategies with science. Add this book to your library. Read it! And apply the ideas. You will have an unfair (yet ethical) competitive advantage in your marketplace."

—**Ed Tate,** principal at Ed Tate & Associates, LLC, and World Champion of Public Speaking

"Most sales advice has little support beyond someone's assumption. By contrast, David Hoffeld's work and practice are grounded in solid behavioral research and focused on core aspects of selling applicable in many markets. This book can help you sell more and, equally valuable, make you feel better about your career."

—**Frank Cespedes,** Senior Lecturer, Entrepreneurial Management Unit at Harvard Business School, and author of *Sales Management That Works*

"David Hoffeld's newest book, *Sell More with Science,* is one every person in sales should read no matter their experience level. The truth and insights found inside will help all sales professionals from complex B2B to transactional consumer-facing roles and everything in between. I love this entire book. I appreciate the way difficult ideas are explained and then broken down into simple and actionable messages. If you want to sell more and sell better, then read *Sell More with Science* and watch your sales growth accelerate."

—**Mareo McCracken,** CRO at Movemedical and author of *Really Care for Them*

"This book is essential reading for anyone seeking to drive improved sales results. It harnesses the power of behavioral science and neuroscience, blended with the art of selling for greater influence and improved sales results. *Sell More with Science* explains the why and how for elevating sales engagement and leadership. David's evidenced-based perspective enables leaders to intelligently and confidently blend art and science together for successful sales transformation."

—**Tony Hughes,** bestselling author and speaker and co-founder of Sales IQ Global

Sell More
with Science

The Mindsets, Traits, and Behaviors
That Create Sales Success

David Hoffeld

Bestselling Author of *The Science of Selling*

A TarcherPerigee Book

tarcherperigee

an imprint of Penguin Random House LLC
penguinrandomhouse.com

Most TarcherPerigee books are available at special quantity
discounts for bulk purchase for sales promotions, premiums,
fund-raising, and educational needs. Special books or book
excerpts also can be created to fit specific needs. For details,
write SpecialMarkets@penguinrandomhouse.com.

Hardcover ISBN: 9780525538738
Ebook ISBN: 9780525538745

Printed in the United States of America
1st Printing

CONTENTS

To my son Joseph, whom I was sold on before he was born.

Selling is a human task that can only be explained satisfactorily in human terms. We must look a good deal further—into the mysteries of personality and psychology—if we want real answers.

Robert N. McMurry, *Harvard Business Review*, March 1961

Use Science to Sell More

WHAT CREATES SALES SUCCESS?

In the past, the factors that enabled some people to sell more than others were a mystery. Some salespeople just seemed to have what it takes, while others didn't. Thankfully, we've since learned that's not the case. Over the past fifty years, scientists have conducted groundbreaking research identifying how our brains process information, perceive value, and decide whether to purchase one product or service over another. Even more exciting, these discoveries have revealed the specific mindsets, traits, and behaviors that salespeople can embrace to achieve success. In fact, of all the innovations to the sales profession in recent years, none has the potential to make a more positive and lasting impact than basing the way we sell on science.

Though this research-backed methodology has repeatedly been proven to boost anyone's performance, many sales and businesspeople are unaware of it. Even worse, many of the most common selling practices today contradict the science. That's why I wrote this book: to provide real-world, actionable, evidence-backed insights that you can use to supercharge your selling—both on the job and out in the world.

Here's a quick overview of how I created this proven way of selling and the benefits you'll receive by adopting it.

How Science Will Transform Your Sales

If you read my previous book, *The Science of Selling*, you'll know that I am fascinated by the science of influence. When I was ten years old, my mother gave me Dale Carnegie's bestselling book *How to Win Friends and Influence People*. I was amazed at how simple words and phrases could inspire people to respond in predictable ways.

It wasn't until many years later that I experienced that in my own career. After graduating with my master's degree, I needed to get a job for what I thought would be just a few months. I naively assumed I would be good at selling and looked in the local classifieds. (Remember when the newspaper was where you went to find a job?) As I browsed the open positions, one caught my eye. The headline read "Make $100,000 a Year." Right below it were three words that made me even more excited: "No Experience Necessary." This was perfect, I reasoned, because I had no experience, and who wouldn't want to make six figures right out of school? I called the number listed and scheduled an interview. The next day I went to the company's office and was interviewed by a sales manager who asked me just two questions. The first was "Do you have reliable transportation?" My confidence grew as I answered that yes, I'd driven there in my own car. He nodded and then asked, "Do you like people?" "Yes!" I exclaimed. The sales manager smiled and said, "Great, you can start tomorrow." And with that, I was ushered into the profession of sales.

What happened next surprised me. As I began selling, I became captivated by it. What I had thought would be a short-term job turned into my life's work. What I had gotten a glimpse of as a ten-year-old when I read *How to Win Friends and Influence People*, I now saw out in the field every day. Salespeople are professional influencers: They inspire someone to take what they say seriously and be willing to act on it.

As I became more and more fascinated by the process of selling, I sought out training on how to do it better. But nearly all the books I read and courses I took were anecdotal—or downright contradictory—in the advice they gave and offered no objective proof that their methods were more effective than others. Dismayed at the lack of evidence, I decided to investigate. I began by looking at the research I had analyzed when writing my master's thesis on how to communicate effectively. And the more I dug into the science, the more I saw how it addressed *every* part of the sales process.

Now, when I say "science"—a term that is haphazardly thrown around in the profession of selling—I mean objective, verifiable research. Specifically, I examined peer-reviewed studies, some by Nobel Prize–winning scientists, in cognitive psychology, social psychology, neuroscience, and behavioral economics. These fields explain how our brains make choices and the factors that influence what we decide to do or buy.

Best of all, as I began applying what I was learning, my sales increased. Armed with the science, I no longer needed to guess the best approach or rely on the opinions of others. I discovered that success was not due to having some indescribable quality or the gift of gab. To the contrary, science revealed the specific factors that produce heightened performance and what each of us can do to achieve it. The key is to guide potential clients through their buying process and into the decision to purchase. In fact, this is the premise of science-based selling: The closer your way of selling is aligned with how the brain creates preferences and forms choices, the more successful you will be. The opposite is also true: The further your way of selling is from how the brain creates a buying decision, the less effective you will be. The good news is that the science provides a straightforward road map that anyone can follow.

As I continued studying and applying this science in my career, my performance continued to grow, and as a result, the organizations I sold for asked me to explain my techniques to their salespeople. When I trained them how to base their sales behaviors on science, they too experienced significant results. It was just as the behavioral scientists Noah Goldstein, Steve Martin, and Robert Cialdini explain: "Everyone's ability to persuade others can be improved by learning persuasion strategies that have been scientifically proven to be successful."[1]

The reason science predictably improves outcomes is that it provides transparency regarding what occurs in a given interaction and accurately predicts what behaviors will positively or negatively influence the decision-making process. Some even described the clarity that science brings as being similar to what people with poor eyesight experience when they put on glasses for the first time. Suddenly everything becomes clear.

At this point, I realized that science could empower sellers to truly serve buyers by helping them feel confident about making decisions in their best interests. So I launched my own sales training firm, Hoffeld Group, which became the leader in science-based selling. Over the years, I've trained some of the most successful companies in the world and helped them sell more by aligning how they sell with how the brain buys. When salespeople embrace a science-backed approach, the outcomes are always the same—client satisfaction goes up and sales skyrocket. They also gain a serious advantage over any competitors who use traditional, anecdotal-based selling methods.

The Number One Benefit of Selling with Science

When I first began reading scientific journals and applying what I learned, I was merely looking for insights that would help me deliver a more compelling sales presentation. However, over time I realized that my point of view was shortsighted. The biggest benefit I experienced was that science gave me a new way of looking at the *process* of selling that was accurate and predictable and that made a profound, lasting difference in my results. This perspective is best summed up by the words of the late Carl Sagan: "Science is more than a body of knowledge. It is a way of thinking."[2] That is the power of a scientific approach. It provides evidence-backed frameworks to guide you in becoming professionally nimble and productively adapting to each unique buyer and situation. In other words, it reveals how to think about the act of selling in the right way, which is the key to long-term effectiveness and results.

For instance, imagine a friend who is the CEO of a small company comes to you and asks for help deciding between two potential candidates for an open position on her growing sales team. The right person will be highly resourceful, have strong problem-solving abilities, and be able to navigate difficult selling situations. She wants you to interview each candidate for these skills and recommend which one to hire.

During your interview with the first candidate, you ask some prepared questions and then present him with the following dilemma to test his adaptability and capacity to think on his feet: Next door, there is a church with a steeple, which he can clearly see through the office window, and you'd like him to determine the approximate height of the steeple. Without a word, he stands up, walks over to the window, and looks out at the church. After a moment he states, "It's around forty feet." You respond, "That's very close. It's forty-two feet. I'm curious—how did you figure that out?" He smiles and says, "I just looked at the steeple and thought it looks about forty feet tall."

The interview with the second candidate begins much like the first. You pose your questions and then ask her to figure out how tall the steeple is. However, unlike the first candidate, she asks to go outside. As she walks out the front door, she notices that the sun is casting a shadow on both her and the steeple. She crudely measures her shadow, compares it with her height, and develops a simple ratio. After measuring the shadow of the steeple, she uses the same ratio to identify its height. She walks back into the office and states, "The steeple is around forty feet tall," and explains her process.

Assuming everything else is equal between the two candidates, which would you recommend for the open sales position? If you are like most people, you know the second candidate is the better choice. Why?

The answer, of course, is because of her approach.

Even though both arrived at the same answer, the second candidate's science-backed perspective gives her a considerable advantage in the long term. By taking a thoughtful, systematic approach to problem solving, versus going on a hunch, she's more likely to consistently reach accurate conclusions. The way she responded to the steeple challenge also gives you insight into how she'll handle complex and challenging sales situations, leaving you with the confidence that her mindset will empower her to adapt effectively, which, in turn, will increase her probability of earning the sale. This is the opportunity we each have today. We can choose to embrace the science that discloses the specific things each of us can do to improve our sales results. In other words, we can set ourselves up for success by "measuring steeples," while our competitors try to guess their way to more sales.

What You'll Learn in This Book

In *The Science of Selling*, I describe how buying decisions occur and the factors that influence them. Specifically, I delve into how buyers think and react during the sales process. This book is different. Now my focus is on you, the seller. The formula I'll reveal will give you everything you need to virtually guarantee you increase your sales. In addition, this book contains exercises designed to help you apply what you learn and begin using it immediately to improve performance. I'll also share with you the scientific studies I used to create these proven strategies, so that, if you choose, you can dive deeper into the research itself.

As I mentioned earlier, science has proved that success in selling is created by embracing certain mindsets, traits, and behaviors. These components are what make someone effective at selling. And if even one of these elements is missing or weak, then the likelihood of achieving lasting success is reduced as well. A simple way to demonstrate this is through the sales-achievement equation:

$$SA = f(M, T, B)$$

This equation states that sales achievement (SA) is a function (f) of the right mindsets (M), traits (T), and behaviors (B). This straightforward calculation is the key to improving your sales and life. Follow it and you will become more effective. What are the specific mindsets, traits, and behaviors that will empower you to grow your sales? That's what you'll learn throughout this book.

I've divided this book into three parts. In part 1, I'll show you what you can do to set yourself up for success. Then in part 2, you'll learn the specific behaviors and strategies that will give you a major advantage over your competition and drastically improve your sales. In part 3, I'll reveal the critical areas that determine whether you will experience lasting, meaningful success that will positively influence those you interact with.

What you'll discover throughout this book may transform more than just your sales. Over the years, I've witnessed how those who've learned these science-backed insights naturally apply them to other parts of their lives and experience greater enjoyment, effectiveness, and fulfillment as a result.

Below is a quick summary of what we'll cover in each chapter. I recommend reading them in order, as their concepts and strategies build on one another. Then you can always go back to review them if you need a refresher on a specific concept or want to practice certain exercises again.

Part 1: Preparing for Sales Success

Chapter 1, "How You Think Determines the Results You Produce," shows you the two mindsets that have been scientifically proven to make a profound difference in the sales outcomes you generate. You'll also find specific things you can do to adopt and strengthen these mindsets so that you experience even more success.

Chapter 2, "The #1 Trait You Need to Succeed," reveals the trait that predicts how long you'll remain in the profession of sales and how skilled you'll become at selling. I'll help you evaluate how much of this trait you currently have and show you what you can do to bolster it.

In **Chapter 3, "The Science of Attaining Your Sales Goals,"** you'll discover seven scientifically validated strategies to boost your chances of reaching a goal. Using just one of these will make a noticeable difference. However, utilizing all seven will have a compounding effect that significantly improves your ability to reach any sales goal.

Part 2: Creating Sales Success

Chapter 4, "Help Potential Clients Form Buying Decisions," explains how you can truly serve your potential clients by aligning how you sell with how their brains create buying decisions. You'll see two powerful science-backed selling principles that will enhance your ability to guide buyers through the purchasing process and compellingly present high levels of value to them.

In **Chapter 5, "How to Reframe Any Sales Situation,"** you'll learn the real science of reframing and discover a revolutionary five-part reframing process that will enable you to help buyers see things in a new, more beneficial way.

Chapter 6, "Supercharge Your Sales Process with Science," gives you a blueprint for increasing the effectiveness of your overall sales process. You'll learn about some groundbreaking science that you can leverage to instantly elevate your sales approach and help you to win more clients.

Chapter 7, "Three Outside-the-Box Strategies That Grow Sales," explores how you can improve your performance and results by utilizing some unusual yet remarkable science to give yourself an advantage over competitors and earn more sales.

Part 3: Achieving Lasting Sales Success

Chapter 8, "Sell with Integrity," provides fresh, scientific insights regarding the important topic of what it means to sell with integrity and the huge benefits of doing so. You'll learn to identify the difference between manipulation and influence, recognize when salespeople are most likely to engage in manipulative behaviors, and find out what each of us can do to protect ourselves, our clients, and others from unethical selling practices.

Chapter 9, "Take Your Sales Career to the Next Level," is a chapter you'll refer to again and again. In it, I'll demystify the process of improving your sales career by disclosing a powerful formula to create positive change and experience a whole new level of success. If you're ready to take a giant leap forward in your career, this chapter is for you.

Today, in sales and business, you need every advantage you can get. The current marketplace is so hypercompetitive that if you aren't actively working to improve and move forward, you will fall behind. You no longer have the luxury of coasting. So whether you are brand-new to the profession of sales or have a wealth of experience, the science-backed strategies shared in this book will provide you with an unprecedented opportunity to stay ahead of your competition and succeed. That's what science offers—a superior, evidence-backed approach that will enhance your work and your career. Let's begin our journey by looking at the two mindsets that determine how much sales you'll produce.

PART 1

Preparing for Sales Success

CHAPTER 1

How You Think Determines the Results You Produce

A HALLMARK OF ELITE SALES PERFORMERS IS THEY HAVE mindsets that prime them for success. In other words, the way they think helps them get results. This shouldn't come as a surprise. After all, our mindsets are the filters through which we perceive, interpret, and respond to the world around us—and they determine our ability to thrive in different circumstances.[1] Too often in sales—and in life—we focus only on behaviors and outcomes, and ignore what is driving them. Decades of research have demonstrated the enormous impact our thought process has on our performance.[2]

Just how powerfully can our mindsets affect our actions? So much that merely *thinking* you slept poorly last night can make you perform worse the next day. That's what researchers Christina Draganich and Kristi Erdal discovered when they analyzed the impact of our beliefs on our actions.[3] At the beginning of their experiment, they told participants that adults generally spend 20 to 25 percent of their time sleeping in deep REM, and that those who spend less than 20 percent in REM often underperform on cognitive tests. Armed with this frame of reference, the participants were then informed that their sleep would be tracked overnight. The following morning, they were told at random that they had either experienced low-quality sleep—with only 16.2 percent of their night spent in REM sleep—or high-quality sleep, with an impressive 28.7 percent of time spent in REM. When participants were given a test to assess cognitive skills most affected by sleep deprivation, those who'd been *told* they'd slept poorly performed significantly worse than those told they'd slept well—regardless of how any of them had actually snoozed. In other words, believing you slept badly has the same mental effect on your performance as actually having low-quality sleep.

This is why mindsets matter; they predispose you to act in predictable ways that will alter your performance for better or worse. I encounter that impact on performance every time I train salespeople. Often, simply by talking with participants prior to the training—and before I witness their skills or abilities in action—I can accurately predict who will become a top performer. Some mindsets set us up for achievement and enable us to exceed our potential and rise to the top. Others stifle growth and curb performance. The latter sabotage salespeople by causing them to behave in ways that drive down the likelihood of the sale.

Before we go into these mindsets and how to cultivate ones that will help you grow and prosper, it's crucial to remember the following: Your mindsets are *yours*, and you can change them. At any given time, you can *choose* to adopt one that will serve you better. Often, we subconsciously adopt the perspectives and attitudes of those around us, rather than actively deciding how we want to approach the world. Perhaps you've assumed a specific way of interacting with others modeled by your parents, teachers, bosses, or friends, or a bad experience prompted you to embrace a defensive or pessimistic approach to protect yourself. Regardless of how you developed your current mindset, science shows that you don't have to be stuck with it. Mindsets are learned, which means you can unshackle yourself from one that's harming you or holding you back and replace it with one that will help you move forward and realize your goals. In fact, you owe it to yourself to analyze your mindsets and discard any that aren't serving you.

How exactly can you do this? That's what we are going to discover next, as we look at two foundational mindsets that will determine your effectiveness and results.

Foundational Mindset #1: The Achievement Mindset

Success begins in the mind. Studies have discovered that people rarely achieve great things if they don't believe they can. So if you believe you won't accomplish a certain goal, you're probably right. When the social scientist Peter Schulman studied how heightened levels of sales performance are attained, he identified that "expectations of success or failure are often self-fulfilling prophecies. The belief that one will succeed is the engine that inspires the efforts needed to overcome obstacles and achieve goals. Research has shown that the belief that one will succeed produces over-achievement and the belief that one will fail produces under-achievement."[4]

What Schulman's research speaks to is the power of an achievement mindset, which is your belief in your ability to produce a desired outcome.[5] There is more than forty years' worth of scholarly research on the achievement mindset (which researchers commonly call self-efficacy) demonstrating that trusting that you can do something is a precursor to actually doing it. One meta-analysis on the connection between an achievement mindset and business performance even found that an achievement mindset does more than influence how much success you will experience; it *predicts* it.[6]

One of the best examples of the achievement mindset's dramatic effect is the story of Victor Serebriakoff. For the first three decades of his life, he struggled, first in school (dropping out at age fifteen) and then to stay employed, even in menial jobs.[7] By age thirty-one, when Victor joined the British army, his life had been marked by disappointment and a deep-set conviction he would never amount to anything worthwhile.

However, soon after entering the army, he was given an intelligence test, and the results came back that he had an IQ of 161.[8] Victor Serebriakoff, it turns out, was a genius! Finding out those results drastically changed Serebriakoff's belief in himself. His achievement mindset grew so significantly that he took on challenges he'd never even considered before, such as training new military recruits. After leaving the army, he turned his life around, going from being unable to keep the simplest of jobs to becoming an acclaimed author, inventor, and businessman. Victor is perhaps best known for being the international president of Mensa, an organization that requires its members to have an IQ in the top 2 percent of the population, and he is widely credited with growing Mensa into the influential international organization that it is today.[9]

Everyone has an achievement mindset; what matters is how strong it is.[10] Behavioral scientists have found that the reason an achievement mindset either enables or limits success is because it creates a strong confirmation bias, which makes us alter our actions in ways that reinforce our beliefs about what we can do.[11] For instance, even though Serebriakoff had a high IQ his entire life, in his early years he thought he was a failure and acted in ways that verified that belief. His weak achievement mindset became a self-fulfilling prophecy.[12] After the intelligence test, his achievement mindset grew, and his newfound trust in himself gave him the confidence to embrace new behaviors and take risks that would make him successful. In a similar way, the power that this bias has on performance is perhaps best illustrated by one of the most celebrated sports achievements of the twentieth century: breaking the four-minute mile. On May 6, 1954, a twenty-four-year-old medical student named Roger Bannister did what everyone thought was impossible: He ran one mile in three minutes and fifty-nine seconds. Prior to Bannister's record-breaking run, most believed it wasn't humanly possible to run a mile in under four minutes; doctors had even publicly stated that if someone were to do so, the stress would cause that person's heart to explode.

Bannister proved them wrong. But as impressive as his record-breaking run was, what's more important is what happened in response to it. A mere forty-six days later, another runner *beat* Bannister's time. The next year, three other runners did too—in the same race![13] Within three years, sixteen additional runners had also beaten the record.[14] Today, well over a thousand runners have beaten the "impossible" four-minute mile.[15]

Runners had been trying to conquer the four-minute mile for decades. It was only after Bannister's run that dozens began breaking that speed barrier with seeming ease. What caused this incredible change? The answer, of course, is their achievement mindset. As Wharton professor Yoram "Jerry" Wind and Colin Crook explain in their analysis of the mental effect of Bannister's accomplishment on the running community, "The runners of the past had been held back by a mindset that said they could not surpass the four-minute mile. When that limit was broken, the others saw that they could do something they had previously thought impossible."[16]

From a selling standpoint, think of an achievement mindset as a mental thermostat that sets the level of success you'll attain. Those with a strong belief in their abilities are more likely to choose larger goals, take more action to reach them, have more resilience when faced with obstacles, and endure until they succeed.[17] As social scientist Albert Bandura says: "People's beliefs about their abilities have a profound effect on those abilities. Ability is not a fixed property; there is huge variability in how you perform. People who have a sense of self-efficacy [the achievement mindset] bounce back from failure; they approach things in terms of how to handle them rather than worrying about what can go wrong."[18] In short, your achievement mindset determines how you perform in every sales or business situation you're in.

Does IQ Predict Sales Success?

Does your IQ influence how likely you are to be successful at selling? There is no doubt that IQ matters (it would be hard to effectively navigate complex sales situations without having at least a moderate amount of intelligence), but beyond that, it matters a lot less than you might think. Study after study analyzing the influence of IQ on one's ability to perform a task or attain goals has found that intelligence is *not* a predictor of achievement.[19] In fact, as economist James Heckman noted, the data on the correlation between income and IQ shows a minuscule 1 to 2 percent influence.[20] What matters more than IQ, research shows, is the mindset that people embrace.

Yet another benefit of an achievement mindset is that it inspires salespeople to have confidence, which makes them more effective at adapting to demanding situations. Because they believe in themselves, they don't shrink when faced with an objection from a buyer, and they confidently communicate their ideas, which encourages their potential clients to respond favorably.[21] Research conducted by behavioral scientist Don Moore found that our brains instinctively trust people who present themselves and their ideas confidently.[22] Demonstrating genuine belief in yourself is a key part of successful selling because it naturally inspires others' confidence in you.

Since having a healthy achievement mindset will determine your success, here's a quick assessment to help you evaluate your current level of achievement orientation.

Achievement Mindset Assessment

To evaluate the level of your achievement mindset, answer the statements below using the following five-point rating scale: 1 = strongly disagree; 2 = disagree; 3 = neither agree nor disagree; 4 = agree; 5 = strongly agree.

1. I am able to achieve most of my sales goals.
   1 = strongly disagree, 2 = disagree, 3 = neither agree nor disagree, 4 = agree, 5 = strongly agree

2. When faced with a challenging selling situation, I'm usually able to solve it.
   1 = strongly disagree, 2 = disagree, 3 = neither agree nor disagree, 4 = agree, 5 = strongly agree

3. In general, I obtain the sales outcomes that are important to me and/or my organization.
   1 = strongly disagree, 2 = disagree, 3 = neither agree nor disagree, 4 = agree, 5 = strongly agree

4. I am able to succeed consistently at the sales tasks I focus on.
   1 = strongly disagree, 2 = disagree, 3 = neither agree nor disagree, 4 = agree, 5 = strongly agree

5. During the sales process, I'm able to successfully overcome
most setbacks.
*1 = strongly disagree, 2 = disagree, 3 = neither agree nor
disagree, 4 = agree, 5 = strongly agree*

6. I believe I will be able to successfully execute any part of the
sales process.
*1 = strongly disagree, 2 = disagree, 3 = neither agree nor
disagree, 4 = agree, 5 = strongly agree*

7. Compared with others, I am very good at selling.
*1 = strongly disagree, 2 = disagree, 3 = neither agree nor
disagree, 4 = agree, 5 = strongly agree*

8. Even when things are challenging, I perform well.
*1 = strongly disagree, 2 = disagree, 3 = neither agree nor
disagree, 4 = agree, 5 = strongly agree*

Add up the points to calculate your final score, which will range
between 8 and 40. Then check the chart below to see where you
currently stand.

SCORE	RATING
35–40	High Sales-Achievement Mindset
30–34	Average Sales-Achievement Mindset
24–29	Low Sales-Achievement Mindset
8–23	Extremely Low Sales-Achievement Mindset

Regardless of where you landed, don't worry; this is simply a
benchmark from which you can improve (yes, even those of you at
the top). In fact, it's likely your rating will shift, because you can
always change and enhance your achievement mindset.

How to Strengthen Your Achievement Mindset

Ken has been in sales for nearly a decade but hasn't advanced much in his career despite wanting to grow and improve. His slow progress is not due to a lack of motivation; rather, he struggles with a low achievement mindset. Throughout his life he's had a hard time believing he can achieve his dreams, ever since he was told as a child by adults he trusted that he wouldn't amount to much. Ken mainly chooses to strive for small goals that he knows he can easily attain. He also often quits when he faces a setback or an obstacle, and he struggles to assert himself when negotiating with clients or handling tough objections. Ken knows his mindset is limiting his career and life, but he doesn't know what to do about it.

All of us have experienced a low achievement mindset at one time or another. Perhaps it's caused by harsh words from someone close to you, negative self-talk, or a toxic environment that makes it hard to maintain self-confidence. Whatever the reason, it is a problem that requires your attention. Like Ken, those who *regularly* have low achievement mindsets see lower sales results, procrastinate, and give up more easily on their goals. In short, our self-imposed limits restrict our ability to accomplish something and make failure more likely. Here's another way to think about it: All of us have also at times been surprised we were able to achieve something we thought was unlikely. Those were cases of breaking through the ceiling that your mindset may have imposed. Unfortunately, going beyond our own limiting perspectives doesn't happen that often, which is why it usually shocks us when it does. That's why it's critical to first focus on growing your achievement mindset, which will empower you to improve your results.

Selling and business present constant challenges that we need to rise above. If, like Ken, you have a low achievement mindset, you're not alone—and you're also not stuck with it (remember our friend Victor Serebriakoff). Here are three scientifically proven strategies to help you adopt the healthy achievement mindset you need to propel you toward your professional goals and improve the quality of your life overall.

1. Grow Your Achievement Mindset by Challenging Yourself

The most potent way to strengthen your achievement mindset is to put yourself in challenging situations that force you to grow in competence and, as a result, confidence.[23] That's the most significant thing to remember about an achievement mindset: It is earned through dedication and hard work, and it has to be grounded in reality. You can't foster it by tricking yourself into believing something that isn't true. So, trying to convince yourself that you're a great salesperson when you know deep down that your sales skills are weak won't change your mindset for the better. As social psychologist David Myers put it, an achievement mindset "grows with hard-won achievements."[24] If it's not earned, it's just overconfidence. This is why embracing challenges that push you outside your comfort zone is the key to developing a healthy achievement mindset.

When I train new hires for a client, I require each of them to take me through their entire sales process as if I were their buyer and "sell" me their product or service. This often intimidates them because they know I'll be a harder sell than their typical buyers. But after they complete this exercise, two things always happen: Their confidence surges, and their sales take off. Through the process of developing new knowledge and skills and putting them to use in a challenging situation, they have earned a robust achievement mindset and improved their sales ability, both of which will benefit them throughout their career.

Sales Training Grows Achievement Mindsets

One of the best ways to improve a salesperson's achievement mindset is through sales training. Effective training will help you master selling, which, in turn, will naturally boost your mindset.[25] So if you're a salesperson, seek out high-quality training to grow your skills. If you're a sales leader, make sure that all your people are well trained, which will benefit them, you, and your company.

Let's take a moment for an exercise that will help you grow your achievement mindset. Think about a sales skill that you don't feel particularly confident in. What is one challenge you can give yourself to improve that skill and your confidence in it? For instance, if you feel that you aren't delivering your sales presentations effectively, you could ask your manager or a colleague to watch you present and give you feedback on how you could improve.

What is one challenge that will take your sales abilities and confidence to the next level?

_____

How and when will you embark on this challenge?

_____

Now that you know what will help you grow your achievement mindset, resolve to do it. Whenever you push past your comfort zone and pursue more challenging goals, you'll find your mindset enriched as well as your career. In other words, don't look for short-cuts. Tackle difficult pursuits and earn your confidence.

2. Reflect and Flush Negativity

The words of others have the power to build us up or tear us down.[26] All of us experience criticism and rejection at some point when selling. And if you don't have a productive way to handle it, negative words and actions can damage your achievement mindset and significantly limit your results. So what should you do when you are criticized or rejected? I recommend utilizing a highly effective strategy I created called Reflect & Flush, which I've taught to thousands of salespeople to help them protect and strengthen their achievement mindsets.

Here's how to implement it: When you encounter rejection, negative feedback, or a sales call that goes wrong, first reflect on what happened and determine what you can learn from it. Once you identify what you can do better and differently and strategize how you'll put that insight into practice, you then proceed to the second part of the strategy—flush.

Flush is exactly what it sounds like: You mentally flush the encounter or comment and refuse to think about it anymore. You've already gathered all the benefits you could when you reflected on it, so continuing to ruminate will only weaken your confidence in yourself and your ability to make positive changes based on what you learned. To move on, refocus on something positive. Remember, you have the ultimate control of what you allow your mind to pay attention to. By choosing to cultivate thoughts that build confidence and competence, you'll naturally strengthen your achievement mindset. When you first use Reflect & Flush, your thoughts may drift back to the negative comment, but keep at it. As with any acquired skill, the more you practice it, the easier and more natural it becomes.

Let's apply Reflect & Flush to a common sales situation: developing new business. Imagine that you meet a potential client who harshly rejects your attempt to connect. After the encounter, you should first reflect on what you might have done differently that could have positively influenced the situation. (If you're not sure how to do this, don't worry. In chapters 4 and 5, I'll show you how to diagnose and correct this.) Then think about how you'll implement that insight in the future. For instance, if you realize from your potential client's response that you didn't demonstrate enough relevant value, you can pinpoint exactly what you should have done and then practice it until you are competent. After that, flush the buyer's discouraging response from your mind and refuse to dwell on it further. Redirect your focus to something positive, such as a recent success or a reminder of how, because of your prospecting efforts, you've surpassed your sales quota for the quarter. This process of Reflect & Flush is both simple to execute and extremely powerful, because it will free you from being demoralized by others' negativity.

Sales Leaders' Words Matter

One of the top ways sales leaders can raise the achievement mindset of their salespeople is through expressing their confidence in them and the work they are doing.[27] So if you're a sales leader, share with your team the confidence you have in them. And if you are a salesperson, be generous in sharing genuine compliments with your colleagues.

3. Practice Positive Self-Talk

One of the biggest reasons salespeople don't have a stronger achievement mindset is because of negative self-talk. Their inner narrative limits their belief in what they can do and, as a result, the amount of sales they produce.

Do you tell yourself things like "I couldn't ever do that" or "I'll never earn that much or have that level of sales success"? This kind of negative self-talk will, if left unchecked, hinder your ability to achieve your goals. It's an easy trap to fall into, but you can change your self-talk so that it strengthens your mindset rather than hinders it. This is mission critical, as the research is conclusive: Talking to yourself in a productive manner will improve performance.[28]

The first step in correcting this is to realize that not all your self-talk is accurate. As researcher Erika Andersen explains, "I've found that the people who evaluate themselves most accurately start the process inside their own heads: They accept that their perspective is often biased or flawed and then strive for greater objectivity . . . The trick is to pay attention to how you talk to yourself about yourself and then question the validity of that 'self-talk.'"[29]

Whenever negative thoughts about yourself pop into your mind, reject them by focusing your attention on why they are not true. Then replace those thoughts with a more accurate, beneficial version. So "I could never be a good salesperson" becomes "Every great salesperson was once new to sales and not skilled. They worked hard to learn how to become a top performer, and so can I." Or "I can't sell five million dollars this year" becomes "People in our company have sold five million dollars in a year, and if I work harder and improve my skills, I will sell five million dollars this year."

Here is an exercise that will help you identify and replace some of the self-talk that may be limiting you. When you think about achieving your big sales goals, what is some of the limiting self-talk that comes to your mind?

Limiting self-talk #1:

_____

Limiting self-talk #2:

_____

Now let's replace that limiting self-talk with a more empowering perspective that will naturally enhance your achievement mindset.

Beneficial self-talk #1:

_____

Beneficial self-talk #2:

_____

Now that we've explored the positive impact of an achievement mindset on you and your sales, let's turn to a related mindset so powerful that it will heavily influence your level of success.

Foundational Mindset #2:
The Growth Mindset

In 1999, then aspiring motivational speaker Craig Valentine achieved his dream: winning the prestigious World Championship of Public Speaking. Organized each year by Toastmasters International, the contest brings top speakers from around the globe to compete for the coveted title of world champion, an honor that instantly propels the winner into the lucrative world of professional and corporate speaking.

But after clinching the goal he had been chasing for years, Craig did something remarkable. As soon as he landed back home in Baltimore, with a trophy nearly as tall as he is, Craig went straight to a bookstore and bought a book on public speaking.[30]

Pause for a moment and let that sink in.

What would compel someone just crowned World Champion of Public Speaking to buy a book on that very topic? The answer is his mindset. Craig has what scientists call a growth mindset. In fact, he has a hypergrowth mindset. It's what enabled him to win the world championship—and then prompted him to buy a book to master it further.

A growth mindset is the belief that through focused effort you can improve your abilities.[31] Stanford University's Carol Dweck, the leading researcher on growth mindsets, states that what makes them so potent is that they are based on the empowering belief that we can change.[32] Those with growth mindsets, like Craig, maintain the conviction that, regardless of their current level of knowledge and skills in any area, they can always learn more and improve their results. Numerous research studies have confirmed that people who possess a growth mindset are far more likely to be successful in sales, business, and almost anything else they put their minds to.

To be clear, a growth mindset is closely linked with an achievement mindset; in fact, a growth mindset is what enables you to harness the power of an achievement mindset. If you have a growth mindset, you'll consistently push yourself to do better. As a result, you'll move closer to accomplishing your goals, which in turn will strengthen your belief that you can achieve them. This is why a growth mindset is so critical: It helps you live out an achievement mindset.

In *The Science of Selling*, I briefly mention the high correlation between having a growth mindset and success in selling, and I advise sales and business leaders to hire candidates who have and demonstrate this mindset. Now let's delve into why growth mindsets are so impactful, how they influence performance, and what each of us can do to cultivate and strengthen our own.[33]

Growth mindsets set you up for success in how they help you perceive and respond to failure.[34] Failure is something we all face at various points. However, those with a growth mindset react differently than the rest of us do.[35] Rather than view it as an indictment against themselves (i.e., they failed, so therefore they *are* a failure), they take it as useful feedback (i.e., they missed the mark this time and will adapt and do better next time).[36] This perspective sets them up for success because they are more likely to learn from their mistakes. One study conducted by business school professors Francesca Gino, Bradley Staats, and Chris Myers found that participants with a growth mindset who took responsibility for their poor performance on an initial task were almost 200 percent more likely to succeed on the next task.[37] They learned from their failure, which helped them adjust and flourish in similar future situations.[38]

Not only does the data support the notion that a growth mindset will help you attain success, I also see this played out in every organization I train. Working with salespeople across the globe and teaching them how to use science-based sales strategies to improve their results, I continually observe how those with strong growth mindsets are the ones who work persistently to develop their skills, view their missteps as learning opportunities, and adapt to overcome obstacles—all of which leads to greater achievement. As a matter of fact, I cannot think of one salesperson (and trust me, I know a *lot*) who has become—and remained—an elite performer without having a robust growth mindset. In the incredibly fast-paced sales and business worlds, it has become a necessity to stay competitive.

Though we all have varying experiences, talents, interests, and skills, the growth mindset reminds us that we can each develop our abilities if we put our minds to it. It's this optimistic focus on continuous improvement that makes the growth mindset (and the related achievement mindset) such a potent force for good in our careers and lives.

The Fixed-Mindset Trap

Of course, everything has its opposite. With the achievement mindset, it's more of a low-to-high spectrum that you fall somewhere along and can move up or down depending on what beliefs you choose to internalize and cultivate about yourself. When it comes to the growth mindset, there is an inverse called a fixed mindset, and it's built on the idea of permanence. While a growth mindset is grounded in the conviction that you can improve your abilities, a fixed mindset is the limiting belief that you can't do much to change your existing skills.[39] People with fixed mindsets see their capabilities as being carved in stone, and they tend to perceive mistakes as evidence that they shouldn't be engaged in whatever they have failed at, rather than as opportunities to learn and improve.[40] It's an unfortunately easy and common trap for even the most talented people to fall into, and I've seen it cost people sales and business and even destroy their careers.

Not surprisingly, as the opposite of a growth mindset, a fixed mindset can significantly limit improvement for one major reason: It triggers people to view failure as a reflection of who they are. As a result, people with this mindset tend to avoid even the most constructive feedback because they interpret it as a statement that they simply aren't good enough.[41] Those with a fixed mindset can be challenging to train or coach; they aren't focused on getting better, but rather on proving they are already good enough. Chris Argyris, the former professor emeritus at Harvard Business School, neatly summarized the negative impact of this mindset on learning, noting that it causes people to "become defensive, screen out criticism, and put the 'blame' on anyone and everyone but themselves. In short, their ability to learn shuts down precisely at the moment they need it the most."[42]

If you frequently fall into a fixed mindset, don't worry. In the following pages I'll show you the specific things you can do to foster a growth mindset. But first let's look at the difference in sales performance between a fixed and a growth mindset.

Is There a Difference in Performance?

If you're wondering whether your mindset will make a tangible difference on the sales results you produce, the answer is a resounding yes! In one study, researchers at Michigan State University analyzed how having a growth or fixed mindset affects performance.[43] They gave participants a test to determine whether each had a fixed or growth mindset, then measured brain activity while the participants made mistakes trying to complete an extremely challenging task. Participants with a growth mindset experienced more neural activity when they made errors than those with a fixed mindset, which demonstrated that their brains were actively processing their errors in an effort to learn from them.

The researchers also noticed that growth-minded participants viewed the errors they made as instructive feedback, whereas fixed-mindset participants perceived them as an inherent lack of ability, which decreased their neural activity and engagement levels. Most importantly, those "growth-minded individuals also showed superior accuracy after mistakes compared with individuals endorsing a more fixed mindset."[44] In other words, their mindsets dictated their improvement in completing future tasks.

The idea that a growth mindset inspires superior performance is not a new one. In 1989, social scientists Robert Wood and Albert Bandura conducted a study that revealed that business outcomes improved when participants embraced a growth mindset and dropped when they adopted a fixed mindset.[45] Social psychologists Laura Kray and Michael Haselhuhn found something similar when they conducted numerous studies to observe the impact that mindset has on the common sales activity of negotiating.[46] In one of their studies, participants who embraced either a fixed or a growth mindset entered into a complex negotiation. Those with a growth mindset were more successful than their fixed-mindset counterparts at a rate of nearly two to one!

Because those with growth mindsets learn from their mistakes, they act in ways that increase their competence and confidence, which naturally strengthens their achievement mindset.[47] In contrast, those with a fixed mindset retreat when they experience a setback, which erodes confidence. It's no surprise then that belief in one's abilities is a primary attribute of top sales performers.

A growth mindset can also enhance the overall performance of a team or even an entire organization, especially when a corporation's leaders embrace and mold culture around it.[48] In 2014, when Satya Nadella became CEO of Microsoft, there was a general consensus that the company needed to make major changes in order to stay relevant. The stock price had stalled, product development was lagging, and employee morale was low. Within seven years, there was little doubt that Microsoft had become a much healthier company under Nadella's leadership. Just take a look at its monthly stock price over that time period.

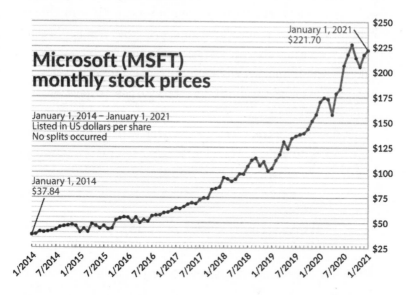

What did Nadella do to transform the company? The *Harvard Business Review* reports he used a single overarching principle to drive the organizational changes he wanted to see: The idea that "a growth mindset, rather than a fixed one, is the key to developing a dynamic, learning-focused culture."[49] In addition to modeling the mindset in his daily leadership, Nadella began rewarding employees for being "learn-it-alls" instead of "know-it-alls."[50] Leaders began to wrap up each meeting by asking attendees, "Was this a fixed- or a growth-mindset meeting? Why?" The fresh focus on living out a growth mindset encouraged collaboration and innovation, which transformed the company, expanded its relevance in the marketplace, and helped it deliver much more meaningful value to its clients and customers.

That's what growth mindsets do. They not only fuel sales growth but also positively transform people, teams, and organizations. Moreover, they inspire the hope that no matter where you are today, you can change, improve, and achieve goals currently beyond your reach. The key to remember is that this transformation starts with you. If you don't change, neither will your results. After all, your sales and success can only grow to the extent that you do. A growth mindset will help you mold yourself into the person you desire to be—the kind of person who can achieve whatever you put your mind to.

Let's do a quick appraisal to uncover your current mindset when it comes to selling. Then I'll share some practical strategies for cultivating a growth mindset.

Growth Mindset Assessment

Which of the following statements do you believe to be true?

1. A person's sales skills can rarely be improved; some just naturally have the ability to sell, and others don't.

2. No matter where you start, you can become better at selling.

3. You can learn new selling strategies, but your sales results are mostly dependent on your innate talent and personality.

4. Regardless of where you are currently, you should continually work to improve your sales expertise.

As you may have guessed, statements 1 and 3 are fixed-mindset statements, while statements 2 and 4 convey a growth mindset. Which are most reflected in your selections?

Here are a few more examples you can use to evaluate your mindset.

Which of the following best describes how you view this statement: Your sales skills are like a muscle you must continuously develop and strengthen.
    A. Strongly agree
    B. Somewhat agree
    C. Disagree

Which most accurately describes the self-directed effort you've put into improving your sales abilities within the last year:
    A. A lot
    B. A little
    C. None at all

Which best describes your belief about this statement: Great salespeople are born, not made.
    A. False
    B. Partially true
    C. True

The As represent a growth mindset, Bs a hybrid of a fixed and a growth mindset, and Cs a fixed mindset. If you found your-self mostly agreeing with the As, nice job, and keep reading to learn how to strengthen your growth mindset even further. If you chose mostly Bs, I'll show you how to move more toward a growth mindset and away from a fixed mindset. If you selected mostly Cs, don't worry, this book will teach you how to embrace a growth mindset and take your sales skills and success to a new level.

On a side note, growth and fixed mindsets also affect our lives beyond selling. So if you'd like to evaluate your approach to other areas, try modifying the statements above by switching out the topics. So instead of "Great salespeople are born, not made," you can say, "Great parents are . . ." or "Successful start-up founders . . ." or "Savvy investors . . . ," for example.

Does Anyone Have a Pure Growth Mindset?

The reality is that *none* of us has a pure growth mindset all the time.[51] Rather, in some parts of our lives we have a growth mindset, and in others we have a fixed one. You may even have a hybrid of a growth and a fixed mindset. The key is to continually evaluate where you're at to make sure a fixed way of thinking isn't creeping into an area you want to improve and holding you back from doing so.

Now that you've evaluated your growth mindset, let's look at what you can do to develop it and perhaps even encourage one in those around you.

How to Cultivate a Growth Mindset

A lot of research shows the specific things you can do to adopt and strengthen a growth mindset and set yourself up for success too. Here are seven strategies to help you get started.

1. Identify Fixed-Mindset Triggers

As you start to intentionally pursue a growth mindset, you'll begin noticing certain triggers prompt you to fall into fixed-mindset thoughts and reactions.[52] The question to ask yourself is not *if* you have these triggers—since we all do—but rather what yours are. By understanding what situations are likely to activate a fixed mindset, you can more easily recognize when they happen and, in turn, reduce their influence over you.

Often, these triggers come in the form of challenges, comparisons with others, criticisms, negative comments, public errors, or mistakes. For me, it's easy to fall into a fixed mindset when I encounter a setback, especially if it's unanticipated. This can be when a major project is suddenly delayed, when business or travel plans are disrupted, or when I'm faced with an unexpected obstacle at work or at home. I figured this out by reflecting on those times I had fallen into a fixed mindset and then thinking back to pinpoint what had prompted it. Since I've identified what leads me into a fixed mindset, I'm now better able to immediately address and get past it.

Pause to identify and think through some of your fixed-mindset triggers. Complete the sentences below to help you mentally prepare so that when they present themselves, you'll be equipped to identify and resist or overcome them.

Fixed-Mindset Triggers Exercise

Example #1: I often fall into a fixed mindset when

_____

Example #2: I often fall into a fixed mindset when

_____

2. Adopt Growth-Focused Self-Talk

As with the achievement mindset, self-talk can also help foster a growth mindset. One study published in the _Journal of Organizational Behavior_ found that participants who engaged in productive self-talk had enhanced business performance, which also benefited their organization.[53]

How can you engage in self-talk that will help you deepen your growth mindset? Each time you find yourself considering a fixed-mindset statement, such as "I can't do this," swap it out with the growth-focused question "How can I achieve this?" Instead of thinking, "This is impossible," ask, "What could I do to make this possible?" As you practice, you will train your mind to adopt this kind of growth-oriented mindset automatically.

Additionally, asking growth-focused questions either after a challenging situation or at the end of each day can strengthen your growth mindset. Here are a few to consider:

- "What did I learn today?"

- "What mistake did I make in this situation, and what did I learn from it?"

- "What is one small way in which I grew, learned, or improved today?"

- "What is one thing I did today that will help me be more successful in the future?"

These questions too extend beyond sales. They can help anyone become more resilient and productive. Posing similar questions to children, for example, will help them adopt a growth mindset, which research shows will positively influence everything from their schoolwork and future careers to their marriages and overall happiness.

Growth-Focused Self-Talk Exercise

Reflect on one of the examples from the previous exercise on what often causes you to slip into a fixed mindset. Write down the fixed-mindset statement you often say to yourself when that happens:

_____

Now write out a growth-focused statement or question you can tell yourself instead:

_____

3. Surround Yourself with People Who Have Growth Mindsets

My first sales manager used to tell me, "David, you can't fly with the eagles if you hang around with turkeys," and he was right. Surrounding yourself with those who have a growth mindset will make it easier for you to have one as well. Seek out friends, family, and colleagues who live out a growth mindset. Ask them about what they are learning and share how you are working to grow your abilities. This is what Dylan, a salesperson for a small software company, does. Every Tuesday morning, he meets a colleague for breakfast, and they both share what they've learned over the last week. Dylan told me that these conversations are a key part of his success because they hold him accountable, since he knows he'll need to report on his progress each week. You can adopt the same approach. Invite like-minded people to join you on your journey of self-improvement and make learning a team sport.

Now, perhaps you're in the situation I was in many years ago, when I found myself surrounded by people who didn't have a growth mindset, or if they did, it was weak. I still figured out a way to seek out the most successful people in sales and business on a daily basis, all of whom had hypergrowth mindsets: I read their books, listened to their audiobooks and podcasts, watched their videos, and took their trainings. Though I didn't know them personally at the time or have direct access to anyone with a strong growth mindset like them, I was able to immerse myself in how they thought and learn from their ideas and advice by engaging with their content.

4. Reject Fixed-Mindset Labels

Throughout our lives people put labels on us. They'll say, "You have a gift for this," or "You're not good at that." Scientific research has repeatedly proved these remarks are incredibly influential in how we perceive ourselves—and how we act on our skills, which can launch us to victory or sabotage our efforts, depending on what we've been told.[54]

But you don't have to be stuck with any label that's limiting you. You can let them go and replace them with a more empowering belief. To do this, you must resolve to reject any negative fixed-mindset descriptions others have put on you. They are not only counterproductive, but they are also often false. If someone tells you, "You're not good at closing," ask yourself, is that really true?

Are you forever doomed to be inept at closing a sale, or are you a human being who can learn any skill, including how to close deals? Of course you can improve. When it comes to selling, embracing fixed-mindset labels will hinder your performance and steal from your future success. This is why I strongly recommend you refuse to accept or even think about the labels others put on you. Instead, when someone attempts to classify you as one thing or another, disregard it in favor of a growth-mindset question or statement. So "You're not good at building rapport" becomes "How can I become better at building rapport?" And "You'll never become successful at selling—it's not for you" becomes "I'm not as great at selling as I could be, but if I invest in good training and work hard, I will be."

5. Embrace the Power of "Yet"

In her popular TED talk, Carol Dweck shares a story about a high school that gives the grade "Not Yet" when students fail a course.[55] Dweck explains that the power of a "Not Yet" grade, rather than an F, communicates to students that they haven't failed (which can be a devastating and debilitating message to receive) and instead that they're engaged in the process of learning, with the opportunity to improve. "Yet" is a potent tool for us as well. Instead of saying, "I'm not skilled at presenting to large groups," add the word "yet" to the end of the sentence so that it becomes "I'm not skilled at presenting to large groups *yet*." Try it! You'll be amazed at how this subtle shift in language will motivate you to keep working to improve and eventually produce amazing results.

6. Act on Your Growth Mindset

The science demonstrates that we not only act on our beliefs but that our actions can also influence them.[56] As a result, behaving in ways that are consistent with a growth mindset will strengthen your growth mindset.

In picking up and reading a book like this one, you are already doing this. By engaging in any sort of activity that helps you learn, you are actively improving. Take it a step further by asking yourself follow-up questions such as "What have I learned so far?" or "From what I've learned so far, what is one thing I can incorporate into my life today?" As leadership coach Kristi Hedges notes in her excellent article "Make Sure Everyone on Your Team Sees Learning as Part of Their Job": "You should come back from every workshop or training with a story about what you learned. Rather than the typical, 'It was interesting,' be specific. For example, you might say, 'I thought I was a good listener, but I can see that this is a growth area for me. The day showed me new ways to interact with others, and though they aren't necessarily comfortable for me, I'm going to try them out.'"[57]

7. Prioritize Growth Every Day

In today's business climate, selling is especially challenging. With more competitors entering the marketplace each year, an increase in copycat products and services, and tumultuous market conditions, salespeople are wondering how to best position themselves to thrive. This is why growth is so critical. Those who continuously improve their abilities set themselves up to adapt well to these ever-changing conditions, while those who don't often struggle. The reality is that salespeople always need to grow to ensure they don't get left behind.

Consider this question: If you hit your sales objectives for the year but you didn't improve professionally, did you have a truly great year? I would say no, as simply achieving a goal without learning anything in the process means your success is likely temporary.

A consistent focus on strengthening and expanding your knowledge and skills is what will set you up for long-term success. And that's why it's important to celebrate and prioritize growth; it's what creates lasting achievement.

What does this look like? It's the salesperson who invests twenty minutes every day in honing her presentation skills; the sales manager who reads one book a month on selling or leadership, looking for the best ways to help his salespeople reach their full potential; and the business owner who rewards her employees' progress in moving closer to a sales goal and provides them opportunities to learn skills and grow both personally and professionally.

Now, celebrating growth and not just outcomes may seem like odd advice from someone who makes his living helping businesses increase their sales results. Yet in my years of experience, I've consistently found that when salespeople focus on continual improvement, sales growth naturally follows. And when they stop focusing on it, their sales suffer. That's because lasting success doesn't happen by accident. It's the work you put into growing that compounds over days, weeks, and months and that improves your effectiveness.

We've covered a lot of ground in this chapter. Together, achievement and growth mindsets lay the foundation we'll build on throughout this book to increase your effectiveness, results, and overall quality of life. Now that you understand these two crucial mindsets, let's look at the number one trait you'll also need to cultivate to accomplish your sales objectives. In the next chapter, I'll show you how to adopt this trait and take your sales to an all-time high.

CHAPTER 2

The #1 Trait You Need to Succeed

IMAGINE IF THERE WERE A WAY TO PREDICT, BEFORE HIR-
ing them, which employees would stay with your company long-
term and which wouldn't. Knowing this would be a significant
business advantage, given that the *Harvard Business Review* reports that the turnover rate of salespeople each year is an alarming
27 percent.[1] It's also expensive; the average turnover costs companies around $600,000.[2]

Thanks to recent scientific breakthroughs, it is now possible to
accurately forecast which salespeople are most likely to remain
with your organization and which will leave. In a landmark research study, four social psychologists analyzed the causal factors
that prompt people to either give up or persevere when things get
challenging. In particular, they looked at whether salespeople remained with their employer or not and at the key reasons for drop-
outs during a grueling twenty-four-day Army Special Operations
Forces selection course.[3] What they discovered stunned them: A
single trait predicted the retention rates for both salespeople and
army candidates—grit.

Grittier soldiers were the ones most likely to complete the Special Operations Forces course, and grittier salespeople were the ones most likely to stick with the job even when it was difficult.[4] The sway of grit is so strong, the researchers concluded, that it influenced retention more than other factors like intelligence, talent, personality, and previous job experience.

So, what is grit? It's sticking with a goal and continuing to work toward it, even when things get tough. Not only have scientific studies demonstrated a clear link between people who have high levels of grit and their personal and professional accomplishments, but the trait itself seems to fuel achievement. Attaining any goal may take longer than you anticipate and require you to persist through obstacles and setbacks. Gritty individuals are much more likely to persevere instead of giving up, and this tenacity often means the difference between realizing their goals or not.

The correlation between grit and performance first came to light back in 1892, when the British scientist Sir Francis Galton examined the lives of successful people and noticed that they each demonstrated "ability combined with zeal and with capacity for hard labor."[5] Since then, behavioral scientists have conducted extensive research that both verifies and adds some nuance to Galton's insight. Today, researchers contend that grit, a noncognitive trait, is an even better predictor of success than IQ.[6]

To prove this point, one study found that grittier contestants in spelling bees practiced harder and longer, which enabled them to outperform their counterparts.[7] In another study in which five behavioral scientists scrutinized high school dropout rates, they discovered that students with higher levels of grit were more likely to graduate.[8] Grit is even a primary predictor of teacher effectiveness in the classroom.[9]

Given its substantial impact on everything from academic

performance to retention rates, it's no surprise that individual levels of grit also heavily influence sales results, as well as job performance and satisfaction.[10] My own assessments of thousands of salespeople, ranging in skills, tenure, and industry, have repeatedly confirmed that grit is the number one trait that sets salespeople up for success.

Here's the science-backed reality: Success is hard enough to attain, and not having grit makes it even harder. Without grit, salespeople will often see their effort and interest in a goal decline when they face failure or adversity or hit a plateau. Gritty salespeople, on the other hand, approach their goals like runners approach a marathon, slowly and steadily building toward them, and their advantage is that tenacity. They don't give up when pursuing their dream clients, they look for solutions instead of quitting when faced with challenges, and they persist until they get the job done. In short, gritty salespeople are far more likely to achieve what they set out to do.

Of course, any discussion of grit wouldn't be complete without referencing the incredible work of Angela Duckworth, one of the leading experts on the trait. This MacArthur Fellow and internationally acclaimed professor of psychology at the University of Pennsylvania dedicated her career to studying grit after witnessing its significant impact on accomplishment in her own life and as a high school math teacher.[11] She published two simple equations that get to the root of the positive effect grit has on performance:[12]

Equation 1: Talent x Effort = Skill
Equation 2: Skill x Effort = Achievement

What these equations mean is that though talent and skill matter a great deal, when it comes to achievement, *effort* matters more.

In fact, effort counts twice. Grit inspires sustained effort over long periods of time, which is the key to accomplishing long-term goals.

Wondering how gritty you are? As with the achievement and growth mindsets we explored in chapter 1, you can grow your level of grittiness. Let's first establish where you currently stand by using the assessment below, which was inspired by the Grit Scale that Angela Duckworth and Patrick Quinn put forth in the *Journal of Personality Assessment.*[13]

Grit Assessment

Read through the following statements and select the answer that best describes how much you agree or disagree with them.

1. I frequently commit to a goal but later lose interest and pursue something else.
   1. *Strongly agree*
   2. *Somewhat agree*
   3. *Disagree*

2. Setbacks don't dissuade me when I'm working toward an important business goal.
   1. *Strongly agree*
   2. *Somewhat agree*
   3. *Disagree*

3. I'm often initially motivated to follow a positive new course of action but soon lose interest.
   1. *Strongly agree*
   2. *Somewhat agree*
   3. *Disagree*

4. I continually find ways to push myself to achieve my sales or business objectives.
   1. *Strongly agree*
   2. *Somewhat agree*
   3. *Disagree*

5. I struggle to stay focused on a sales target for more than a short time.
   1. *Strongly agree*
   2. *Somewhat agree*
   3. *Disagree*

6. I am able to stay motivated to attain a goal, even if it takes longer than expected.
   1. *Strongly agree*
   2. *Somewhat agree*
   3. *Disagree*

7. I'm easily distracted from my current objectives.
   1. *Strongly agree*
   2. *Somewhat agree*
   3. *Disagree*

8. I often lose interest in goals I set for myself within a small amount of time.
   1. *Strongly agree*
   2. *Somewhat agree*
   3. *Disagree*

9. Once I commit to a project, I typically complete it.
   1. *Strongly agree*
   2. *Somewhat agree*
   3. *Disagree*

10. I don't give up because of the challenges I face when working toward a big goal.
    1. *Strongly agree*
    2. *Somewhat agree*
    3. *Disagree*

Did you find yourself gravitating toward the same option for most of the statements, or were you varied in your answers?

Rate your current level of grit by adding up the numbers that designate the selection you chose. On questions 2, 4, 6, 9, and 10, the lower your score, the higher your grit. Whereas on questions 1, 3, 5, 7, and 8, the higher your score, the grittier you are. Remember, we are just getting started in our exploration of this important trait, and over the rest of this chapter, I'll share scientifically proven ways to boost your grit. So whether you are satisfied with your current level or not, the strategies you'll learn throughout this chapter will help you improve it as you put them into practice in your career and life.

There are two main components of grit: passion and persistence. In fact, as you may have already realized, the Grit Assessment is testing for both. Questions 1, 3, 5, 7, and 8 are focused on helping you determine your level of passion, while questions 2, 4, 6, 9, and 10 gauge your level of persistence. Let's dive into why they both matter and how you can use them to increase your level of grit and therefore your likelihood of achieving greater success.

Persistence Drives Performance

In one of the most well-known behavioral science studies of the twentieth century, Stanford University social scientist Walter Mischel led a series of experiments famously called the "marshmallow test."[14] The research focused on presenting three- to five-year-old children with a single marshmallow and informing them that they could either eat the marshmallow now or, if they waited a short time, receive a second marshmallow to enjoy along with this one. Many children couldn't resist temptation and scooped the marshmallow into their mouths immediately. But some were able to wait in order to receive the second one, distracting themselves by playing with their hands, closing their eyes, or singing songs.

After the test, Mischel noticed that those children who were able to delay gratification and wait for the second marshmallow were doing better in school. With his curiosity piqued, he began to monitor their progress throughout their teenage and college years. The data showed that those who were able to control their impulses as small children were also far more likely to experience academic success, be healthier, and even do better on their SATs. Incredibly, this trend continued into adulthood. Those adults who had shown self-control as small children tended to earn more money, more effectively pursued their goals, and were generally happier than those who hadn't resisted the lone marshmallow. Here's how Mischel summarized his findings some forty-two years after his initial research was published: "What the preschoolers did as they tried to keep waiting, and how they did or didn't manage to delay gratification, unexpectedly turned out to predict much about their future lives."[15]

Most worthwhile goals require sacrifice, hard work, and patience. This means fixing your eyes on your objective and sticking with it, even when it's hard—which is no small feat for children or adults.[16] As Mischel's and others' research has shown, delaying gratification and being persistent is linked with success, but how important is it in sales?[17] In perhaps the biggest analysis of sales performance ever conducted, researchers examined 268 different studies that evaluated 79,747 salespeople across 4,317 organizations.[18] They found that one of the most significant predictors of performance was high levels of engagement resulting from a gritty drive to work hard and continually improve. In fact, over forty years of sales research has proved that continual effort is a main factor in performance.[19] Here's why. The ability to persist through a difficult sales call, a rejection, a deal falling through, or any other setback requires that you don't give in to the emotions that often arise during those situations. This kind of self-regulation is no small thing. It's what allows you to rise above your impulses to quit or take the easy way out and to keep at it through challenging circumstances.[20] It's also what allows you to be nimble and adapt well to whatever environment you're in.[21]

What's more, delaying gratification is not only a critical part of grit; it's also a foundational component of integrity (a topic we'll explore more in chapter 8). In an illuminating study, social scientists observed that the ability to postpone enjoyment or satisfaction in pursuit of a goal is linked with ethical consistency, which is living out what you say you believe.[22] Think about it: If you can continue on with what you know is right, then most likely you'll also be strong enough to not compromise in other areas of your life. This is why grit isn't solely a trait that will help you sell more. It's an essential part of true and lasting success.

Being able to delay gratification and persevere is a hallmark of highly effective people—and it can be practiced and mastered by anyone. Get acquainted with these three strategies to help you fortify your persistence and achieve your goals.

1. Recognize That the Price of Success Is Paid Upfront

When I work with sales teams, sales managers, and business leaders, helping them use science to change their behaviors and grow their sales, I've found that they're more likely to live out grit if they embrace this concept: "There's a price for success, and you pay that price upfront." By that I mean, before you can achieve your desired outcome, you must first earn it through the hard work, practice, and sacrifices needed to create the success you seek. After all, if it were easy to achieve your goals, you would have already done so.

Adopting the attitude that you must pay the price of success upfront will inspire you to act in ways that will lead to increased performance and results, rather than focusing on what you're sacrificing in the short term to get to your goal. Here are two perspectives that will help you create and maintain this mentality through the hardest parts of the journey:

- **Embrace the challenge:** Though we all know in theory that meaningful accomplishments usually involve hard work, the reality of that hard work often demotivates people and prompts them to quit. This is why I'm encouraging you to persist through the obstacles between you and what you want to achieve; it will set you apart from the rest of the pack. Think about it like this: There is a wall around success. Simply *seeing* the wall keeps most people from attempting to climb it. But with good training, continued dedication, and a lot of effort, it can be scaled. So embrace the adversity, because it's the challenges that make the success you're after worth achieving.

- **Remember that the pain is temporary:** Years ago, when I was launching my sales training firm and just beginning my massive, yearslong research applying science to improve the process of selling, one thing that helped whenever I found myself overwhelmed or discouraged was remembering something my uncle Paul used to say: "It's just temporary." His words were a much-needed reminder that the struggles I was going through at that moment would eventually pass, and they helped me muster the motivation to continue chipping away at my objectives. Let my uncle Paul's words be an inspiration to keep you motivated too. And remember, the pain is just temporary, so don't quit.

2. Have Strong Whys

One of the secrets of staying the course is having clear reasons for doing so. This is what seven researchers found when they investigated how the reasoning behind a particular aim affects whether we attain it or not. Their experiments uncovered that motives predicted persistence and engagement levels and ultimately made a noticeable impact on whether or not the goal was reached. They even nodded to that conclusion in the title of their study: "When the Going Gets Tough: The 'Why' of Goal Striving Matters."[23]

Having compelling whys is paramount because all significant undertakings involve big hurdles. And it hardly takes a scientist to tell you that overcoming them isn't easy. There will be times when you'll want to abandon your goals. Having whys that inspire you to continue can be the difference between quitting or persevering.

Thinking back to when I launched my firm, I had a few key reasons for doing so. First, I believe that science has answers that will enhance the profession of selling. It provides clear insights that allow us to base our work on how our brains are influenced and form buying decisions, which I believe will elevate the profession. Second, I believe that sales training changes more than behaviors; it changes people too. It provides them with new mindsets, knowledge, and skills that can help them transform their lives and better serve others. Third, I have a passion for sales training. I genuinely enjoy training salespeople and thinking about how to apply science to the selling process. These whys helped me stay the course during the tough early years when I was building my company and keep at it until it turned into the thriving business it is today.

How about you? For your major goals, why do you want to achieve them? How will they enhance your life and career? In what way will accomplishing them positively impact others? Will attaining them move you further away from what you don't want to experience and closer to what you do? Thinking through and answering these questions will help you stay focused when the going gets tough and increase the likelihood that you'll persist to the finish line.

Let's stop for a moment and think through your whys for two main goals you have. Write down a goal and then three reasons why it is important to you. Remember, the stronger your whys, the more likely you'll be to actually achieve that goal.

Goal 1:

_____

Why achieving this goal matters:

Reason 1:

_____

Reason 2:

_____

Reason 3:

_____

Goal 2:

_____

Why achieving this goal matters:

Reason 1:

_____

Reason 2:

_____

Reason 3:

_____

This is a valuable exercise and one we'll come back to in the next chapter, where we'll dive deeper into goals and the powerful, science-backed ways to make yours a reality.

3. Don't Settle for the Easy Way Out

What is the top thing that will keep you from achieving what you want? Settling for _good enough_. That's right: What keeps most people from the life they want isn't some insurmountable obstacle. It's that they settle for an easier substitute that's not nearly as good but, well, good enough, they suppose. Jim Collins summarizes this idea in his bestselling book _Good to Great_: "Good is the enemy of great. And that is one of the key reasons why we have so little that

becomes great . . . Few people attain great lives, in large part because it is just so easy to settle for a good life."[24]

As you embrace grit and move closer and closer to your goals,
you will face this dilemma: Should you continue on to the finish
line, or stop and settle for what you've already obtained? The way
you respond to that dilemma will determine whether you accomplish what you want or settle for something ultimately less satisfy-
ing. This gets to the heart of what it means to have grit. Gritty people
don't stop chasing their goals because those goals are challenging
or they've come close enough. They relentlessly pursue what they
want and say no to anything that will cause them to veer off course.

Not settling can change both your life and the lives of others
for the better. For example, on March 24, 1975, legendary boxer
Muhammad Ali, then the reigning Heavyweight Champion of the
World, fought journeyman fighter Chuck Wepner. What happened
during the fight was, to many, a miracle. Wepner survived till the
last round, before being knocked out in the final seconds. Many
were moved by Wepner's performance, including a struggling
young actor who, after witnessing the fight, went home to his
apartment and began frantically writing a screenplay that encom-
passed the emotions he felt. He showed the script to two producers
who wanted to buy it and make it into a movie—with one condition:
They wanted to cast an A-list star for the main role instead of the
unknown actor. But he persisted, insisting that if he wasn't allowed
to play the lead role, he wouldn't sell the script. Hoping more money
would change his mind, the producers made a series of escalat-
ing offers, capping out at a whopping $360,000 (an unheard-of
amount at the time for an inexperienced screenwriter), but each
was rejected.[25]

Eventually, they gave in and allowed the actor to play the lead
in exchange for accepting a major reduction in compensation for

the script, and they assigned a meager budget to the film. The movie *Rocky* became a breakout hit, won the Academy Award for Best Picture in 1977, and went on to become one of the most iconic films ever made.[26] Perhaps most importantly, it launched the career of Sylvester Stallone, and all because he had the grit to pursue his dream in the face of huge obstacles and not settle.

Now, you may never have to say no to a movie contract as you chase your goals, but you will likely need to say no to something enticing along the way that threatens to derail you. What should you do when you're tempted to take the easy way out? Here are three ways that you can fight off the urge to settle.

1. **Make a Commitment to Your Goal:** Commitments matter because they shape future behavior. The science tells us that committing to an objective makes a huge difference on whether or not you'll attain it. In fact, one study found that without a robust commitment, it's unlikely you'll stick with a goal or put in the necessary effort to attain it.[27]

   Pause for a moment and think of one of your goals. Evaluate how dedicated you are to it by thinking through what you would give up in order to reach it. If your willingness to sacrifice for a goal is weak, most likely so is your resolve to accomplish it. However, if you are willing to let go of things you value (say, free time, hobbies, or entertainment) so that you can attain it, then you can feel good about the strength of your resolve.

2. **Ask Yourself Whether You Will Regret It If You Settle:** An effective way to strengthen your resolve is to ask yourself, "If I settle, will I regret it?" This question will help you think through how you'll feel if you give up

now. Many of my clients have found that asking this type of question was pivotal in pushing forward and remaining committed to their target. As you read about Stallone's persistence, you may have wondered how he was able to resist the temptation to take the producers' offer. Stallone has shared that, in that moment, he asked himself what would happen if *Rocky* became a hit and he wasn't the star. He said that he wouldn't be able to live with himself, and this realization gave him the courage to stand firm.[28] How about you? When you make progress, you'll be tempted to stop and take the easy way out. By thinking through the regret you'll feel if you settle, you'll be equipped to resist the urge and continue the hard work.

3. **Focus on Next Steps:** Quitting on your goals doesn't typically happen in a flash. Instead of focusing on what you should do to move closer to your target, you may find yourself thinking more frequently of settling. Over time, these thoughts can chip away at your resolve and lead you to veer off track. Yet, the process of how you get drawn away from a goal also reveals what you can do to stay motivated. Keep your focus on your next steps, not on why it would be easier to stop pursuing your objective. For instance, it can be overwhelming to think about how much work it will be to accomplish a large goal, and this may cause you to become discouraged. By concentrating on the specific task you can do *right now* to move you closer to the goal, you'll be more likely to act on it even in a small way. In doing so, you'll make a bit more progress, which naturally will foster your motivation to keep going.

There's no doubt that persistence is a critical part of grit and, thus, of sales success. However, there is still another essential part of the trait to explore. In this next section, you'll discover how living out your passion will also increase your grittiness and put you in a peak performance state to launch you to new heights.

Passion Drives Performance

Let's be honest: It's hard to be successful at anything if you aren't passionate about it. When it comes to sales, sure, you may be able to make a living, but it's unlikely you'll be a top performer. Why? Selling is challenging and at times stressful. You'll often have to go through a lot of nos before you get a yes, which can be demoralizing and demotivating. There is also constant pressure to perform: to generate business, outsell competitors, and exceed your quota. It takes a lot of hard work—not to mention long hours—to create and sustain a high level of performance. In the end, if you aren't passionate about sales or about what you are selling, you'll constantly be tempted to turn your focus to things you like better, and you'll have limited motivation to improve.

Passion is a major part of grit, and for that reason, it has been shown to increase the likelihood of heightened levels of achievement. This particularly applies to our careers. Behavioral scientists have found that to flourish in any skill-based profession, like business or sales, you need to be intrinsically motivated not solely by money but also by enthusiasm for the work itself.[29]

In other words, when it comes to whether you should follow your passion or follow the money in terms of your career, science has definitively answered the question: By pursuing your passion, you are much more likely to experience success—and be well compensated financially. But don't take my word for it, let's look at the evidence. When behavioral scientists evaluated the specific factors that influence sales performance, they found that task enjoyment was a major driver of success.[30] A meta-analysis that looked at sixty years of research came to the same conclusion: People perform better when they are passionate about their work.[31] Another meta-analysis, which scrutinized twenty-six years of studies on what creates high-achieving salespeople, identified the same phenomenon: Those who were enthusiastic about selling were far more likely to rise to the top.[32]

Thought Experiment:
Why Passion Improves Performance

Imagine a family member needs to undergo a risky medical operation that could save her life. Due to the delicate nature of the procedure, the skill of the surgeon will make a big difference in the success of the surgery. You have a choice of two doctors. The first makes it clear he doesn't really like being a surgeon and, as a result, seldom thinks about how he can improve the care he gives his patients. In fact, when performing an operation, he counts down the moments until he can be free to pursue his real passion—golf. Surgery is simply a way to support his family and pay for the golf trips he takes each year. The second doctor, on the other hand, loves being a surgeon and considers it a way to serve others. As a result, she is constantly working to improve her knowledge and ability. She studies the latest medical breakthroughs and attends the top conferences, striving to find ways to create better outcomes and provide better care. Instinctively, you recognize that the best option is the second surgeon because her passion produces behaviors that are more likely to achieve a successful outcome.

Not surprisingly, our brains naturally focus on our passions because we like them. And we instinctively recognize that people who are passionate about something are much more likely to put in the time and effort to develop their abilities in that area, which is why passion matters in everything we do, from relationships and hobbies to jobs and careers. And if you're excited about selling, you'll be much more likely to become a top performer, as learning and improving your expertise won't feel like a chore. Enjoying the process makes it more likely you'll keep at it until you triumph, even in the face of setbacks.

How to Identify and Pursue Your Passions

Perhaps the most significant reason why you should pursue what you are passionate about is that it puts you in a peak mental and emotional state that allows you to perform at your best. Scientists refer to this as *flow*.

The leading researcher on flow is Mihaly Csikszentmihalyi, a renowned psychologist whose work has captured the attention of world leaders, business experts, and professional sports coaches. The insight that made Csikszentmihalyi famous was uncovering the "flow state," which is when people are so immersed in an activity that it naturally puts them in the optimal state for doing it. Athletes often describe it as "being in the zone," and people who experience flow regularly report that they are completely present in the moment, experience joy throughout the process, and are deeply focused on the task at hand.[33]

Csikszentmihalyi stumbled on the concept of flow when he was studying people in a variety of occupations (chess players, doctors, businesspeople, musicians, farmers, dancers, and artists, to name a few) in an effort to identify what made them both successful *and satisfied*.[34] Across the board, they described a state of mind in which they were so carried away by an activity that nothing else seemed to matter. That's actually where the term "flow" came from: People explained their experiences as being similar to being swept away by what they were doing, as if water were carrying them along.[35] As a result, flow is linked with activities you are intrinsically motivated to do. No one goes into a state of flow doing something they hate.[36]

One of the most fascinating things about flow is that time seems to fly by because you are so absorbed in what you are doing. This often happens to me when I speak about science-based selling. I'm so immersed in the moment, so excited to share ideas that I know will truly help my audience, that I don't notice how much time is passing. Can you remember being so engaged in an activity that an hour flew by but it felt like only a few minutes? If so, then you've experienced flow.

Yet flow is more than just an enjoyable feeling; it also increases grit and, correspondingly, success. When Csikszentmihalyi analyzed the factors that contributed to whether or not art students became professional artists, he discovered that those who were passionate about painting and regularly experienced flow were grittier and more likely to remain in the profession. In contrast, those who were drawn to the profession for potential money and fame, who rarely experienced flow, abandoned their careers in the face of obstacles.

Entering into a flow state also enhances performance, especially skill-based ones, which is why social psychologist Daniel Goleman calls it a "prerequisite of mastery."[37] It also seems to improve some behaviors more than others, making the most significant impact on activities that require you to grow your skills in order to achieve competence, such as selling.[38] This is why salespeople who regularly are in a state of flow generally outperform those who aren't. One study that measured the influence of flow on sales outcomes found that it helped salespeople perform at their best and be more likely to earn the sale.[39]

And what's more, flow doesn't just influence the effectiveness of individuals; it can also transform an entire company. One prime example of this impact is the Swedish state-owned logistics company Green Cargo.[40] Its sales had become so stagnant that the business had not made a profit since 1889, surviving only on the support it received from the government. When new leaders took over in 2003, they introduced a program for employees based around the concept of flow. The goal was to help workers enter into this peak performance state more often, which would boost morale and production. Managers regularly met with workers to craft motivating goals, provide useful feedback, and create positive challenges that helped workers experience flow. Only a year later, the company became profitable for the first time in 115 years.

If flow sets you up for success by helping you tap into your potential, you're probably wondering what you can do to enter into it more often. Take a look at these three proven ways to foster your flow.

1. Seek Out Challenges That Strengthen Your Skills

When do you think you'd be more likely to experience flow, at work or leisure? You may be surprised to learn that, if you're like most people, you are far more likely to enter into a flow state at work than while having fun.[41] This is because a key requirement of flow is a balance between the demands of an activity and your skill level; it occurs when the situation demands a high level of performance and you are able to stretch your skills to meet that challenge.[42] If the task isn't challenging enough—like if you're watching TV or chatting with a friend—you'll relax instead of reaching your edge. On the flip side, if you're attempting to do something well beyond your abilities, you'll feel pressure and stress, which is equally detrimental to flow.

Think about times when you're presented with a challenge that forces you to stretch your skills. Identifying those opportunities and creating more of them will naturally improve the likelihood that you'll enter a flow state.

2. Minimize Anxiety to Achieve Peak Performance

Many sales and business professionals say that one of the things they like most about their work is experiencing flow. As we've discussed, it boosts morale, motivation, and happiness. However, there is a major killer of flow: anxiety. It's hard to get in the zone when you are anxious, especially about your performance.

Sometimes when you're concerned about an upcoming interaction or presentation, you have a good reason to be anxious. Worry can be a signal that you are not prepared or confident about what you're about to do or what's going to happen. This is why one of the ways to set yourself up for peak performance is to practice with a colleague or a manager, or on your own. Early in my career, I practiced my presentations in front of the mirror just to get comfortable with them. Even now, after conducting thousands of sales calls and trainings, I still practice. Why? I want to prepare so that I will be able to enter into a flow state and perform at my best. Effective practice allows you to try new things, make mistakes, receive immediate feedback, adapt, and try again. So if you feel nervous about *any* activity, practice ahead of time. You'll find it lowers your anxiety, increases your confidence, and enables you to rise to the challenge.[43]

A second way to calm your nerves is by rethinking your

response. Researchers have found that when faced with fear, denying or dwelling on it are both counterproductive.[44] Instead, reframe it. Harvard Business School's Alison Wood Brooks identified that when most people feel apprehensive about an upcoming presentation, they instinctively try to calm themselves down, which rarely works. It is far more effective to reframe your anxiety by saying, "I am excited" or telling yourself, "Get excited!"[45] This counterintuitive tactic lowers anxiety and improves performance, so give it a try next time you're feeling those butterflies.

3. Focus More on Actions Than on Outcomes

I met Paul at my second sales job when we went through new-hire training together. Paul was a jovial guy who, unfortunately, wanted so badly to sell that he came across as needy, which eroded his credibility with potential buyers. This tendency also prevented him from entering into flow, where his skills and confidence would come across and help him win the sale. He was so fixated on the outcome he wanted that he didn't focus enough on the behavior necessary to achieve it.

If I could go back and talk to Paul, I would tell him to pay attention to his mindsets and behaviors first, because if you have the productive mindsets and execute the right actions competently, the results will take care of themselves. As we've discussed, your mindsets influence your behaviors and your behaviors shape your outcomes.

One way to experience a flow state is through developing your ability to focus.[46] In selling, this means that you are fully present during each part of the process and attentive to only what you're doing at that point in time. You aren't worried about what will happen at the end of your presentation or even whether you'll get the sale; you are so immersed in what's right in front of you that you automatically perform your best. Here's how you develop that focus: Whenever you find yourself getting distracted—as you inevitably will—try to gently guide your attention back to the task at hand. With practice, you'll find that becoming absorbed in your work happens more naturally, easily, and frequently. You will also notice that this increased focus will produce better results, boost efficiency, and enable you to enjoy being in a flow state more often.

Throughout this chapter we've focused on the lasting impact grit can have on your success, and we've discussed the two main components of the trait—persistence (strategically delay gratification to succeed) and passion (find your flow)—and three strategies you can use to grow in each.

Now that you know how to strengthen your mindsets and level of grit, it's time to expand our focus and dig into the science-backed recipe you can follow to consistently reach your goals. Turn the page and let's get started.

CHAPTER 3

The Science of Attaining Your Sales Goals

WHAT SCIENCE HAS SHOWN IS THAT SUCCESS DOESN'T happen just because you're smart or you're lucky; it is the result of the goals you create and how you pursue them.[1] That's why goals matter: They are a precursor to action, and action leads to results.[2] Goals direct your mental focus and physical efforts toward the accomplishment of a specific outcome.[3] This channeling of attention and effort, in turn, intensifies your motivation to succeed, which makes it more likely that you will.[4]

And here's the most remarkable thing about goals: They not only determine how effective you'll be day-to-day but also impact the trajectory of your whole career. In particular, the way salespeople perceive and respond to goals shapes their activities, behaviors, and overall sales performance.[5] One meta-analysis of decades of empirical evidence on what makes salespeople effective concluded that those who are goal-oriented are more likely to thrive.[6] Another concluded that those who create specific, challenging objectives before entering a negotiation consistently realize higher profits than negotiators with none.[7] Mark Roberge, senior lecturer at Harvard Business School and former chief revenue officer at HubSpot, agrees, stating in his bestselling book, *The Sales Acceleration Formula*, that top salespeople have clearly defined goals that allow them to measure what that success looks like.[8]

When I first started my career in selling and was taught to set sales goals, no one ever explained (or knew, for that matter) what determined whether you reached them. So attaining them seemed like the result of luck or a fortunate accident. But it doesn't have to be left up to chance. Thanks to more than a thousand scientific studies that have uncovered why some salespeople accomplish their goals and others don't, we know there are specific steps you can take to achieve yours.[9]

In this chapter, I share seven science-backed strategies that have been proven to radically increase the likelihood you'll reach your goals. Using just one of these will help you pursue your goals more effectively, and implementing all seven has a compounding effect that will supercharge your ability to reach any goal.

Strategy #1: Create Goals That Captivate You

When you first establish a goal, your enthusiasm to achieve it is usually at an all-time high. But as time passes, you may feel your motivation decline. Though you still want to make it happen, you find yourself doing less in your quest for it. Many salespeople struggle with this problem; it's one of the key reasons they fail to hit the targets they've set. Motivation is vital to success because it drives you to take the actions necessary to reach your goal.[10] Without it, your goal-directed behaviors will decrease and so will your chances of accomplishing it.

If motivation is vital, what can you do to make sure yours stays strong? Again, science can help. Multiple studies on motivation have uncovered that the way we *state* our goal heavily impacts our motivation. That's because the way something is presented shapes how we perceive and respond to it. The following are three science-backed principles that will help you implement this strategy and stay motivated throughout the process.

1. Make Your Goals Specific

Creating clear, specific goals is linked to achieving them. When behavioral scientists Edwin Locke and Gary Latham examined thirty-five years of empirical research on goals, one of their primary findings was that *specificity* led to putting forth more effort than generic objectives or vague guidelines that urged people to "do their best."[11] This was true even when the targets were difficult to achieve. In fact, Locke and Latham found that when people were told to "do their best," they rarely did. The reason, they explain, was because that directive has no external reference point, so it is unclear what achieving it looks like.[12]

Defining your goals helps you establish what you will need to do to make them a reality. A detailed objective, such as "I will improve my monthly sales volume by twenty thousand dollars," is far more likely to be acted on than an ambiguous one, like "I will improve my sales each month." Similarly, saying, "I will get better at delivering my sales presentation" is not nearly as effective as "I will spend four hours this week analyzing my delivery of the sales presentation and identifying at least three specific things I can do to improve." Notice how the details establish what needs to be accomplished and how to go about doing that, and thus are far more motivating. And much like in our discussion of grit, an additional benefit of setting specific goals is that they clearly define what you want to achieve, making it less likely that you will quit or settle for "good enough."

2. Focus Your Goals on Learning and Improving

In particular, learning-based goals are associated with enhanced performance in many areas, including selling. Anytime you are focused on improving, you're leveraging the power of a growth mindset, which, as we saw in chapter 1, equips you to interpret and respond more effectively to the failures and challenges you will inevitably face when pursuing your goals.[13] In addition, by concentrating on developing your skills, you naturally improve your results.[14]

Let's look at a few examples. In one study, behavioral scientists Don VandeWalle, Steven Brown, and William Cron observed 153 salespeople who were responsible for selling over two thousand different lines of medical supplies and equipment.[15] The salespeople who had goals centered on learning new skills or enhancing existing ones had higher sales than their colleagues whose goals centered on showcasing their abilities and receiving recognition for them. In fact, the stronger the emphasis on learning and improving, the more sales they produced.

Another study reached a similar conclusion.[16] The salespeople with goals oriented toward learning were much more effective and outsold those whose goals were focused primarily on being applauded for their performance. The conclusion is clear: Grow your knowledge and skills and you will be more likely to achieve the success you desire.

I encourage you to think through your goals and ask yourself: Are they framed around improving your skills and expertise? If not, how can you make them more learning-based? Remember, how much you sell is the result of *how* you sell, which is why goals directed at developing your abilities always produce the biggest and best results.

3. Determine How to Frame Your Goals for Best Results

You probably won't be surprised to learn that framing a goal positively can both improve performance and increase the likelihood of achieving it. One study found that when participants were presented a task with a positive frame ("Try to solve at least twelve of these anagrams") they were more successful than when a negative frame was used ("Try not to miss answering more than three of the fifteen anagrams").[17]

But is there ever a situation where a negatively framed goal can boost your performance and help you attain it? As a matter of fact, yes. In certain situations, it can signal a lack of progress and prompt greater effort in the pursuit of an objective.[18] Whether you should go with a positive or negative spin depends on where you are in relation to achieving your objective. A positive framing fosters a deeper commitment to your goal, so keep that in mind when you're in the beginning stages of pursuit, or when your goal is in an area you're not skilled at.[19] Negative framing is useful when you have already made progress and are close to the finish line, or when you are experienced in the area and just need a bit of a boost to get to where you want to be.[20]

For example, let's say you want to make fifty calls each day to existing clients to connect with them and look for upselling opportunities. When you set your target, frame it positively ("I will make fifty calls to existing clients by five o'clock today"). Then, once you've made thirty-five or so calls and feel your motivation fading, reframe your goal negatively to give yourself an extra burst of energy to get to the end ("I've already made thirty-five calls and have only fifteen more to go, so I can't stop now").

Or let's imagine you've just joined a new team. Perhaps your initial goal is "Learn how to present the new sales process competently and gain an understanding of the product offering within the next three months." This positive framing will get you off to a strong start (and it's specific and learning-focused too). However, at the beginning of your third month, after you've worked hard pursuing this goal, you can push yourself to finish strong by reframing it as "I've already invested two months pursuing this goal. To make sure I don't waste that effort, I need to finish learning the sales process by investing just twenty more hours over these final four weeks to improve how I demonstrate the value that our digital platform delivers to customers."

Now that you've learned how to create compelling goals, let's look at the second strategy, where I'll show you how to deepen your commitment to them.

Strategy #2: Commit to Your Goals

When you look at the scientific research on goals, one fact repeatedly emerges: Commitment is predictive of attainment.[21] In other words, your dedication to your goals directly influences whether you'll achieve them. And as we saw in the previous chapter when we discussed persistence, goal commitment matters, especially when what you're pursuing is challenging and requires high levels of consistent effort.[22] Without a robust commitment, it's unlikely you'll put in the sustained effort needed to accomplish it.[23] Behavioral scientists Murray Barrick, Michael Mount, and Judy Strauss discovered exactly this when they monitored the performance of ninety-one salespeople. Their research revealed that those salespeople who made resolute pledges to their goals far outperformed their colleagues.[24]

There are many factors that influence goal commitment, including the achievement mindset, which I addressed in chapter 1.[25] As a reminder, those with a healthy achievement mindset feel confident embracing tough but worthwhile goals and, as a result, are able to make deep commitments to them.[26] The opposite is also true: If you don't believe you can achieve a big sales target, you won't commit to it, which makes your odds of attaining it very low.

Having an achievement mindset is just one of the ways to help you stick with your goals. Here are two others.

1. Tell the Right People About Your Goals

One powerful, yet simple way to boost your commitment to any goal is to tell others about it so they can help hold you accountable.[27] The reason, research suggests, is that it makes pursuing the goal a matter of personal and public integrity.[28]

That said, your success largely depends on *who* you tell as well. There are times when telling others *won't* improve your commitment. The deciding factor comes down to what you think about the people you are sharing your target with, per fascinating research published in the *Journal of Applied Psychology* in 2020.[29] If you hold their opinions in high esteem, then informing them about your goal will amplify your resolve to achieve it. However, if you don't value their opinions and aren't swayed by what they think of you, then it won't. So make sure you talk to folks whose opinions matter to you. Doing so can give you the added incentive you need to push forward.

2. Choose Authentic Goals

Goals are personal things. With each one you set, you are determining who you want to become, what you want to achieve, and the life you want to create. This is why goals that trigger commitment and effort are always authentic, in that they are aligned with your desired future.[30] That's what social psychologists found when they examined which factors influenced whether or not eight hundred participants achieved their objectives.[31] The researchers identified that those who were most likely to commit to and realize their goals were the ones whose goals moved them closer toward the life they wanted.

The opposite is equally true: You will struggle to stay committed to a goal if achieving it won't move you closer to what you truly value and desire. It is only when your vision of who you want to be and the future you want to create is so aligned with your objectives that you will be compelled to forgo your short-term comfort to achieve long-term satisfaction in them.

Goal authenticity matters even when it comes to sales, where often money is thought to be the primary motivator. Though it is true that money can enhance your commitment to any particular goal, financial incentive actually matters far less than authenticity when it comes to motivation. As a widely acclaimed *Harvard Business Review* article by business experts David Mayer and Herbert Greenberg concluded, top salespeople sell not merely for "the money to be gained" but also because it improves their "self-picture."[32] In other words, they sell because serving others through the act of selling connects with who they desire to be and what they desire to achieve. If you ask them why they go the extra mile, it's not just because of the commission they may receive. It's because selling is part of their identity and thus a part of their goals.

Let's do an exercise that will help you either strengthen your commitment to your existing goals or reveal that they are not aligned with your vision of what you truly want. If you discover they're the latter, it will free you to create new goals that better support what you value.

Write down a goal:

_____

_____

Is the goal aligned with who you want to be?
Yes No Somewhat

Explain why or why not:

_____

_____

Is the goal aligned with the results you want to be known for and produce?   Yes No Somewhat

Explain why or why not:

_____

_____

Is the goal aligned with the life you desire to create?
Yes No Somewhat

Explain why or why not:

_____

_____

Going forth, as you create your goals, use this short exercise to ensure they are authentic and will inspire lasting commitments. One of the worst feelings is to create a target, work hard, and achieve it, only to experience disappointment when you realize it wasn't something you really wanted in the first place. This strategy will help you avoid that.

Let's move on to an effective approach to overcome any obstacles that come between you and your goals.

Strategy #3: Apply Mental Contrasting

Does thinking positively about your goals help you accomplish them? Contrary to what many self-help books promise, upbeat thinking is not always the answer. In fact, a large number of studies have proved that in certain cases, it can actually work against you.[33] An overly optimistic "Dream it, believe it, achieve it" mentality, for example, has been shown to *not* motivate the behaviors necessary to achieve an objective.[34] Rather, it can produce a dangerous false sense of confidence that can cause you to underestimate the barriers you need to overcome.[35]

So, if positive thinking won't help you accomplish your goals, what will? The answer is mental contrasting. This highly effective strategy helps you identify the gap between where you are and where you need to be—and then think through how you'll bridge that gap. The four-part process involves imagining your goal, focusing on the outcome if you achieve it, identifying potential obstacles, and planning how you'll overcome those. Scholarly studies have verified the proven track record of mental contrasting, whether your objective is to lose weight, quit smoking, get better grades, enhance communication skills, find a job, improve sales performance, or something else entirely.[36] One of the benefits of mental contrasting is that it deepens your commitment to whatever you set out to do. And as we have learned, your dedication to your goals is a vital part of realizing them. Because mental contrasting inspires people to think through how they'll accomplish an objective, it naturally strengthens their commitment to it.[37]

Mental contrasting also improves goal motivation, grit, and energy, and it boosts your resistance to discouragement from negative feedback.[38] Last but not least, it guides you in thinking through and preparing for any challenges you may come up against, so when you do face these hurdles, you're more likely to overcome them since you've already determined how to respond to each.[39]

How to Use Mental Contrasting

To utilize mental contrasting to move you closer to your goals, let's look at the four-step process based on the cutting-edge research of social scientist Gabriele Oettingen:[40]

- Step 1: Establish the goal you desire to accomplish.

- Step 2: Visualize the outcome that will occur if you achieve it.

- Step 3: Identify all obstacles that may prevent you from attaining your goal.

• Step 4: Determine a plan you will follow to overcome each
  obstacle.

Note that the order of these steps here is important. If you do
them backward (known as reverse contrasting),[41] and focus on
your obstacles first and then your goal, many of the benefits are
diminished or canceled out.[42]

Here's an example of how mental contrasting works. Kim is a
salesperson who was struggling to generate consistent new business. After she learned about mental contrasting, she created a
new goal: For the next three months she'll invest one hour each day
reaching out to potential clients (Step 1). Then she thought about
how a steady stream of clients would set her up for long-term success with her employer and make it likely she'd earn a performance
bonus, which she was planning to use as a down payment on a new
car (Step 2). As Kim contemplated the obstacles that may pop up,
she identified that she has a tendency not to think about prospecting until late in the day, and by then she is already busy responding
to current clients and completing her daily administrative tasks
(Step 3). Her plan to overcome this was to begin each workday by
reaching out to potential clients instead. She also spotted a second
barrier, which was that her coworkers and manager often interrupt
her to ask for reports or assistance or to chitchat. To avoid disrup-
tions, Kim created an appointment on her shared calendar to show
that she was occupied for the first hour each day. Additionally, she
informed her colleagues that she had this blackout period each day
because she'd be reaching out to new business leads (Step 4). By using the process of mental contrasting, Kim was able to design a
system to enable her to finally accomplish a goal she had been
grappling with for a long time.

Now that you understand how to engage in mental contrasting,
let's do a quick exercise so that you can begin reaping the benefits

right now with a goal of your own. Below are the four steps. Select a goal you have for yourself and let's boost your ability to achieve it.

Goal:

_____

Outcome:

_____

Obstacles:

_____

Plan to Address Each Obstacle:

_____

_____

Our next strategy will show you how to take the necessary action to keep moving ahead. In fact, it is one that I used to accomplish a major goal of my own.

Strategy #4: Keep Your Attention on Your Goals

Perhaps you can relate to an odd experience I had a number of years ago. I purchased a car for what was, at the time, the most money I had ever spent on a vehicle. Afterward, everywhere I went I began noticing cars of the same model as the one I had bought. I found this peculiar because, before buying the car, I rarely spotted others driving them. Now I couldn't help seeing them all over the place. What was going on?

The answer is found in the strange workings of our human brain. Though weighing only around three pounds, our brains consist of more than ten billion neurons and ten trillion synapses that are able to perform remarkable feats.[43] Yet, in spite of this, our brains have one big limitation: attention.[44] As neuroscientist Daniel Levitin explains, "To pay attention to one thing means that we don't pay attention to something else. Attention is a limited-capacity resource."[45] Sure, you can focus on a few things at once—if they are cognitively undemanding.[46] But the more difficult the task, the more incapable you are of giving your full attention to it and to something else at the same time.[47] In other words, you can ponder what you've just read or how much you enjoyed the last meal you ate, but not both at once.[48]

Our brains still function amazingly well even with this limitation because they are able to filter out most of the stimuli we come in contact with, bringing to our attention only what is most important to us.[49] This is why after spending money on a car, I began seeing that model everywhere I went. Before the purchase, my brain filtered out the vehicles I saw on the road, as they weren't relevant. Once I had made buying a car a priority and then settled on that specific model, my brain began bringing them to my awareness.

Understanding the science of how your brain decides what it will (or won't) call to your attention is vital because it reveals how to set yourself up for victory. When you make a strong commitment to your targets and begin focusing on them, you are informing your brain that they are significant. As a result, when it encounters something relevant to your goals, it knows to bring that to your attention. For instance, many people have found that once they begin to think about their goals every day, they start to see new ways of accomplishing them. What they are "seeing" may have always been right in front of them, but their brains filtered it out. Once their brains realized that it was significant, it alerted them to the insight.

Even more impressive is that continually focusing on your goals actually rewires your brain by creating synaptic connections associated with them. And these new neural links boost your ability to accomplish your goals because they improve your brain's capacity to think productively about how you'll achieve them and even enhance your performance of goal-related tasks.[50] So to say that it's good practice to focus on your goals daily is an understatement. Doing so is *essential* to attaining them.

The following are three simple things you can do on a daily basis to keep your attention centered on what you desire to achieve.

1. Write Down Your Goals

Writing down your goals deepens your commitment to them and makes it more likely you'll act on them.[51] That's what social scientists Delia Cioffi and Randy Garner found when they conducted an experiment in which some participants responded to a request with a verbal commitment while others were asked to write down the commitment after agreeing to it. Those who wrote down the commitment were nearly 200 percent more likely to follow through.

When you write out your goals, you are both documenting your commitment to them and actively focusing on them.[52] The very act of putting a goal in your own words prompts you to think it through and frame it in language that resonates with you. It's also important that you keep your goals concise. If you've written more than one sentence, condense it. This will ensure that you are staying specific and to the point.

Writing out your goals doesn't have to be a onetime endeavor. Anytime you feel your commitment begin to weaken because of a setback, a challenge, or general discouragement, center your mind back on the significance of your goals by writing them out. Many also find it beneficial to focus on their goals each day by writing them out in the morning and again just before bedtime.

2. Look at Your Goals Every Day

In addition to writing down what you want to achieve, another effective approach is to review your goals on a daily basis. The easiest way to do this is to put them in a conspicuous place where you can't help but see them. I post my goals next to the mirror in my bathroom, which prompts me to look at them at the start and end of each day. Because they are right in front of me, I never forget to focus on them, and I've found this extremely helpful in keeping them top of mind. If you think posting your goals in your bathroom (or anywhere that is visible) seems extreme, think again. Your goals are what you want out of life. If concentrating on them will improve your chances of accomplishing them—and it will—then investing that time, even for just a few minutes, is a worthwhile endeavor.

3. Reflect on Your Goals

At the end of a day, how do you judge how productive you were? I ask myself, "Did I move closer to my goals today?" Some days you may focus on your professional targets, some days you may dedicate to your personal ambitions, and other days you may attend to both. Regardless, at the end of each day, reflecting on what you did that moved you closer to your objectives is a powerful exercise that will help reinforce goal-producing behaviors. Additionally, thinking through what you did or didn't do that kept you from making progress can help you course-correct.

Another effective way to reflect on your goals is to consider how accomplishing them will improve your life and the lives of those around you. This will strengthen your commitment and foster the motivation you'll need. It's a particularly worthwhile exercise to do when you feel your motivation beginning to fade.

Strategy #5: Break Big Goals into Subgoals

Manuel was a good salesperson, but he was frustrated. After I delivered a training to the sales team he had joined a year earlier, he approached me and asked if we could meet to discuss a problem he was facing. He shared that he was disappointed because he was falling short of many of his sales targets and didn't understand why. He proudly told me he had both short- and long-term goals, which he'd written down and reviewed nearly every day. As further incentive, he had calculated how much additional commission he would make if he reached each of them and had even cut pictures out of magazines of the things he was planning to buy with these extra earnings. Yet, in spite of all this, Manuel was still struggling to make tangible progress. I told him, "This sounds great—so what is your plan to achieve these goals?" Surprised, he paused, unsure how to respond. In that moment, the real issue Manuel was facing became clear to both of us: He had done all the right things to create strong goals, but he hadn't mapped out the steps to take to make them a reality.

Manuel isn't alone. It's easy to fall into the trap of designing goals you are passionate about but then not taking the necessary action to move closer to achieving them. And of course, when you do this, little will change. Goals are not attained by hope, but through careful planning and continued action. So how do you map out the route? The answer is to focus on what researchers call subgoals.[53] Think of subgoals as the building blocks of larger objectives: small steps or actions, which, as you complete them, will help move you closer to realizing your big aspirations. And this consistent, incremental approach is what makes subgoals so powerful—they propel you toward your ultimate target much more viably than if you try to attack it all at once.[54]

Breaking big goals down into actionable subgoals is what social scientist Karl Weick recommends, after he analyzed what behavioral science research says is the best way to pursue a significant aspiration.[55] One of the reasons that subgoals are so impactful is because they deliver easy wins, which will energize you to stay motivated while also helping you advance in the direction of a significant aim.

As you pursue subgoals you will also receive the clarity you'll need to judge how you are doing in your progress toward a large goal.[56] This fresh perspective may come in the form of new insights or discovering unforeseen obstacles that will prompt you to adjust your approach to work more effectively.[57] Getting this feedback, researchers affirm, is a critical part of your success because it will allow you to be nimble and quickly adapt if something isn't working.

After Manuel learned about subgoals, he began using them to help him take the action needed to attain his larger objectives. One of his aspirations was to improve his win rates by 20 percent. To accomplish this, he designed the following subgoals and executed them:

- Record at least one of his sales presentations per day and analyze it to identify what he could improve.

- Create three stories (something we'll discuss in chapter 6) that he could leverage when presenting his product to help potential clients perceive more value.

- Spend at least two hours each week practicing how he responds to potential customers' objections.

- Meet weekly with his sales manager to work on improving his ability to obtain incremental commitments from buyers and move the sale along (something I'll show you how to do in chapter 4).

Manuel's subgoals helped him make real progress: Within a mere six months, his win rates grew by an impressive 27 percent. Now that you understand the power of subgoals, let's create some. Write down one of your big goals and then jot down three subgoals you can accomplish in the next month that will move you closer to it.

Goal:

_____

_____

Subgoal #1:

_____

Subgoal #2:

_____

Subgoal #3:

_____

Strategy #6: Use Action Triggers

All of us can relate to committing to a goal, but when it comes time to implement the behaviors that will move us closer to it, we struggle to do so. Indeed, the biggest obstacle you will face when pursuing your goals is taking the action necessary to achieve them. For instance, imagine you desire to become fitter and healthier, so you decide to begin getting up earlier each day to exercise. In the moment you make this decision, that seems easy enough. But the next day, when the alarm clock rings an hour earlier than normal, instead of getting out of bed, you find yourself reaching over and hitting snooze, while promising yourself you'll begin the program tomorrow.

It's an all-too-common problem: In the pursuit of your goals, you will experience times when you won't feel like behaving in ways that move you ahead on the journey, whether it's health or business or sales-related.[58] This is what many salespeople are talking about when they say that the hardest thing about developing new business is taking that first step to reach out to a prospective client. Even though they know it's imperative they cultivate relationships with potential clients, they procrastinate and push it off till later, as we saw in the earlier example with Kim.

Sometimes, you may find it challenging to pursue your goal

because you are bombarded with other tasks that seem equally urgent. Many salespeople have told me they want to improve their sales skills, grow their sales with existing clients, or finally pursue a dream client. But despite their best intentions, each day keeps them busy responding to new or unexpected requests—problems and situations demanding their immediate attention. As a result, they grow discouraged as they fall further and further behind.

I know this feeling well. For years, I wanted to write a book that would finally reveal and explain the scientific and psychological factors that influence and create buying decisions. Yet as I began the daunting task of writing the book that would become *The Science of Selling*, I was struggling. A heavy workload, family responsibilities, and a host of time-consuming activities were making it a challenge to find the time to write. In my frustration, I began to scour scientific journals, looking for a solution. What I found transformed my productivity and enabled me to carve out a few hours each day to write what became a bestselling book. What's more, I realized that the scientific insights I was using could help anyone increase the likelihood of accomplishing a goal—and eventually led me to write this very chapter you're reading.

What I'm about to say may seem almost too good to be true, but it's not: You don't need more willpower; you simply need to change your environment. A wealth of studies have shown that willpower is a finite resource—one that can get you only so far. So the key is not to muster up more willpower but instead to create prompts within your environment that make it easier for you to do what you need to do.[59]

The way you do this is to use action triggers. These preloaded decisions pass control of a goal-producing behavior to your environment.[60] It says that when A occurs, you'll do B. Most importantly, action triggers (which researchers refer to as "implementation intentions") unconsciously *trigger* you to do the behaviors that will help you progress. And because they put your decision to act on autopilot, they significantly reduce the amount of self-discipline (a.k.a. willpower) you need to perform those behaviors.[61] Social scientists call action triggers "instant habits" because of the consistent and predictable outcomes they generate.[62]

In one study analyzing the difference that action triggers and traditional motivation strategies make on exercise frequency, participants were divided into three groups. The control group was given no guidance or resources. The second group read motivational material extolling the benefits of exercise. The third group was instructed to create action triggers prompting them to identify the day, time, and place they would exercise. So instead of trying to find time to exercise in the spur of the moment, the third group had a predefined plan, such as "On my way home from work, when I drive by the gym, I'll go in and exercise for thirty minutes." At the end of the study, the researchers observed, 35 percent of those in the first group and 38 percent of those in the second had exercised. However, the third group, which had created the action triggers, had a dramatic surge in participation, with a rate of 91 percent.[63]

The power of action triggers to spark goal-producing behaviors is well documented,[64] on everything from reducing binge drinking and remembering to take medication to boosting voter turnout, as well as increasing flu vaccination and colonoscopy rates.[65] In fact, one meta-analysis found that action triggers not only had a significant impact on goal attainment but also shielded people from influences that would thwart their ability to achieve their goal.[66] Social psychologist Heidi Grant Halvorson summarized the data of more than two hundred studies on action triggers by stating that those who use them are "300% more likely than others to reach their goals."[67]

You can use action triggers to give you an edge when pursuing any ambition, and especially when you're working to achieve a challenging one. To circle back to my own example, that's what I did when writing my first book. Once I created the action trigger "After I put my kids to bed each night, I will write in my home office for at least three hours," I found that nearly every night I would write and make progress. No longer was I relying on willpower alone. The action trigger ensured that I didn't have to think about when I would write because I knew that the behavior (writing) would happen when an external stimulus (putting my children to bed) was completed.

Now that you understand action triggers, let's look at how to create and implement them.

Create Your Own Action Triggers

Action triggers are not only powerful but also easy and straightforward to construct. Once you learn how to form them, you'll be able to use them to accomplish a variety of goals, from contacting new potential clients to improving your sales presentations and win rates. To develop your own action triggers, you can follow the *What*, *Where*, and *When* method, a three-part framework that will help you establish the essential components of your action trigger by answering the following three questions:

- *What* activity or behavior do you want to accomplish?

- *Where* will you engage in this activity or behavior?

- *When* will you carry out this behavior or activity?

The *What*, *Where*, and *When* method guides you to form highly influential action triggers that will move you closer to your goals each day. You can answer them in any order. If you want to dedicate one hour each day to reaching out to new leads, you could design an action trigger like the one Kim did: "When I arrive at the office [*Where*] at nine o'clock [*When*], I will spend one hour reaching out to new prospective clients [*What*]." If you aspire to improve your negotiation skills, you could create an action trigger along these lines: "Every day on my way home from work [*When*], in my car [*Where*], I will listen to an audiobook on negotiating [*What*]." You can even use action triggers to implement a rebuttal when you're faced with a challenging objection from a potential client, along the lines of "After I ask a buyer to purchase [*Where*], if she says, 'I want to think about it' [*When*], I will respond by answering her objection with the story I've practiced on why our product is superior to others and solves her needs [*What*]."

One final tip: The more specific the action trigger, the better.[68] Generic action triggers ("Make twenty-five calls to potential clients this afternoon") aren't as influential as specific ones ("When I arrive back at my office at two o'clock, I'll begin making calls to potential clients and continue until I've made twenty-five calls").

Let's start leveraging the power of action triggers by creating a few. To begin, define what activity or behavior you want to accomplish, where you will do it, and when you will carry it out.

What:

_____

Where:

_____

When:

_____

Now put all the pieces of the framework together and construct an action trigger. Don't worry about the order you convey each of the parts (*What, Where,* and *When*), just make sure all three are present.

Action trigger:

_____

_____

To ensure you are comfortable developing your own action triggers, let's create one more.

What:

_____

Where:

_____

When:

_____

Action trigger:

_____

_____

Excellent! Start using your action triggers, and you'll find they'll enable you to make rapid progress toward your goals.

Strategy #7: Look to the Future

Imagine you learn that you've won $1,200 in a lottery at your local bank. The bank offers you a choice: Take the winnings now or wait for one year and receive $1,500, a gain of 25 percent. Which would you choose?

If you are like most people, you'd take the $1,200 now rather than wait a full year for an extra $300.

The Nobel Prize—winning behavioral economist Richard Thaler conducted an experiment in which he presented participants with this scenario; however, he asked them how much compensation they would need to receive in order to be willing to wait to claim their winnings for three months, one year, or five years.[69] Participants said they would be willing to wait three months if given $1,500, one year if their money doubled to $2,400, and a whopping $5,000 (an increase of over 300 percent) to wait a full five years.

This is what behavioral economists call "temporal discounting," which is a bias we all have to give more weight to something in the present than to the possibility of receiving something greater in the future. Temporal discounting is the opposite of delayed gratification (which we explored in the last chapter); it causes our brains to focus on what feels good now rather than make a small sacrifice in the short term to hold out for an even better future. It has a lot of sway on human behavior, much of it not good. For example, it has been shown to lead to overeating, unsafe sexual activities, gambling, the abuse of tobacco, drugs, and alcohol, and other risky behaviors.[70] It's also been proved to adversely affect income, education, retirement savings, and overall prosperity.[71] All of this is because temporal discounting makes us minimize our understanding of the negative impact our choices today will have in the future and encourages us to act on our immediate impulses rather than our best interests long term.

As you've probably figured out by now, temporal discounting is a major reason why we don't achieve our goals. It causes us to give much less care and emphasis to our future selves and underestimate the pain our choices will inflict.[72] If you've ever given in to a behavior that you know isn't good for you and will negatively impact you in the future, then you know what I mean. This lack of psychological connection is a problem when it comes to achieving our goals, because to realize an objective, as we discussed in chapter 2, you must sacrifice now to earn the goal later.[73] Yet, as we've already established, with temporal discounting you don't care as much about your future self as you do your current self.

If this situation seems hopeless, it's not. One potent way to reduce the effects of temporal discounting is to engage in what social scientists refer to as *elaboration on potential outcomes* (EPO). EPO triggers you to focus on what you want in the future, which helps you say no to a present temptation that will prevent you from following through on your goals. In one study, participants who struggled with the aim of regularly investing for retirement were prompted to think through the future outcomes they would experience if they contributed to their retirement plan now versus if they did not. These participants invested almost twice as much as those who did not think through the potential outcomes.[74]

As you imagine how actively pursuing your goals will positively impact your future self, you'll find the effects of temporal discounting diminish. In fact, the more vividly you imagine this, the better.[75] For instance, when pursuing a challenging sales goal, picture your life once you achieve it. How will it improve your career, family, and finances? This is what Jon, a salesperson for a shipping provider, did when he began pursuing a dream client. Though it took over three years of hard work to earn the sale, Jon never gave up. Instead, he focused on what landing this large client would mean for his career (a massive promotion) and for his family (the raise would help him and his wife pay the tuition for their twin sons' first year of college, so they wouldn't have to take out extra loans). Jon persevered even when it was challenging because he was clear on the *outcome* he desired.

Take a minute to write down two goals you want to achieve, and then think about how accomplishing them will positively influence your future self.

Goal:

_____

Outcome(s) achieving that goal will produce:

_____

_____

Goal:

_____

Outcome(s) achieving that goal will produce:

_____

_____

Writing out and thinking about your goals and the positive outcomes of reaching them will help you decrease the perceived gap between your current and future self, making it more likely you'll sacrifice now to achieve the goals later.

In this first section of the book, I've shared how to prepare yourself for sales success. In chapter 1, we covered how a growth mindset and an achievement mindset are the foundations that your sales performance is built on. Chapter 2 revealed how fostering the trait of grit will empower you to act in ways that will set you up to reach new levels of success. And in this chapter, I disclosed seven science-backed strategies that will help you achieve your goals. Now let's continue on our journey. In the next section, you'll discover how to sell in ways that are proven to create sales success. We'll begin by exploring how you can align how you sell with how your potential clients form their buying decisions.

PART 2

Creating Sales Success

CHAPTER 4

Help Potential Clients Form Buying Decisions

WHAT IS THE MOST CHALLENGING PART OF SELLING? Believe it or not, the answer is buying. That's what recent research published by the advisory company Gartner discovered. As Gartner vice president Brent Adamson explained, "As hard as it has become to sell in today's world, it has become that much more difficult to buy. The single biggest challenge of selling today is not selling, it is actually our customers' struggle to buy."[1] As a result, "sales organizations shouldn't be solving for a sales problem, they should be solving for a human problem."[2] The research firm CSO Insights agrees. It reports that, in spite of all the recent technological advancements created to help sellers close deals more effectively, the number of salespeople who met their quotas declined by 15 percent in 2018–2019 compared to five years earlier. Plus, more than half of the sales that they forecasted would close didn't.[3] The solution, CSO Insights contends, "is to map selling actions to the buyers' processes, rather than the reverse."[4] In other words, no longer can we try to make potential clients conform to our way of selling. We must instead align how we sell with how our potential clients form their buying decisions.

While it's great that established research and advisory firms are finally recognizing that selling should mirror how customers make purchasing choices, if you've read my previous book, *The Science of Selling*, you'll know they are a bit late to the party. The goal of selling has always been to help prospective clients through their decision-making process and into a positive buying decision. It's the very reason salespeople are needed. For a long time, however, many in the field were taking a seller-centric approach (i.e., a way of selling based on the seller's preferences, not the buyer's) because the marketplace wasn't as competitive, and buyers weren't as well informed. With fewer product or service options available to buyers, it was harder for them to be choosy, and information about products, services, and competitors was not easily accessible. However, in today's hypercompetitive business climate—with an excess of nearly identical products and services to meet every need, and vast amounts of information just a click away—the power has shifted back to buyers, and they are rightfully demanding more from their sellers. This is why you can no longer afford to embrace the old practices or even sell the way you did a few years ago. The marketplace keeps evolving, and so must your strategies if you want to stay ahead of the competition.

Serve Buyers Through *How* You Sell

The fact that your potential clients are struggling to make the right purchasing decisions presents an opportunity for you to serve them in a uniquely meaningful way. They need sellers who can help them navigate the buying process and put their needs at the forefront. So one of the primary ways you can differentiate yourself is through *how* you sell, not just what you're selling. Contrary to traditional sales wisdom, people don't choose between competing products and services solely based on which will serve their needs best; they choose based on their *perceptions* of those products and services. And their choices are heavily influenced—indeed, often determined—by the salesperson. In fact, when buyers reject a product or service (as in, the sale is lost), it's usually not because of a concern they have about the product or service itself but rather because of how the salesperson presented it to them. In other words, how you convey your product or service will determine how buyers will perceive its value and respond to it.

This highlights an important principle of selling supported by thousands of scientific studies: Buying, and therefore selling, is not a purely logical exercise but a psychological one.[5] And what science has also confirmed is that success in selling is predictable: The closer you align your selling methods to how the human brain forms a buying decision, the more successful you will be at closing each deal. (The opposite applies as well: The further your strategies diverge from the way our brains make choices, the less effective you will be at guiding buyers to a yes.) This explains why some salespeople can sell more of the same product or service to nearly identical customers or clients than their colleagues on the same team. The difference isn't what they're selling, but *how*.

I have a large client in the ultracompetitive electronics industry that sells products identical to their competitors'. But they consistently outperform their competition in winning new business and retaining their existing clients year after year, all while charging higher prices than everyone else. How do they accomplish this? During the sales process, they focus on helping their prospective and returning clients make comfortable, confident buying choices by engaging them in the way their brains naturally perceive value. Their approach is such a measurable differentiator and so appreciated by clients that it gives them a significant competitive advantage.

In this chapter, I will show you how to align how you sell with how people buy in order to increase the number of sales you successfully close and improve your relationships with your customers. Each of the science-backed principles I share will give you a substantial edge over your competition and, more importantly, equip you to help your potential clients feel good about their choices.

Get Commitments to the Six Whys®

As we've seen, the key to success is to sell the way the brain buys. When I began studying the scientific research around how buying decisions occur, I was struck by the fact that small commitments consistently lead to larger ones. Studies have shown over and over that when we're faced with an important choice, the small commitments we make early on in one direction or the other predispose our brains to make larger commitments in that same direction later.[6] These small commitments are the essential reference points our brains use to come to their ultimate decision.[7] One study of cigarette smokers illustrates this concept well. Certain participants were first asked for the small commitment of answering a few questions about their smoking habits in order to qualify for the study. Once they agreed to that, the researchers informed them that to participate, they would also be required to not smoke for eighteen hours. Remarkably, those who had made that initial small commitment to answer questions were over 500 percent more likely to agree to participate than the control group, which consisted of smokers who were only informed that the study would require them to not smoke for eighteen hours.[8] As this study shows, the most effective way to guide people into a large commitment (like a buying decision) is to first ask them to make smaller agreements that are aligned with and inspire the larger one.

Exactly what commitments make possible the choice to purchase? I call them the Six Whys®. They are six questions that represent the mental steps our brains go through when forming buying decisions. As buyers make strong commitments to each of the Six Whys®, they go through a natural progression of consent and into the decision to purchase. Your ability to answer and gain their commitment to the Six Whys® will determine how successful you will be. That's right, if you (or any salesperson, for that matter) have a qualified buyer with the financial means and authority to make a purchase, and you can get these buyers to commit to all Six Whys®, the sale will almost always close. If they do not commit to each of the Six Whys®, their decision process breaks down, and they will be unable to make a positive buying decision, so the sale *cannot* occur. This is why the Six Whys® are the building blocks of the sale, and attending to them gives you a significant competitive advantage.

In *The Science of Selling*, I devote an entire chapter to explaining the Six Whys® and the six-year research process I used to develop my science-backed methodology based on them. Here, I'll briefly review the Whys and then share new material and practical exercises for strategically applying them. I will also help you identify which commitments you need to focus on regardless of where you are in the sales process and reveal how to use every won or lost sale as a stepping-stone to greater success in the future.

Before we get into them, a quick note to keep in mind: The brain's decision-making process isn't linear. Each Why can come up at various points during the selling process. In fact, your potential clients may enter initial conversations having already committed to one or more of the Whys. If that's the case, confirm those previous commitments and then focus on answering and obtaining commitments to the rest of the Whys.

Why #1: Why Change?

Your biggest challenge will likely be overcoming a "status quo bias." This bias is the strong tendency to remain in one's current situation because it is familiar, even if it is problematic.[9] It's what makes change so daunting for most people.

This is the foundational Why, and the one that you'll need to concentrate on early in the process, or the sale will likely die. Think about it: Why would prospective clients spend time with you talking about a change they don't care about making? They wouldn't. So how do you speak to and gain their commitment to Why Change? First, focus on addressing the specific problem or pain point they have and how your product or service will solve that. Then make a strong case for why doing nothing about it (in other words, sticking with the status quo) is much riskier for them than moving forward with a positive change.

Why #2: Why Now?

You have addressed why your potential clients should make a change, but why should they do it now? Why can't they wait a week, a month, a year, or longer? This Why, like Why #1, is crucial and challenging to address because our brains naturally procrastinate. Even if you make a compelling case for change, if you don't speak to why that change needs to happen *now*, your prospective clients will likely drag their feet.

The most effective way to create a convincing case for Why Now? is to help potential clients realize how much pain their problem (which your product or service will solve) is causing them already and how badly it will continue to cost them if they don't make a change *fast*. Remember, pain creates urgency. If there is no pain, there's no rush to resolve it—and ultimately, no reason, in their eyes, to say yes to you.

Why #3: Why Your Industry Solution?

This Why is often the sneakiest because many salespeople don't think about addressing it until it's too late. First ask yourself, Can your potential client create an effective and cost-efficient solution on their own or go outside your whole industry to meet their needs? If so, this is a Why to focus on proactively, as you can safely assume your buyers are considering those alternatives.

Answering Why Your Industry Solution? requires you to expand your thinking regarding whom you view as your competitor. I define a competitor as anything or anyone that can take business away from you. So this includes not only direct competitors (companies like yours) within your industry but also nontraditional competitors outside your field, your client's internal resources and capabilities, and even their status quo bias. (After all, if you can't convince them that making a change is far better than sticking with their current situation, they will always resort to maintaining the status quo.)

To answer this Why, you need to show potential clients the

problems that may arise if they attempt to choose a solution outside your industry, as well as the results your industry provides that they cannot duplicate on their own. One of my clients frequently finds that their buyers consider creating their own solution rather than buying from my client or a direct competitor. By clearly demonstrating why the buyers' internal solutions don't adequately address their needs and will actually cost them more in the long run, my client is able to obtain a strong commitment to Why Your Industry Solution? and continually secure their business.

Why #4: Why You and Your Company?

With so many competing options, why should buyers choose to do business with you and your company instead of with other similar providers? Obtaining a strong commitment to this Why is vital because it makes getting commitments to Why #3 (Why Your Industry Solution?) and Why #5 (Why Your Product or Service?) that much easier. When buyers commit to you and your company, they are both less likely to consider going outside your industry for a solution (or creating one internally) and much more receptive to learning about your product or service.

Often salespeople attempt to answer this Why by talking about how great their company is and the accolades it has collected over the years. Let me be blunt: Your potential clients don't care about your company, the awards it's received, or how wonderful its employees are. What they *do* care about is how you and your company can help them in ways that matter deeply to them.

The reality today is that there are so many seemingly identical companies in the marketplace that buyers confess they can't tell them apart. So the way to distinguish yourself is to *sell* differently. As I've noted, research shows that buyers will judge both you and the company you represent by how you interact with them. There are so many bad sales practices being used out there that by simply leveraging the strategies in this book, you will set yourself apart in meaningful ways. When it comes down to it, the biggest reason why prospective clients choose to buy from your company is because of *you*.

Why #5: Why Your Product or Service?

Even if your prospective clients determine that they can't make a solution themselves and they want to do business with you, you still must answer why the specific product or service you are selling is right for them. How will it meet their needs better than your direct competitors' products or services, or even related services offered by other departments within your company? There are numerous science-backed strategies you can deploy to help clients see the unique value your product or service provides. I'll share many of these throughout this chapter and book, but for now, here's a look at one proven way to set yourself apart.

Imagine sitting through two presentations on similar products delivered by two salespeople from the same company. The first salesperson launches into a generic presentation about the strengths of his products. The other salesperson first asks about your situation, your priorities, and the problems you want to solve. She then customizes her presentation to connect her products to what matters most to you and shows exactly how they will address each of your needs and pain points. It's not a stretch to imagine that, as a buyer, you'd be more likely to purchase from the second salesperson over the first. Even though she may have shared much of the same information as her colleague did, because she tailored it to you, it helped you perceive more value in her products.

When you clearly communicate how your product or service will positively affect your buyers and address their needs, you make it easy for them to recognize the high value in what you're offering.[10] This is what elite salespeople do. They tailor their presentation to their buyers, and those buyers love them for it.

Why #6: Why Spend the Money?

The final Why addresses the reasons your potential clients should invest in your product or service. In today's selling climate, you'll often need to show your buyers why purchasing from you is in their best interest, versus spending their money on something else. Imagine that a potential client informs you they may wait to purchase your product and instead buy a software upgrade they think they may need. To earn the sale, you must prove to them why investing now is a wiser business choice than the software upgrade.

To persuasively answer this Why, you have to convey clearly what your potential clients may lose by not moving forward—as well as what they stand to gain if they do. This will help them think through and understand why they should commit to investing in your product or service.

Now that we've reviewed each of the Six Whys®, here are three ways you can leverage them.

1. Align Your Sales Process with the Six Whys®

As I noted earlier, a sales process that mirrors the brain's decision-making process will always outperform one that doesn't. And it's here that the Six Whys® can help: You can use this framework to accurately evaluate the effectiveness of how you sell and how you can improve. I have trained thousands of salespeople from companies of all shapes and sizes—from small businesses to Fortune 500 organizations—to actively use the Six Whys®. They consistently report two positive outcomes:

- **The buying process speeds up.** By helping prospective clients through the mental steps of the choice to purchase, you naturally help them make that decision faster. This is a major benefit of the Six Whys®; it significantly reduces what I call "sales time," which states that the more time it takes for the sale to occur, the lower the probability it will happen. When the buying process drags out longer than needed, challenges crop up: Buyer turnover and budget cuts occur, priorities shift, new problems and/or competitors emerge, etc. Salespeople who have sold in long sales cycles know this to be true. Consider one of my clients whose average sales cycle was nine months. By restructuring their selling process around the Six Whys®, they naturally reduced the friction between their selling and their buyers' purchasing processes, which cut down the average time it took to close each deal by almost six weeks. Not only did their efficiency increase, but so did their sales—by an impressive 32 percent—because they improved buyer engagement and satisfaction.

- **Sales increase overall.** I've worked with salespeople around the world who have used the Six Whys® to significantly boost their sales. For example, after redesigning its entire process around the Six Whys®, one medium-sized company with around two hundred salespeople grew its sales by 27 percent the next year. Another smaller company with only six salespeople nearly tripled its sales. And within ten months of training its salespeople to focus on the Six Whys®, a Fortune 500 company's sales rose by 16 percent. These organizations reported receiving fewer objections as well as having deeper buyer interactions and more success outselling their competitors.

They achieved these results by leveraging the science, which gave them an advantage over their competitors who didn't. And you can too. To begin the process of aligning how you sell with the Six Whys®, take a moment to complete the following exercise. Think through each of the Six Whys® and assess how confident or unsure you feel about your ability to address each during the sales process.

Note: You may identify several you could improve at. For now, focus only on the one you believe you are the *least* effective at and what you can do to address it. Once you've made improvements on that Why, you can begin to tackle any others you would also like to become better at.

THE SIX WHYS®

Why Change?	*Why Now?*
Why Your Industry Solution?	*Why You and Your Company?*
Why Your Product or Service?	*Why Spend the Money?*

Which of the Six Whys® are you least effective at answering?

_____

What are three things you will do to strengthen your sales process to better address that Why?

1. _____

2. _____

3. _____

2. Evaluate Where You Are and How to Move the Sale Forward

As noted earlier, each sale will involve commitments to the Six Whys®. In today's complex selling environment, it will also usually involve numerous decision-makers (those who have the authority to say yes or no) and influencers (those who hold sway over the decision-makers' choices). In addition, the process potential clients go through when evaluating whether to purchase often involves internal discussions among everyone (influencers and decision-makers) in the buying group. As a result, the process can stretch out over many interactions.

So how do you know what to focus on in each of these interactions? For example, if you have had an initial discussion with a potential client and are about to go into your second meeting with them, what should you share? This is another instance where you can utilize the Six Whys® to set you and your buyers up for success.

As you think through what to concentrate on in your next interaction, use the framework of the Six Whys® to identify which commitments you've already received and what you still need to address. For instance, let's say you are about to meet with a potential client for the third time. In the previous two meetings, you've gotten their commitment to three of the Whys (Why Change? Why Now? Why Spend the Money?). Now you should assess how you can best answer and obtain a commitment to the remaining Whys (Why Your Industry Solution? Why You and Your Company? Why Your Product or Service?).

Let's apply the Six Whys® to one of your potential clients to practice how you can determine where you are in the sales process and what you should do next.

Name of Potential Client:

_____

Have you received commitments to any of the Six Whys®? If so, which ones:

_____

Of the remaining Six Whys®, what are some potential challenges you may face from your prospective client, and how will you address each of those?

_____

_____

What is your plan for obtaining commitments to the remaining Six Whys®?

_____

_____

As you strategize how to answer and gain commitments to each of the Six Whys®, don't forget your secret weapon: your colleagues and team members. In my years of experience training salespeople and corporations to use this proven methodology, I've noticed one of the biggest benefits of the Six Whys® is that when sales teams embrace them, they get a common language to collaborate around. They begin asking one another questions like "How do you address Why Change?" Or "How do you obtain a commitment to Why You and Your Company?" This fosters an atmosphere of creative innovation that helps everyone grow, improve quickly, and experience more success.

3. Conduct a Win-Loss Analysis of Every Sale

Here is a nonnegotiable rule I adhere to and teach to my clients: Whether you win or lose a sale, always know why. And the best way to understand why you got the result you did and how to improve in the future is by conducting a win-loss analysis using the Six Whys®. When you center your win-loss analysis on the Six Whys®, you'll find they are a powerful blueprint for accurately assessing why you won or lost a sale and revealing exactly what you need to improve to increase your win rates.

The main reason to conduct win-loss analyses with the Six

Whys®: it will make you "antifragile," a term that was popularized by Nassim Nicholas Taleb in his bestselling book *Antifragile: Things That Gain from Disorder*. Taleb describes antifragility as a characteristic that allows something (or someone) not only to bounce back after experiencing a stress or an adversity but to *grow stronger* in the process.[11] Antifragility goes "beyond resilience or robustness," according to Taleb. "The resilient resists shocks and stays the same; the antifragile gets better."[12] One example of antifragility is building your muscle strength through exercising. When you work out, your muscle fibers become damaged from the stress, and your body repairs itself. Done repeatedly, this process causes your muscles to grow in size and strength because they are antifragile. If your muscles were fragile, per Taleb's definition, a bicep workout would permanently damage your arms. If they were merely robust or resilient, your biceps would recover to only their pre-workout level of strength. Instead, they grow stronger than they were from the workouts because they are antifragile.

In a similar way, you can make your sales "muscles" antifragile by conducting win-loss analyses using the Six Whys®. Here's how: For a lost sale, ask yourself which of the Six Whys® you obtained a commitment to and which you didn't. That lack of commitment reveals where and why you didn't earn the sale. After conducting win-loss analyses, most salespeople see a pattern that the majority of their sales are lost because they didn't receive a commitment to the same one or two Whys. Once you identify which Whys you aren't getting strong commitments to, focus on strengthening the parts of your sales process in which you address those. (The exercises in the previous two strategies can help you do this.) Taking the time to understand why you lost the sale and identify what you can do better will help you bounce back and improve your skills and tactics, increasing your odds of future success.

For each sale you win, it's also wise to perform a win-loss analysis. As sales expert and senior lecturer of business administration at Harvard Business School Frank Cespedes explains, "Wins are as important as losses: they provide information about your strengths, competitor weaknesses, buying behavior, and elements of the selling firm's business model or positioning pitch—all factors that can be used to measure and increase the odds of success."[13] Ask yourself, What were the main reasons you won that sale? What did you do particularly well? Which part(s) of your sales process really resonated with the client? Recognizing your strengths will often lead to insights into how you can make them even more persuasive. Also, even though you won the sale, no presentation is ever perfect. That's why I always recommend identifying at least two things you could have done that would have improved your performance. Otherwise, you are missing an opportunity to stay antifragile, which will help you keep winning sales.

A major bonus benefit of conducting a win-loss analysis after every won or lost sale is that it will help you avoid or get out of a slump. In fact, over time, this practice can make you immune to such slumps. Before you can fall into one, you'll already be working to improve on whatever might have caused one. You'll also be staying attuned to what matters most to your clients, so you won't accidentally make changes to your process that would stop serving their needs and sabotage your success (something I see happen when salespeople experience a little success and get overconfident).

I hope I've convinced you that using the Six Whys® when you sell is mission critical. Let's now turn our attention to another key part of effective selling: presenting high levels of value to your buyers.

To Convey More Value to Buyers, Ask the Right Questions

Helping buyers perceive the value that your company, product, or service offers them is one of the most significant things you can do to ensure a positive buying decision. In fact, your ability to convey meaningful value is what keeps potential clients engaged and motivated throughout the process and thus more likely to say yes.

If you ask salespeople whether they are effectively communicating the value they will deliver to their buyers, most will say that they are. Yet 80 percent of buyers state that the meetings they have with salespeople provide no value to them and waste their time.[14] Sales leaders agree. In a recent survey asking them what their top priority was for their salespeople, their number one response was to improve their salespeople's ability to communicate value.[15]

Why is there such a disconnect between how buyers and sales leaders perceive salespeople and how sellers perceive themselves? It's due to a powerful bias known as the false consensus effect, which is our natural tendency to overestimate the extent to which others agree with our point of view or what we're saying.[16] The false consensus effect particularly misleads salespeople as they are presenting the central value proposition of their product to obtain a client's buy-in, which the success of the sale hinges on. In their eagerness to close the deal, they frequently misinterpret a buyer's nod, silence, or ambiguous statement, like "That makes sense," as a signal that the buyer understands and agrees with the value they're sharing. In fact, one of the main reasons why buyers *don't* assign value to what they're being presented with isn't because the salesperson didn't convey the value, but because buyers didn't recognize it.

As I share how to present the value you can provide in ways

that will help buyers recognize and appreciate it, here are two principles to keep in mind.

1. **The brain's assessment of value is flexible and easily influenced by a variety of factors.** A research study by Richard Thaler demonstrates this brilliantly. Thaler first asked participants to imagine relaxing at the beach on a hot summer day. Then he told them to imagine becoming thirsty and asked how much they would be willing to pay to get a cold beer at an upscale hotel and at a small, run-down grocery store, each by the beach. Participants were willing to pay 76 percent more for the same beer from the ritzy hotel than from the grocery store simply based on the description of each.[17] What this study and others confirm is that the way something is conveyed influences the amount of value we perceive in it and how much we are willing to pay for it.

2. **The key to ensuring that potential clients understand the value your company/product/service will provide is to make it easy for their brains to recognize it.** The more cognitively demanding it is for buyers to perceive value, the less likely it is they will. This is why your job is to communicate that value in ways that are clear, concise, and easily understood. As Neil Rackham and John DeVincentis explain in their book *Rethinking the Sales Force*, buyers "increasingly place value on how the product is sold to them rather than on the product itself. The sales process itself plays an increasing role in creating customer value."[18] As I said earlier, it's not what you're selling but how you're selling it that makes all the difference.

You can present this value in a way that potential clients can easily grasp by asking them questions that prompt them to assess it. In chapter 5 of *The Science of Selling*, I explain a layered model with three levels of questions to get to the core of buyers' needs and concerns. The questions I'll discuss in the rest of this chapter are "second-level assessment" questions, which actively engage potential clients in thinking through and voicing their responses to the information you've shared. This neutralizes the false consensus effect by ensuring that you never assume your buyers understand or agree with an important value proposition you've shared unless they confirm it verbally.

Here's a look at a few examples of assessment questions that prompt buyers to contemplate and share their thoughts on a value proposition you have presented:

- As you think about what we've discussed, what do you believe would be the biggest benefits you would receive from our service?

- If your employees went through our virtual training, how do you think it would help improve their efficiency?

- Would you ever consider investing in a product that did not include this feature?

- Does what I've shared address your concerns about whether we are the right company to partner with on this project?

- Does our five-step installation process give you the peace of mind that if there are any issues, we can catch them early and correct them right away?

Researchers have identified that when a credible presenter delivering a persuasive message—such as at a sales presentation—asks these types of questions, people are more convinced by what's been presented.[19] That's because these questions prompt people to think about the value behind the message; and because they are contemplating it, they are naturally more persuaded by it. In the same way, asking assessment questions, which inspire buyers to think about and affirm a statement of value essential to the sale, will greatly improve the likelihood they'll choose to do business with you.

Another unexpected benefit of these questions is that people enjoy answering them. In a study published in the prestigious *Proceedings of the National Academy of Sciences*, researchers asked participants to choose between receiving a small monetary reward or answering an assessment question and not receiving any financial compensation for doing so. Amazingly, a large number chose to forgo the money to answer the question.[20] Their findings concluded that participants were willing to give up the money because answering the question, which required them to share their opinions, was more intrinsically rewarding.

As a general rule, you should pose these kinds of inquiries anytime you present a value that a commitment to one or more of the Six Whys® is based on. This is why these assessment questions are so vital; they allow you to gauge accurately whether your potential clients agree with and buy into the value propositions the sale is built on. If buyers won't recognize and affirm the value your company, product, or service would provide them, then they aren't going to commit to Why #4 (Why You and Your Company?) or Why #5 (Why Your Product or Service?). And if they won't commit to who you are and what you're selling, then they probably aren't going to purchase from you, no matter how persuasive you are.

Regardless of how your potential clients respond to your assessment question, you are always better off having asked it. If they endorse the value you've conveyed, then you can move confidently to the next step in the process. If they don't agree with it, you now know their concern and can immediately address it to get the sale back on track.

One final tip on posing assessment questions: Make sure you frame them positively so that the process of answering helps buyers think through and recognize the value you are presenting, and then respond by agreeing with it. For instance, after explaining the value of your product, you wouldn't want to ask something like "Do you have any concerns about the product I've shared?" That prompts buyers to think negatively about your product and focus their attention on why it may not be right for them. It could even cause them to find or invent a reason not to purchase, even if your product is exactly what they're looking for. Instead, you want to ask questions like "Of the features I've shared, which do you think would have the biggest positive impact on your business?" or "If you had this product, what are some of the benefits you'd experience from it?" See the difference? Always make sure you frame your questions to guide your buyers to consider what you've presented and offer their perspectives on it in a way that moves the sale forward.

I can't emphasize enough the power of these questions and their ability to help you earn more sales. Here's an example from my own experience: I was presenting to a CEO of a potential client I'd been pursuing for a while. I had already obtained buy-in from everyone involved in the buying decision but the CEO, who had recently joined the company and had the power to kill the deal. From the start of the meeting, he was standoffish. He rebuffed my attempts at building rapport, wouldn't make eye contact, and replied to my questions in a terse manner. As I presented the proposed solution and showed how it would provide high levels of value to his organization, he remained expressionless. However, things changed after I asked him the following assessment question: "If you were to adopt this training solution, how do you think it would benefit your company?" He was silent for a moment as he pondered it. Then, to the amazement of everyone in the room, he proceeded to state the many ways our solution could positively impact his organization. And—here's the exciting part—the more he shared his thoughts, the more engaged he became. In fact, by the end of his response, his entire demeanor had changed. He was looking directly at me, and he did something he hadn't done before—he smiled. For the rest of the meeting he was jovial, focused, and actively participating. A few short weeks later, the sale closed.

Did that one assessment question change the trajectory of that meeting and likewise the sale? You bet. And the reason that question had such influence was because it prompted this decision-maker to take a moment to think through the value I had communicated and then publicly share how *he* believed my solution would help his company. Stating his thoughts also encouraged him to begin to take deeper ownership of both the problem his company faced and the solution I was offering.

I'm not alone. Many salespeople have reported that when they begin using questions to help potential clients mentally digest the value they could deliver, sales skyrocket. Developing the skill of using assessment questions takes practice, but once mastered, it will significantly improve your effectiveness. To get you started, I'll share some examples of how these questions can be applied in real sales situations, and then I'll take you through a few exercises to practice using them.

Example #1

A salesperson is going to use assessment questions to help the buyer think through the value her product offers.

> **SALESPERSON:** Now that you understand our reporting, does it make sense why so many companies are choosing to invest in our software because of the in-depth reporting it provides across all media platforms?

> **BUYER:** Sure. It certainly provides a lot of clarity and seems useful for evaluating what's working and what isn't.

> **SALESPERSON:** I hear that from a lot of our clients. May I ask, now that you've seen the advances we've made in making reporting more "useful for evaluating what's working and what isn't" and how it "provides a lot of clarity," is it a functionality you'd want to have as part of any software you invest in?

> **BUYER:** Yes, I really think we need this level of reporting. It's something we'll definitely want.

Example #2

A salesperson has presented an overview of his company and wants to use assessment questions to inspire the prospective client to commit to Why #4 (Why You and Your Company?).

> **SALESPERSON:** One of the main things you shared on our last call was how frustrated you are with your current pro-

vider's lack of support. You also wanted to make sure that you'll be happy with the level of support your new provider offers so you don't need to migrate to another system ever again. As we've discussed, we meet all your service requirements, we don't lock you into long contracts like many providers do but instead earn your business with our great customer support each month, and we have a high client-retention rate. Does that give you the peace of mind that if you chose to work with our company, you would not have to migrate to another provider again?

BUYER: Yes, I like what I've heard so far about your company. It all sounds great.

SALESPERSON: Based on what you know about us, are we the company you'd feel comfortable having as your provider?

BUYER: Definitely. Your company is much better than my current provider.

Example #3

A salesperson is presenting her solution and asks for buy-in from the buyer but gets a noncommittal response. She'll need to use some assessment questions to get the sale back on track.

SALESPERSON: As I've explained, our platform is used by many of the top companies in the world to help them manage their performance across social media. Based on what we've discussed, does what we offer meet what you said you were looking for in a platform?

BUYER: Maybe. It sounds interesting, something for me to think about.

SALESPERSON: It seems like you are interested in our platform. May I ask, if you did have it, what do you think would be the biggest advantages your company would experience?

BUYER: Well . . . I like the visibility it provides and how it would give us a consistent way to measure performance across all social media channels.

SALESPERSON: That makes sense. Because of the visibility our platform provides and how it would allow you "a consistent way to measure performance across all social media channels," do you feel it is the right solution for you?

BUYER: Yes, when you put it like that, it does seem to provide everything we need.

Now that you've witnessed the power of assessment questions, let's practice using them. In the following examples, you'll be introduced to a scenario and given two options of possible assessment questions to ask. Choose the one you believe is the best. (You'll find the answers to both situations beginning at the bottom of the next page, but try to decide on your own first without looking.)

You've just presented your product and the value it would provide to a potential client. Which of the following is the best question to ask?

Option 1: Based on what I've shared, do you have any concerns about what your experience would be with our product?

Option 2: Based on what I've shared, what do you think would be the biggest benefits you would experience from our product?

Your potential client has experienced problems in the past with their current equipment provider's service. When a machine breaks down, the provider will often take a week or more to fix it, which is very costly to the client. You've disclosed that your technicians respond to service issues quickly, often within forty-eight hours. Which of the following is the best question to ask?

Option 1: Does the fact that we are often able to fix machine breakdowns within forty-eight hours give you the peace of mind that if you do experience a problem with a machine, you'll receive a quick resolution?

Option 2: Does the fact that your current provider often takes a week or more to fix a machine breakdown help you see why we are the better choice and should be your provider?

Example #1 answer: Option 2 is the better choice. It inspires your potential client to think through and share what they believe will be the biggest benefits they'll experience from your product. Option 1, on the other hand, is a poor choice because it asks them to think of any concerns they might have about your product, which discourages them from wanting to commit to it.

Example #2 answer: Option 1 is the best choice. It reminds them of the fact that you'll provide service within forty-eight hours, helps them digest that information and the potential benefits of that service, and projects how it would make them feel if they were your client. Option 2 is weaker because it attacks their current provider and then clumsily asks the potential client to affirm that you are the better choice, without reminding them of why this is the case.

Now it's your turn. Take a moment to identify two ways your company, product, or service provides meaningful value to your clients. Then create a question you can begin asking prospective clients after you present that value to help them think through and respond to what you've shared.

Value your company, product, or service offers:

_____

Question to obtain client buy-in to the value:

_____

Value your company, product, or service offers:

_____

Question to obtain client buy-in to the value:

_____

Asking these assessment questions immediately after you present buyers with an important value proposition will ensure that you know whether they understand and agree with what you've shared. In addition, the questions will improve your ability to help buyers perceive and appreciate the value you bring to the table, since you'll be engaging them in the way their brains are wired to respond.

We've covered two key science-based selling principles in this chapter: implementing the Six Whys® and asking the right assessment questions to ensure that your buyers recognize and respond to the value you've presented. As you begin applying these, you will be mirroring the way your clients' brains form buying decisions, which will naturally boost your effectiveness and results. That said, there will no doubt be times when your buyers are stuck in a point of view that's hindering them from moving forward. In the next chapter, I'll share a revolutionary reframing process that will help you guide your buyers into new, mutually beneficial perspectives that will advance the sale.

CHAPTER 5

How to Reframe Any Sales Situation

AS WE LEARNED IN THE LAST CHAPTER, THE WAY SOME-thing is presented heavily affects our impression of it and the decisions we make about it. This applies to every aspect of our lives. Behavioral science research has discovered that when consumers tasted ground beef labeled "75% lean," they rated it as less greasy and better tasting than when it was described as "25% fat."[1] Another experiment, published in the *New England Journal of Medicine*, examined how physicians decide on treatments for a life-threatening disease and found the same thing: When one treatment was presented as having a 90 percent survival rate, 84 percent of the doctors chose it.[2] However, when that same treatment was said to have a 10 percent mortality rate, only 50 percent chose it.

Business decisions are not immune to this framing effect. In research published in the *Journal of Applied Psychology*, executives gave higher performance evaluations to a project team described as having a 60 percent success rate than when the same team was portrayed as experiencing a failure rate of 40 percent.[3] In another study, researchers instructed buyers to imagine their companies were going through a merger, and during that process, they had to choose between two service providers.[4] The catch was that, because of the merger, they didn't know how much they would need to purchase and, as a result, couldn't identify which supplier had the best price. The first provider offered fixed pricing regardless of how much or little was purchased. The second offered a riskier, tiered pricing model, which could benefit the buyers if they purchased a large amount, but would cost them more if it turned out they needed to purchase only a small amount. When researchers presented the choice in a way that emphasized not missing out on savings, 79 percent of buyers chose the risky provider with the tiered pricing. When they presented it in a context emphasizing certainty and stability, 56 percent of buyers chose the provider with the fixed price.

The way you frame an idea, a behavior, or a situation during the sales process shapes whether your potential clients will choose to embrace it or not. Consider the following situation from a research study conducted by the acclaimed cognitive psychologists Amos Tversky and Daniel Kahneman:[5]

You have decided to see a play where admission is ten dollars per ticket. As you stand in line to purchase a ticket, you discover that you have lost a ten-dollar bill. Would you still buy a ticket and see the play? Yes or no?

If you're like 88 percent of people, you probably decided you would purchase the ticket without a second thought. Now read the slightly modified situation below:

You had paid ten dollars for a ticket to a play. However, as you arrive at the theater, you realize that you have lost your ticket.

Will you purchase another ticket so you can see the play? Yes or no?

Was this decision more challenging for you to answer yes to? It was for most who encountered it. In fact, presented with this situation, 54 percent of people say they would *not* purchase the ticket. Yet, if you think about the two scenarios, mathematically they are the same (in both cases, you have lost $10), and therefore, logically, they should elicit the same response from you. Again, it's all about the framing. Spending $10 to replace a ticket we already bought and lost causes our brains to perceive the second ticket as costing $20. In contrast, the loss of the $10 bill in the first situation wasn't linked with the ticket purchase and is therefore perceived as a separate loss, even though purchasing the ticket—as most people said they would—still puts you out the same $20 amount. As Kahneman explains, "Unless there is an obvious reason to do otherwise, most of us passively accept decision problems as they are framed and therefore rarely have an opportunity to discover the extent to which our preferences are *frame-bound* rather than *reality-bound.*"[6]

This likewise applies to sales situations: Each person approaches the sale from a certain point of view or framework. So it's important to realize that potential clients are not responding objectively based on the information you've given them—even if they may think they are. Instead, they are reacting to the point of view they came in with, which may cause them to get stuck in a frame of mind that's damaging to the sale. It's therefore crucial to acknowledge and address their viewpoint to keep the sale alive. If you are not able to nudge them out of this frame, they will reject what you are presenting—not because it wouldn't benefit them, but because it doesn't align with how they perceive it.

Consider how you would approach the following three situations in which the buyer is caught in a negative frame:

- You have done research and identified that the potential client is in desperate need of your product. You reach out to share how you can help them in meaningful ways, but before you are even able to disclose how you can provide value, they tell you, "We are not interested." How can you respond in a way that gets the sale back on track?

- You are selling to a prospective client who is considering leaving their current provider. However, they've set a budget that is far too low to purchase a solution that will meet their needs. How can you address the situation in a way that helps them realize their budget will prevent them from getting the results they want—regardless of whether they go with your services or another's—without giving the impression you're trying to push them to spend more than they want to?

- You are about to close a sale and your potential client says, "We need to think about it. We aren't sure that we should move forward now." How can you address their concern and show them that moving forward now, instead of waiting, is indeed in their best interest?

In each of these situations, success hinges on your ability to help buyers embrace a new way of looking at their circumstances. To do this, you'll need to engage in what is known as *reframing*, which is the process of guiding buyers from their current perspective into a new, more beneficial one that will inspire a different response. Reframing is an incredibly powerful skill you'll need to develop to become a top performer.

How to Reframe

Years ago, after I realized the importance of reframing, I began looking for ways to become skilled at it. What I discovered was that most salespeople who try to reframe do so by memorizing phrases they've heard other salespeople use to respond to a specific situation. Yet it's rare that words designed for one scenario will work equally well for a range of others, so it wasn't surprising to see that this strategy yielded hit-or-miss results. I knew that to be truly successful at selling, I needed to be professionally nimble and able to address and reframe each unique situation I encountered. After scouring sales literature and finding little to help me learn how to reframe effectively, I began studying what the science had to say.[7]

Everyone from behavioral scientists and Nobel Prize–winning researchers to psychologists and psychotherapists has conducted experiments proving that reframing can shift people's perspectives and developed techniques to do this in a positive way.[8] The scientific research revealed three key concepts that helped me figure out a process for reframing during the sale. The first is that, even though your potential clients have a certain point of view, you can often nudge them free from their frame into a more productive one by offering a new perspective on it. For instance, take a look below at the picture of a rabbit.[9]

When people view this image, they will initially see either a rabbit or a duck. Look again. Notice the duck now? When you first glanced at it, you were looking for a rabbit because that is how I framed what you were going to see. After I reframed the image by informing you it could also be interpreted as a duck, you saw the duck. Now you probably see both easily. The point is, the frame determined what you initially perceived, and your perception changed once I gave you a nudge. That's what reframing does in sales as well: gives potential clients a new way of looking at and responding to something.

The second concept I uncovered is that "reframes" have a compounding effect. So in order to effectively move buyers out of their current point of view, you'll usually need to share at least two new frames back-to-back that emphasize the fresh perspective. When you use two related frames in a row, it amplifies the influence of each and makes the overall reframing process more impactful. To demonstrate an example of this, read in consecutive order the following four frames about a house that is for sale.

- Frame #1: The outside of the house is painted an odd color brown.

- Frame #2: The house is 3,600 square feet and has many luxurious features.

- Frame #3: The house is located in a very desirable neighborhood and likely won't be on the market long, as numerous potential buyers have already expressed an interest in making an offer for it.

- Frame #4: The house is in move-in-ready condition, and because of a job transfer, the current owners have priced it 17 percent below market value.

Did you notice how each frame alters how you perceive the house? When the first frame introduces the house, it focuses your mind on the unsightly brown exterior color, which makes it seem unattractive. However, as each new frame redirects your attention toward the house's positive features, your overall assessment changes and it becomes more and more desirable. This exercise demonstrates the compounding effect that sharing similar frames in sequence can have on our perception of something. With each new perspective, the original frame seems less significant and, in turn, is less likely to sway a person's decision. And within the context of selling, it is especially effective to share more than one new, positive frame when attempting to guide potential clients out of a negative point of view that is hindering their ability to commit to the sale.

The final breakthrough concept I discovered is that not all frames are equal in their persuasiveness. Certain frames are more influential than others and are therefore more likely to be embraced by someone with an opposing point of view.[10] Certain frames are also more impactful in the sale than others. These frames make up the reframing process you'll learn in this chapter.

Armed with knowledge of these three concepts, I began creating a reframing process for salespeople and testing it with numerous clients in diverse selling situations across many industries. The researching and testing process took more than three years and revealed several key insights on how to reframe things most effectively when selling. Once my methodology was finalized, I began training salespeople on how to apply it, and I consistently observed that after only a few hours of practicing the techniques, they drastically improved how they responded to challenging situations. The approach gave them the structure they needed to come up with a strong response when facing buyers whose perspectives were hindering the sale. It also provided them the flexibility to adapt that response to each unique situation they encountered. These salespeople even began applying the frames to their normal processes at work, which helped them improve how they presented their ideas, company, product, and service in routine interactions.

The process consists of five proven frames. Though you will rarely use all five within one sales situation, you should strive to use at least two back-to-back to maximize the effectiveness of each. Which of the five you use will depend on the circumstances, but once you learn all five and practice using them, you'll find that the process will guide you in coming up with compelling responses to any challenges you face.

Reframe #1: Social Proof

"How can I increase the sales at my stores?" Sylvan Goldman asked himself after he purchased several small grocery stores in 1934.[11] Within a short time, he identified the bottleneck he believed was costing him sales: the baskets his customers were using. While shopping, customers would put their groceries in little handheld baskets; once the basket was full, they would stop shopping even if they needed more items. Goldman recognized that the size of the basket was limiting how many groceries his customers could purchase at one time. To solve this problem, he invented the shopping cart and proudly put his new invention in all his stores, expecting sales to skyrocket. But shoppers thought the cart was odd-looking and refused to use it. Undeterred, Goldman had signs posted clearly explaining the benefits of using a shopping cart. Still, customers insisted on the handheld baskets they were accustomed to. How did Goldman finally persuade his customers to make the switch? He reframed the experience of using a shopping cart by hiring male and female actors to walk around his stores pushing shopping carts and putting items in them. So now when customers would enter his stores, they would see lots of "shoppers" happily using shopping carts, and they began using them too. (On a side note, you may be wondering if the shopping cart actually improved sales at Goldman's grocery stores. Yes, it did. However, where he made the bulk of his fortune was in licensing his invention around the world.)

Goldman gained market acceptance for the shopping cart through reframing it with a powerful psychological trigger known as *social proof*, which connects the persuasiveness of an idea with how others are responding to it. It's the reason Goldman's customers were open to using the shopping cart once they finally saw others using it. Social proof is so influential because "people's behavior is largely shaped by the behavior of those around them," writes social scientist Steve Martin in his *Harvard Business Review* article that humorously uses social proof in its title, "98% of *HBR* Readers Love This Article."[12] Another example of the sway of social proof is a famous study a group of behavioral scientists conducted on a busy sidewalk in New York City.[13] The researchers had an assistant stand on the sidewalk for one minute looking up toward the sky. Though many people noticed the odd scene, only a few stopped to see what the assistant was staring at. However, when five assistants stood on the sidewalk gazing upward for a minute, over 300 percent more people passing by stopped to see what they were looking at.

Social proof is extremely important in selling too. As your potential clients are forming judgments, they'll instinctively look at how others like them are responding in the same or similar situations.[14] When they see others engaging in the same behavior, it makes the behavior seem less risky and more appealing. And one of the benefits of reframing with social proof is that our brains naturally trust what a lot of people similar to us are doing. This is why the Wharton Business School contends that social proof is the *most*

important way modern businesses can establish trust with potential clients.[15]

One of the best times to use social proof is when you're introducing a new frame. Doing so predisposes buyers to trust what you
are sharing, naturally increasing their receptiveness to what you're
saying and setting you up for success. Let's look at the difference
that social proof can make.

Here's a basic statement that does not use social proof: "What I
recommend to those who purchase this product is to also invest in
our service plan. The reason is because . . ."

Now let's upgrade the statement by framing it with social proof:
"Companies who purchase this product almost always invest in
our service plan. The reason is because . . ."

Notice how framing the recommendation with social proof
boosts its trustworthiness and makes it far more persuasive. Here
are a few more examples of ways to use social proof to introduce a
new frame:

- "When companies have the concern you mentioned, they will
  almost always choose to invest in our product because of two
  specific reasons . . ."

- "This next feature I'm going to share with you is the one that
  our clients tell us is the most important to them . . ."

- "When most people consider a purchase like this, the number
  one thing they say they want is . . ."

- "I'm glad you brought up that issue, because it's the reason
  that our most successful clients say they continue to do
  business with us . . ."

- "The reason so many companies are choosing to work with us is because . . ."

- "What many of my top-performing clients do to successfully correct this issue is . . ."

As you begin using social proof, it can be helpful to try general phrases such as "many companies," "most people," or "our most successful clients," as buyers know that your clients' collective experiences are a good indicator of what theirs will be. Where appropriate, you can also share the names of specific satisfied clients or customers who are in a similar situation as your prospective buyers to further solidify your case.

Now let's apply social proof to your sales process. Take a moment to think of a time when you often need to reframe during the sales process. Maybe it's when you repeatedly receive a specific objection from your buyers, encounter a common misunderstanding about your product, or must make the case for why your service is priced higher than one of your competitors' products. Then write out how you can use social proof to introduce the new frame.

What you are reframing:

_____

How you will use social proof to introduce your new frame:

_____

_____

Reframe #2: Contrast

What should you do to help a buyer when they're struggling to make a decision on their own? This was the dilemma an investment banking firm faced with one of its existing clients. The firm had identified that the client's business was vastly underinsured, and if something unexpected happened, it would jeopardize the client's entire company. After doing an extensive amount of research analyzing the business's liabilities, the firm crafted an insurance policy that provided the right amount of protection for the business without any unnecessary extras. Out of concern for their client, a sales leader at the firm, whom we'll call Mark, presented the insurance policy to the client. The client was grateful for all the work the firm had put into creating a thoughtful new policy and stated that he believed it was what his business needed but that he wanted some time to think about it. Over the next few months, every time the client was contacted, he would say that he still needed more time to decide. This situation was not good for the client, whose business was at continuous risk, nor for the investment bank, which wanted to earn the sale, of course, but, more importantly, wanted to ensure the ongoing financial health of one of its valuable clients.

Around this time, Mark went through Hoffeld Group's sales training, where he learned how our brains use contrast to reduce the perception of risk and create clarity when forming judgments. Inspired by this insight, Mark realized why his client was having such a hard time making the much-needed decision to purchase the policy: He had nothing to compare it with. Plus, before the business's recent growth, his client hadn't needed to purchase an insurance policy of this size. No wonder the client was apprehensive about the decision, even though he knew it was critical for the sustainability of his company.

Mark decided to reframe the situation with contrast by putting together a second policy option for his client to consider in addition to the first. Mark opened the meeting with his client by reviewing the first policy and explaining why it provided the right amount of coverage to protect the business. He then presented the new policy, which offered slightly less coverage than the first but was still far better than the alarmingly low coverage the client currently had and also came with a cheaper insurance premium. When the presentation concluded, the client leaned back in his chair and after a moment of thoughtful silence, remarked, "I like that the new policy is less expensive, but I agree, it doesn't provide enough coverage. Let's go with the first policy." And just like that, the sale—which was $4 million, by the way—closed.

Why did contrasting the two policies help Mark's client finally make a buying decision? Because our brains are comparison machines; it's something we do instinctively. So when the brain has a hard time identifying a point of comparison, it struggles to make a confident assessment. And as we saw in the previous chapter's section on the status quo bias, when our brains lack confidence in deciding one way or another, we instinctively default to not making a decision at all, even if that inaction costs us more in the end. In the same way, your prospective clients need you to provide comparisons to help them feel confident about why they should choose your product or service. This doesn't mean you need to offer every buyer numerous options, but you should give them at least one alternative to your initial proposal. It can be a minor choice between, say, your standard product features and an additional optional feature, or between twelve- and twenty-four-month service contracts, for example. But by presenting a selection for them to pick from, it makes their chosen option more attractive and boosts their confidence in it.

Contrasting is also one of the primary ways the brain creates certainty, a major factor in successful selling. Numerous studies have shown that buyers are willing to pay more and purchase sooner when they feel certain a product or service is right for them.[16] For instance, if I told you I had recently purchased a regular stapler for $75, would you consider that a good purchasing decision? Probably not. You instantly realize that I paid too much, which you know because your brain immediately compared that $75 with what you've paid for a stapler in the past or the prices you've seen at stores. That comparison helped you easily determine that I massively overpaid for the stapler.

Many studies have also shown that in addition to bringing clarity to the decision-making process, reframing with contrast can also increase buying behaviors. Consider an experiment conducted at Northwestern University in which shoppers were asked to choose between two nearly identical sofas, except that one had sturdy cushions while the others were soft.[17] The sofa with the sturdier cushions was the clear winner, chosen 58 percent of the time. However, when researchers reframed the decision by adding three additional sofas with durable cushions, giving consumers five sofas to select from, a shocking 77 percent of the shoppers preferred the lone sofa option with soft cushions. Why did potential customers choose that sofa at a much higher rate *after* the additional sofas were added to the set of choices? The four similar sofa options with sturdy cushions made the lone sofa with soft cushions stand out by comparison, which increased sales by 83 percent. In another study, when the seller reframed the price of a product by contrasting it with the higher price that past customers had paid for the same thing, sales increased by 65 percent.[18]

Now let's look at some practical examples of how reframing with contrast can earn you more sales. I'll share three ways you can use contrast to reframe the common objection of "Your price is too high" and, in doing so, help potential clients embrace a more productive perspective of your price.

- **Contrast your price with the risk of underinvesting:** "You are right: Our price is higher than some other options, and there is a reason for that. We both agree that our solution will deliver the results you need. [*Mention those specific outcomes.*] What many companies in your situation find is that if they underinvest in a solution, they will miss out on some of the outcomes they wanted to attain, which ends up costing them far more. Wouldn't you agree that it's better to spend a bit more to ensure you get the results you need?"

- **Contrast your price with the problems associated with cheaper options:** "What our clients tell us is that we are not the cheapest option, but we are the least expensive. The reason they say that is because, yes, there are cheaper options out there, and there's a reason they are cheap. Their machines break down more often and are expensive to fix. With a cheaper option, you pay for them over and over again. In contrast, with our machines, you buy them once and, with our quality guarantee and upfront maintenance contract, you will never have to put any more of your valuable time or money into them again. Doesn't it make sense to invest a little more upfront to save time and money later on?"

- **Contrast your price by breaking it down:** "One thing to remember is that, though you are paying for our service once, you will have it for the next three years. In fact, when you look at the costs over the three years and factor in all of your employees who will have access to the service, it comes down to an investment of only a few dollars per day, per employee."

Think of a time you can use contrast to help your potential clients see a situation from a new perspective by reframing it with contrast, and write out below how you'll do it. See if you also can amplify the power of your new frame by combining contrast with social proof. (For a quick reminder of how to do that, take a look at the first and second examples above when responding to the objection "Your price is too high." Both leverage social proof when using contrast to reframe.)

What you are reframing:

_____

How you will reframe with social proof and contrast:

_____

_____

Reframe #3: Positive Outcomes

The positive outcomes buyers hope to attain from a product or service are a major driver of every purchasing decision. So let's look at how to frame these results so that they resonate with potential clients and inspire them to act. In a noteworthy study, behavioral scientists Adam Grant and David Hofmann analyzed the most productive way to present to health-care workers the benefits of washing their hands prior to caring for patients.[19] Alarmingly, physicians wash their hands less than half as often as recommended, which puts both doctors and patients at risk for spreading and contracting diseases. Attempts to improve hand hygiene have mostly focused on promoting the benefits of protecting oneself from illness and have largely proved ineffective.[20] Grant and Hofmann wondered if the way the results of hand cleanliness had been framed could be the reason health-care professionals weren't more receptive to following protocol. To test their hypothesis, they went to a U.S. hospital and randomly posted one of the following signs above each of the soap and hand-sanitization gel dispensers.

Sign #1: HAND HYGIENE PROTECTS YOU FROM CATCHING DISEASE.
Sign #2: HAND HYGIENE PROTECTS PATIENTS FROM CATCHING DISEASE.

A mere one-word difference between the signs produced a major change in the workers' behaviors. Sign #1 had no effect on usage, whereas Sign #2—which framed the positive outcome for patients rather than for health-care workers themselves—increased soap and hand sanitizer use by 45 percent. The reason for this difference in behavior, the researchers identified, was due to a common overconfidence (something we examined in chapter 1) among health-care workers to overestimate their own immunity to disease. (And even when they do become ill, there is rarely a clear, causal link to their poor hand hygiene, so they assume they became sick for other reasons.)[21] However, the majority of health-care professionals are very concerned about the well-being of their patients and are highly motivated to do everything they can to make their patients' lives better, which is consequently why Sign #2 had such a positive impact.

This study shows that often what *we* assume is most important to others doesn't necessarily motivate them to action. Rather, the more a message aligns with what actually matters most to that audience, the more persuasive it will be. This pattern of assuming we know what matters to others is a trap that many salespeople fall into. One study revealed a disturbing 77 percent of executive-level buyers believe the salespeople they work with don't understand their problems and therefore are unable to present solutions that buyers need.[22] In other words, the way the benefits of purchasing were presented to these buyers missed the mark so badly that the buyers decided those salespeople's offerings did not offer any meaningful value to them. This disconnect between sellers and buyers is caused by a lack of awareness. Many salespeople do not obtain an adequate understanding of what truly matters to their buyers, so they are unable to explain how they can deliver positive outcomes in a way that resonates with potential clients.

Ensure you don't fall prey to this by focusing on developing an accurate knowledge of what your buyers value first and foremost. And over a long sales cycle or when selling regularly to an existing client, you'll want to make sure you continue to be aware of their evolving needs and perspectives. This will help you reframe the results you deliver in ways that matter to them. You can do this by obtaining an understanding of the following:

- Specific problems your buyers have and/or want to avoid, which your product/service addresses well

- Costs of those problems in time, money, growth, resources, employee morale, and/or market share

- Solutions for those problems and their positive effect

- Relevant internal or external drivers or business objectives that are linked either to a problem or to solving it

Once you know this information, you can then reframe the positive outcomes you can deliver in a way that will motivate your prospective clients to act on what you're suggesting. To give you an example, I have a client whose products are priced higher than those of its main competitors, but my client still outsells them. The company's salespeople ask questions that draw out the problems their prospective clients have, the pain those are causing, and the results the clients are looking to achieve instead. Then the salespeople convey how their products will solve those problems. For instance, if they identify that a buyer's problems are excessive, time-consuming product maintenance and expensive product failures, the salespeople focus on describing the high quality and durability of their products and explaining their lifetime warranty, which guarantees buyers won't be burdened with the unplanned expense of a product failure. They also present how their products require little maintenance, which is also simple and quick to perform.

Because the salespeople know what matters to their buyers, they focus on it and communicate the positive outcomes they can supply in ways that engage buyers and inspire them to purchase. Remember, buyers do not necessarily care about or want to buy your product or service, per se. They care about achieving the results that matter to them with whatever product or service will do that best. As the legendary Harvard Business School marketing professor Theodore Levitt put it, "People don't want to buy a quarter-inch drill. They want a quarter-inch hole!"[23] When your potential clients believe that you will deliver *their* desired outcomes, then they will be motivated to buy from you.

Let's go through an exercise that will help you practice customizing how to reframe the positive outcomes buyers will experience if they purchase from you.

What are the most significant problems that your product or service solves for your clients?

_____

_____

What questions can you ask in order to identify if your buyer has those problems and how much it's costing them in time, money, growth, resources, morale, and/or market share?

_____

_____

_____

Imagine a past client answered the questions you just wrote down. Based on that, write out how you would present two positive outcomes they would experience if they purchased from you.

Positive outcome #1:

_____

_____

Positive outcome #2:

_____

_____

Reframe #4: Loss Aversion

Though it's critical to emphasize the positive outcomes you can generate for potential clients, it's also vital that you help them understand what they may lose if they *don't* make a change. And guiding them in thinking through what they stand to lose is incredibly persuasive. To illustrate this, consider the following decision problem.

Imagine being offered a gamble that involves a coin toss. If the coin lands on heads, you win $120. However, if it shows tails, you must pay $100. Would you choose to take part in the coin toss?

This decision problem derives from the research of Daniel Kahneman, who says that, in spite of the fact that you stand to gain more than you lose in this situation, most people choose not to participate at all.[24] To our brains, losses are more influential than gains, so the pain of losing $100 is far greater than the joy of winning $120.[25] In fact, neuroscientists who have studied the persuasive clout of loss aversion have discovered it would take a gain of around double ($200) the potential loss ($100) to compel people to participate in the coin toss.[26] If we apply these findings to the act of selling, it means that, though showing the benefits prospective clients will experience after they buy from you is persuasive, revealing how they will avoid losses equal to the potential gains is *twice as powerful*.

The research backs up the idea that loss aversion has a strong sway on decision-making.[27] One study published in the *Journal of Applied Social Psychology* compared the effect that loss aversion and positive outcomes have on buying decisions.[28] One group of buyers was given a sales presentation stressing how fully insulating their home would save them a certain amount of money. Another group was given the same presentation but with a focus on how if they didn't fully insulate their home, they would lose the identical amount of money as the first group saved. Not surprisingly, the buyers informed they would lose money if they did not purchase the insulation had a 150 percent higher closing rate than those told that purchasing it would save them money in the long run. The prospect of losing money hurts far more than the possibility of gaining an equal amount.

In addition, research published in *Econometrica*, a journal of the Econometric Society, demonstrated that loss aversion can make people much more open to taking risks when making decisions—if those decisions are motivated by their desire to avoid a loss of any kind.[29] Every buying decision contains risk, so this is of course incredibly relevant to sales. Buyers won't know if purchasing a product or service is right for them until *after* they experience the results of their decision, and everyone has experienced making a purchase they later regretted. Yet, in spite of the risk inherent in the buying decision, your potential clients need your product or service. Your job is to help them navigate that risk, understand what they will be losing by not purchasing it (as well as what they stand to gain by purchasing), and make a confident choice they'll feel good about.

That said, although research shows fear of loss is one of the most potent ways to reframe, salespeople still vastly underutilize this technique, often because they aren't sure how to do so. Here's an easy two-step process you can use to leverage loss aversion.

Step #1: Identify what your potential clients stand to lose if they don't purchase from you. Will they lose revenue, time, resources, or productivity? Will it significantly lower employee morale? Could not investing in your product or service cause them to lose market share or miss out on a growth opportunity?

Step #2: Help your potential clients understand what this loss means to them. Show your buyers how the loss will impact them by either quantifying or monetizing it. This will help you develop a strong case that will motivate potential clients to consider making a change. For instance, imagine a salesperson who identifies that her software is less complicated than the buyer's existing software and, as a result, would save the buyer's employees an average of ten minutes per day. That salesperson could show that because of the existing software, the two hundred employees who use it are collectively losing two thousand minutes of productivity each day. Then the salesperson could monetize that loss by revealing that since the average employee is paid $40 per hour, the buyer is losing over $1,330 per day and more than $315,000 per year by sticking with its current software instead of switching to hers.

Let's continue exploring how you can reframe with loss aversion by looking at the following three challenging sales situations.

- **When you receive an objection that your product is expensive:** "What really matters isn't what you pay for a solution like ours, but what you get out of it. With the analysis we've done, which you agreed with, the data indicates that not moving

forward will cost you around two million dollars in lost revenue. Given that our fees are a fraction of the two million that
we would save you, wouldn't you agree that moving forward is
a wise financial investment?"

- **When a buyer is thinking of not purchasing from you and
just ignoring their problem instead:** "From what you've
shared, not having a well-trained sales force is costing you
around two sales per month per salesperson. You currently
have ten salespeople with an average sale of around $30,000,
which means that this lack of training is costing your organization twenty sales per month—a loss of $600,000 approxi-
mately every thirty days. If we zoom out and look at the sales
you are missing over a whole year, this is costing the organization $7.2 million in annual revenue that should be yours.
Based on the heavy losses you're experiencing by not having a
well-trained sales staff, isn't this an issue that you'd want to
address immediately?"

- **When working with an existing client who is considering
looking for another provider:** "When you went through the
long process of choosing a provider three years ago, you selected us. Since then we've accomplished a lot by increasing
your manufacturing efficiency and reducing costs by 4.8 percent. Our contract expires in four months, and as you consider
renewing with us, it's important to recognize that we are at a
critical point in our journey together. Our concern is that if we
didn't continue to work with you, it could cause a loss of some
of the success we've achieved together. What's more, we believe that we can continue to help reduce your costs by another 3.2 percent over the next three years with some of our
new systems that will build onto the existing ones we've

already put in place. We don't want you to miss out on that cumulative savings of 8 percent."

Let's practice using what you've just learned. Fill out your answers to the questions below to reframe the common objection "Your price is more than we want to spend."

What is one thing your potential clients stand to lose if they don't purchase from you?

_____

How can you quantify or monetize that loss so that it resonates with your potential clients?

_____

_____

Write what you will say to reframe the objection with loss aversion in a way that reveals the strong business case for investing in your product or service.

_____

_____

Reframe #5: Existing Beliefs

One of the most compelling ways to reframe anything is to leverage the existing beliefs of those you want to influence. An example of this is the fascinating research that behavioral scientists Matthew Feinberg and Robb Willer conducted on how to reframe your message to appeal to people with opposing points of view.[30] They ran six experiments—involving more than 1,300 participants in all—seeking to identify how to make the most effective political arguments to those on the opposite side of an issue. They identified that our natural inclination when presenting a political argument is to frame it around our own beliefs and challenge the other person's point of view. However, Feinberg and Willer observed that people were far more receptive to a political message presented to them if it was reframed to align with their existing beliefs, rather than challenging them.

In one of their experiments, which dealt with the topic of same-sex marriages, politically liberal participants were in greater agreement if an argument for same-sex marriage focused on fairness (all citizens should be treated equally). In contrast, conservative participants were more persuaded when the message was reframed to emphasize how same-sex couples were loyal, patriotic Americans who contribute to the economy and society.

In another experiment, they examined the topic of the United States maintaining current levels of military spending. When the argument was framed to emphasize that citizens should take pride in the military because it unifies the country at home and abroad, conservative participants agreed more strongly. However, when the message was reframed to focus on how military spending ensures that the poor and disadvantaged can attain equal standing and a promising future they would not have access to otherwise, liberal participants were more convinced.[31]

Feinberg and Willer concluded the key takeaway from their experiments and research was that, in order to win someone over to your position, it's often best not to challenge their beliefs but instead reframe your argument to connect to those beliefs. Doing this will help others see the value of your position and reduce the perceptual gap between your viewpoint and theirs.

This doesn't work just for politics, of course; it's equally effective when selling. To reframe what you are presenting to align with your buyer's existing beliefs, you must first get into their heads and identify what they believe about the critical aspects of the sale. This will then enable you to speak to the specific things that matter to them. And because this way of reframing is customized, it resonates with your buyers and helps align their position more closely with yours, resulting in a win-win.

Consider a large corporation that hired my client to monitor the brand's reputation online (brand safety) and fraud protection but used a competitor's platform to track how often a digital advertisement was actually viewed (viewability). When questioned why it chose to use the competitor, the customer stated that it believed the competitor was stronger in viewability and it wanted to have "the best." What did my client do? They reframed the situation by explaining to their customer that it wasn't getting "the best" because the insights generated in the viewability function enhanced brand safety and fraud protection. Because the customer was using the competitor for the former and my client for the latter, it wasn't able to maximize this protection. And since my client reframed the situation around their customer's existing belief that it wanted the "best," the customer was receptive to making a change. The corporation promptly switched all its business to my client and was thrilled with the immediate improvements it got in its digital advertising.

As you reframe your product or service to address your potential client's existing beliefs, use phrases like "Earlier you mentioned," or "When we met last time, the group shared . . ." to introduce the new frame. Then link their belief with what you are recommending. Consider a few examples of what this looks like.

- "Earlier you shared that the number one goal of the training is to improve client loyalty [*existing belief*]. The training solution I've laid out is designed to equip your employees with the knowledge and skills they'll need to better serve your existing clients, which will naturally improve loyalty and increase repeat business."

- "When we spoke on the phone you mentioned that your new bars would be places where customers will come to relax, enjoy great food, and watch sports [*existing belief*]. Investing in commercial TVs will help make your vision a reality because they are designed for continuous use and will ensure you'll always be able to provide your customers with a great experience."

- "A little earlier you shared that one of your main problems with the kitchens in your apartment complexes was the lack of storage and poorly functioning drawers [*existing belief*]. You mentioned that not fixing those issues was the primary thing your tenants were complaining about. Because of that, I wouldn't recommend painting or refinishing, because they won't solve your storage issues or correct how your drawers function. Instead, I'd recommend permanently correcting these problems by remodeling the kitchens."

- "Last time we met, you all agreed that your production needs to increase so the company can meet its new objectives for the year [*existing belief*]. My concern is that if we underinvest in these upgrades, you'll limit your ability to grow your output, which will cost you a lot in lost production. The solution is priced to strengthen production capabilities and ensure that we can achieve the new objectives."

It's your turn to reframe with your buyer's existing beliefs. Go through the following exercise to practice using this powerful way of reframing.

What is one common belief many of your prospective clients have that is important to the sale?

_____

How could you link that belief with something meaningful that your company, product, or service offers?

_____

_____

Write what you will say to leverage that existing belief as you reframe what your company, product, or service provides the buyer.

_____

_____

_____

Anytime your potential clients have become stuck in a point of view that is detrimental to the sale and to their own interests, you'll need to reframe the situation. With the five frames I've shared in this chapter, you'll have a proven way of presenting that will enable you to compellingly demonstrate to clients how you can meet their needs. As I've mentioned, you probably won't need to use all five frames in one discussion, and they can be used in any order and at any point during the sales process. Just remember to try to use at least two back-to-back to maximize their impact.

Here's a quick recap of each of the ways to reframe and what they do:

- **Social proof:** Connects the persuasiveness of an idea with how others are responding to it.

- **Contrast:** Provides buyers with another perspective or option to consider.

- **Positive outcomes:** Focuses buyers on the benefits they'll experience by embracing your recommendation.

- **Loss aversion:** Shares what buyers stand to lose by not acting on your suggestions.

- **Existing beliefs:** Links what you are suggesting with buyers' existing beliefs.

Now that you've learned how to successfully address any concerns or unproductive viewpoints through reframing, you're ready to take your skills to the next level. In the following chapter, I'll show you how to supercharge your sales by leveraging four powerful scientific principles.

CHAPTER 6

Supercharge Your Sales Process with Science

WE'VE COVERED HOW TO HELP CLIENTS MAKE BUYING DE-
cisions and ways to reframe any sales situation. Now in the next
two chapters we'll focus on helping you build on that foundation
and achieve even more success. And that starts with understanding how your behavior affects whomever you're selling to. All of us,
even those who have been in the profession for years, have a natural bias known as the fundamental attribution error, which causes
us to underestimate how much buyers are influenced by our sales
process.[1] This tendency is something you need to be aware of, because if you devalue the impact your actions have on an outcome,
it reduces your motivation and effort.[2]

Thousands of studies have proved that the way salespeople interact with buyers heavily influences and often determines how
buyers behave during the sale. Yet because of the fundamental attribution error, we all misjudge the major impact that seemingly
minor behaviors can have. Thankfully, that's where science comes
in. Much like a pilot depends on a plane's instruments to fly and
land safely, we can rely on behavioral principles that scientists

have uncovered to best navigate each part of the sale and avoid common pitfalls. In this chapter, I'll share how you can apply the science to supercharge your sales process and inspire your potential clients to purchase from you. Let's begin by looking at a simple technique that will instantly improve your effectiveness and translate into better results.

Begin with a Warm-Up

Early in my sales career I rarely used a warm-up when selling to clients. A warm-up occurs at the beginning of a sales interaction and is when the salesperson and buyer(s) greet each other and engage in a few minutes of informal pleasantries. At the time, my rationale for not utilizing warm-ups was that I liked getting right down to business and didn't want chitchat to get in the way—an approach I have since realized was wrong. Time and again, I have uncovered scientific studies proving that when selling or negotiating, even a brief warm-up humanizes the encounter and increases your likelihood of success.

Selling is relational. Even in today's marketplace where buyers glean information about their options online, the buyer-seller relationship is still a major influence in their decision. In fact, that relationship is often even more of a factor than the product or service you're selling or even the price you're offering. Consider a study published in the *Journal of Consumer Research* concluding that the amount of rapport and trust between buyers and sellers impacts the likelihood of the sale even more than the product or service itself.[3] Another experiment, published in *Management Science*, analyzed the effect that the relationships between buyers and sellers had on sales when the seller raised prices by 20 percent.[4] Buyers who had a strong rapport with sellers were an astounding

376 percent more likely to agree to the higher charges and remain loyal to the seller, compared with buyers who didn't have that rapport. In other words, relationships still matter. In fact, they matter a lot.

The positive feelings generated during the warm-up permeate the rest of the sale, which naturally improves your influence.[5] As researchers Amy Cuddy, Matthew Kohut, and John Neffinger explain, "A growing body of research suggests that the way to influence—and to lead—is to begin with warmth. Warmth is the conduit of influence: It facilitates trust and the communication and absorption of ideas."[6] A few minutes of informal conversation predisposes people to share information and comply with a request.[7] A study conducted by social scientists from Stanford, Columbia, and Northwestern, fittingly titled "Schmooze or Lose," identified that when you don't use a warm-up, you are more likely to underperform. In one experiment, before beginning a challenging negotiation, half of the participants were told to have a brief casual conversation (the warm-up) with those they were negotiating with. The rest of the participants were told to get down to business right away. Those who "schmoozed" first generated more rapport and trust with the other party and were 20.1 percent more likely to negotiate a favorable outcome.[8]

Needless to say, after I discovered the science, I was convinced. And because I always strive to follow what science has proved when it comes to how to sell—regardless of my own preferences (an approach I wholeheartedly recommend to everyone)—I started every buyer interaction with a warm-up. It immediately improved my results.

That said, simply incorporating warm-ups into your sales process isn't enough; *how* you do so is what makes the difference. Here are five rules that will help you conduct effective warm-ups and set you up for success.

Rule #1: The Warm-Up Should Evoke Positive Feelings

The warm-up sets the tone for your interaction with buyers, which is why it should be a positive, enjoyable experience for them. Steer clear of any potentially offensive or controversial topics. Instead, think sports, family, hobbies, vacations, things in common, or the weather. I live in Minnesota, which gets extremely cold during the winter months. When my warm-ups focus on the weather, it puts my potential clients in a good (and sometimes gleeful) mood, since they are almost always experiencing warmer weather than I am. If you are unsure what to discuss, do your research ahead of time. A quick online search will likely yield topics they've commented on, which you can use as conversation starters to kick off the sales call in an agreeable manner.

Rule #2: The Warm-Up Should Be Brief

The warm-up is when you present yourself as an engaging, competent, likable, and trustworthy person. That said, it is just one part of your sales process, so it should also be concise. One of the most common questions I am asked about the warm-up is how long it should be. As a general rule, I suggest two to five minutes. Be careful going longer, as you never want to be forced to rush through a discussion or presentation because you let the warm-up run too long.

Rule #3: The Warm-Up Should Focus on the Buyer

A warm-up ideally centers on buyers. That is not to say that it shouldn't be a back-and-forth conversation; it should. But this is not the time for you to tell a story or be long-winded. Keep your remarks brief, because successful warm-ups are the ones in which buyers do most of the talking. If you are dominating the conversation, then most likely you are getting the most out of it, which defeats the purpose.

Rule #4: Don't Confuse the Warm-Up with the Discovery

One common mistake that salespeople make is confusing the warm-up with the discovery. What is the discovery? It's when you ask deep-dive questions to uncover your buyer's problems, buying motives, and decision criteria. (For information on how to conduct an in-depth discovery, check out chapters 5 and 6 of *The Science of Selling*.)

The warm-up prepares buyers for the discovery by generating the rapport and trust you'll need to inspire them to disclose information in an honest, thoughtful manner. In other words, a good warm-up increases your chances of having a successful discovery.

Rule #5: Don't Conduct a Warm-Up When Prospecting

There is one time you shouldn't conduct a warm-up: when prospecting (i.e., trying to develop new business). When you first reach out to a potential client, you will usually have less than thirty seconds to generate enough interest to earn the right to continue the dialogue. In this case, a warm-up is counterproductive, as there simply isn't time. So, with the exception of this very first interaction with buyers, a warm-up should be a regular part of your sales process.

Now let's look at another way to boost the effectiveness of your sales process—through sharing influential stories.

Bring Sales Presentations to Life Through Stories

Something odd occurs when people are asked to donate money: They often feel more compelled to help a single victim than to help millions suffering from the same problem. To explain this dilemma, behavioral scientists Deborah Small, George Loewenstein, and Paul Slovic conducted an illuminating study in which they showed potential donors one of the two descriptions below about victims of starvation and asked for a donation to a hunger-relief organization.[9]

- Rokia, a seven-year-old girl from Mali, Africa, . . . is desperately poor, and faces a threat of severe hunger or even starvation.

- Food shortages in Malawi are affecting more than three million children. In Zambia, severe rainfall deficits have resulted in a 42 percent drop in maize production . . . As a result, an estimated three million Zambians face hunger as well.

As heartbreaking as both the situations are, logically we should feel more obliged to donate to help millions of children than to help just one. Yet participants who learned about Rokia gave 140 percent more than those who learned about the millions of other children facing hunger. So why are we more affected by the story of an individual? People are more influenced by what researchers refer to as "identifiable victims" than "statistical victims." In other words, sharing statistics is good, but it's rarely as impactful as bringing those statistics to life with a real example or story.

Whether you're a nonprofit trying to appeal to donors or a salesperson trying to appeal to a group of decision-makers, your ability to persuade will increase if you can demonstrate relevant facts, statistics, and value propositions through relatable stories and case studies. And conveying this information via narratives benefits your buyers as well. Sharing real-world examples will keep potential clients engaged, improve their levels of trust in what you're presenting, and boost their comprehension and recollection of your presentation.[10] I can't tell you how many times clients have told me a year or two after I closed a sale with them that one of the things they remember best—and were most swayed by—were the stories I shared.

What makes stories so persuasive is the way our brains process them.[11] When you embed your facts or value propositions in a story, it bypasses the brain's typical resistance to a persuasive message by reducing its inclination to create counterarguments.[12] This is why stories and anecdotes are able to influence people, even when facts and statistics fail.[13] As scientists Rebecca Krause and Derek Rucker explain, "Because people produce fewer negative thoughts about a message delivered as part of a story, people should be more persuaded when facts are embedded within a story as opposed to presented alone."[14]

Despite the positive impact stories have in the selling process, most salespeople underutilize them or don't use them at all. In fact, this is one of buyers' biggest complaints about salespeople. Research and advisory firm Forrester reported that 78 percent of the buyers it surveyed stated that salespeople don't share enough examples or case studies that help them think through the value of what's being presented.[15] Your potential clients need more than just hard facts. They want you to share anecdotes that reveal the results others like them have experienced from your company, product, or service. This also activates the power of social proof (which we covered in chapter 5), making them more likely to choose to go with you too.

To practice incorporating compelling and authentic examples into your presentations, let's use one of the Six Whys®, which we covered in chapter 4. To refresh your memory, here are the Whys again. Pick one that you feel a real-life example would help you more effectively answer, and then we'll work on creating a narrative to address it.

THE SIX WHYS®

Why Change?   *Why Now?*

Why Your Industry Solution?   *Why You and Your Company?*

Why Your Product or Service?   *Why Spend the Money?*

If you're having trouble deciding on a Why, consider the following three questions:

- If you've ever had a client who struggled with answering one of the Whys, what was the result?

- Is there a past client whose situation clearly answers one of the Whys?

- What impressive results have you achieved for past clients that answer one of the Whys?

Now that you've selected the Why you want to address through a narrative, answer each of the following questions to help you craft a powerful story around it.

Which of the Six Whys® will the story answer?

_____

What is the point of the story? How do you want your
buyers to respond?

_____

_____

How will you introduce the story?

_____

_____

What are the key points that will be included in the
story?

_____

_____

How will you conclude the narrative?

_____

_____

After you refine this narrative, I'd encourage you to confer with
your colleagues and see what stories they have and how they implement them when selling. I have clients whose salespeople have
each documented one or two real stories and then shared them
with one another. As a result, everyone has a plethora of authentic

examples and case studies to choose from, which enables the entire team to bring their presentations to life.

Three Tips for Crafting Compelling Narratives

1. **Keep your stories concise.** Ideally, you want to share narratives that are between thirty seconds and two minutes long. If yours are longer than two minutes, trim them. The best examples are short and sweet.

2. **Tell stories strategically.** Where in your presentation do you share important data that may not be compelling but is critical for clients to understand? This is a great place to use an anecdote or hypothetical situation to bring that information to life. Or is there a meaningful value proposition you can wrap in a real example so that buyers can fully comprehend and appreciate it? A good way to do this is to link your stories to at least one of the Six Whys®.

3. **Make sure each story conveys a singular point.** Often, salespeople will tell stories emphasizing so many points that they fail to make any of them well. Your stories should present one important idea. To determine what that should be, ask yourself, What do you want your potential clients to believe or do as a result of hearing it? This will help you eliminate excessive or confusing information and deliver a powerful, focused narrative.

Nudge Your Buyers into the Sale

A third way to take your sales process to the next level is to focus on how you present choices to buyers. For instance, if someone offered you a free sample of a new beverage in exchange for your email address, would you do it? If you are like most people, you'd probably refuse the request. That's how 67 percent of participants responded in an experiment by social psychologists San Bolkan and Peter Andersen.[16] However, when they prefaced the request with the question "Do you consider yourself to be somebody who is adventurous and likes to try new things?" an astonishing 75 percent of people agreed to give their email address in exchange for the free sample. That initial question, to which nearly everyone responded yes, predisposed them to want to act on what they had just affirmed. Another experiment in their study produced similar results: When Bolkan and Andersen inquired whether people would contribute to a survey, only 29 percent consented. Yet when they first asked them, "Do you consider yourself a helpful person?" before inviting them to complete the survey, 77 percent agreed to participate.

Why does asking certain questions right before making a request have such sway on the response to the request itself? These questions are what scientists refer to as nudges; they unconsciously encourage people toward a certain decision. The term was coined and made famous by Richard Thaler, who defines "nudge" as something that alters human behavior in a predictable way without restricting one's ability to make a free choice.[17] The effect on decision-making is so powerful that nudges are used in everything from finance and health care to education and government. (The British government even created a "Nudge Unit" focused on improving its citizens' health, wealth, and well-being.)[18]

In the sales process, nudges can help you guide potential

clients.[19] One way to implement nudges is by preparing buyers to interpret and respond to subsequent information in a favorable way. For instance, after sharing information about your company in your presentation, you can utilize a nudge before asking buyers for a commitment to Why #4 (Why You and Your Company?). This nudge could be deployed in the form of an assessment question like "Does it make sense why so many companies like yours have chosen to work with us because of our partnerships and the results we produce?" After your potential client says yes, you can then ask for a commitment with a question such as "Based on what you know about our company, do you feel that we are the right provider for this project?" And because you've prepared your potential client for the commitment with the nudge, by helping them think through and verbally affirm the value that the commitment is based on, you will be much more likely to receive it.

Here's another example of what this combination of a nudge and commitment could look like:

NUDGE: "Do our strong customer service, which we've discussed, and high client-satisfaction ratings meet your expectations concerning what you are looking for in a provider?"

(BUYER AFFIRMS THEY DO.)

COMMITMENT QUESTION: "That being the case, are we the provider you feel comfortable recommending to your board?"

Now it's your turn. Imagine you are speaking with buyers and have already shared the primary value that your company can provide them. What is a nudge you can share in the form of an assessment question to prepare your buyers for a commitment to your company? Remember, this nudge should guide them in confirming the value the commitment is built on.

Nudge:

_____

_____

Now let's leverage the momentum you've gained from the nudge by asking buyers for a commitment.

Commitment question:

_____

_____

Now that you've created one nudge and combined it with a commitment question, look for additional instances where you can insert a nudge to prepare your buyers to commit.

Another way you can use a nudge is through creating defaults, which are preset courses of action that take effect unless one opts out.[20] This type of nudge aligns with the natural human tendency toward inaction (remember that status quo bias we discussed in chapter 4). You can use the nudge of a default to grow your sales as well. For instance, rather than allowing potential clients to choose between features of your product or service, design packages that bundle certain options together and give them the choice of a package. Or rather than trying to upsell buyers on a service contract after they purchase your product, have twelve months of service included with the product and let buyers choose if they would like to upgrade to a twenty-four-month contract. This will allow you to build the twelve months of service into your purchase price, which will raise your average sale and set your clients up for greater success by providing more value to them. These are just two examples of how defaults can be used.

To begin utilizing defaults, ask yourself where you could link a product to a service or bundle a product with services or options. Give this some thought, because the payoff can be huge; I've seen clients create defaults that grew their average sale size between 9 and 43 percent.

Nudge Your Way into a Successful Retirement

Nudges have all sorts of uses beyond sales. One of my favorite examples comes from a research study led by Shlomo Benartzi and Richard Thaler in which they used a financial nudge to increase employee savings for retirement through a program they fittingly named Save More Tomorrow.[21] The program asked people to allocate future salary raises to retirement savings. Since people could defer saving until after they received a pay increase, 78 percent joined the plan. And because the saving was set up as a default (i.e., when you earn more money, you'll automatically have it set aside for your retirement), people remained in the program because they didn't have to take additional action in order to save. Most importantly, the nudge worked to their benefit. Over the course of the forty-month study, the savings rates of participants increased by nearly 300 percent!

Inspire Feelings of Ownership in Your Buyers

The final way to supercharge your sales process is through making your buyers feel a sense of ownership over their decision to buy (or not to buy). A sense of ownership of something causes you to perceive more value in it, even more than it may be worth. In one classic experiment, some participants were given a coffee mug that they could keep or have the option of "selling," while the rest were told they could purchase a mug from the "sellers."[22] The sellers were then asked to name the lowest price they would accept for their mugs, while the "buyers" were asked how much of their own money they would spend to acquire a mug. The sellers' minimum asking price was twice what buyers were willing to pay, because they assigned a much higher value to these mugs they now felt they "owned." Two social scientists came to a similar conclusion when they found that people were willing to purchase a hunting permit for $31 but, once they acquired it, were not willing to part with the permit for less than $143.[23]

The influence that ownership has on our financial decisions can be explained by a behavioral economics principle called the endowment effect, which is the natural bias we have to place more value on something that we possess or feel a sense of ownership over.[24] The endowment effect isn't limited to what we buy; it also applies to things we create.[25] For example, behavioral scientists Michael Norton, Daniel Mochon, and Dan Ariely conducted an experiment in which they instructed some participants to assemble a box, while others were told to inspect the constructed boxes.[26] They then asked every participant to state how much they would pay to acquire the box. Those who assembled the boxes were willing to pay 63 percent more than those who had only inspected them.[27] What this study clearly reveals is that merely participating in creating something prompts feelings of ownership and significantly influences how much value creators assign to it.

Which leads us to selling: An easy way to inspire prospective clients to feel a sense of ownership is to ask assessment questions (which I discussed in chapter 4) that prompt them to describe what the right product or service looks like to them. Some examples:

- "When you compare the two service options we've discussed, which one do you feel is the best for your organization?"

- "Earlier you mentioned the importance of in-depth reporting; this feature set can be added to give you advanced reporting capabilities. Should I include it in the proposal?"

- "Most companies will sign up for our maintenance plan for two years, but there is also a three-year option. Which do you lean more toward?"

Assessment questions, like the ones I just shared, help buyers define what they need or want, and thus increase their feelings of ownership in the right solution—which ideally will be your product or service.

To take this a step further, you can encourage even stronger feelings of possession in what you're selling by helping clients create what I call their "buying criteria." This is the list of their specific requirements and how they'll identify which company, product, or service is right for them. Once they've established this list of criteria, they will use it to judge every potential solution they consider, including the one you put in front of them.

If you're wondering why buyers would need you, the salesperson, to help them define their buying criteria, there are several reasons. Your buyers know they need a solution of some sort, but rarely know what the right one looks like. They're relying on you, as their trusted salesperson, to help them understand which elements they want and which they don't. Other times, they may have already formed a partial criteria list, but may not have thought through every feature or condition that must be met for them to move forward with the purchase. Either way, this presents an amazing opportunity for you to help them define their requirements. And because you'll be aiding them, you can provide insights to guide them toward criteria that fulfill all their needs—and show them that your product or service satisfies them.

Assisting buyers this way does three essential things. First, the process activates the endowment effect. Since your potential clients have played a key role in defining what *they* want in a solution, they naturally feel a greater sense of ownership of it. Second, it sets you apart from every other salesperson they meet with because you'll now be able to customize your presentation in a way that clearly communicates how your company, product, or service fulfills their exact requirements. Finally, it produces one of the most important feelings that you can inspire in buyers: certainty. Once someone feels certainty about your company, product, or service, they'll feel confident in their decision to purchase from you.

Following these three steps will help potential clients develop and take ownership of their buying criteria.

1. Introduce the Buying Criteria and Ask for Buyer Input

When you introduce the buying criteria into the sale, you will want to explain why you are doing so and ask for input, so buyers can contribute what they've already identified the right solution must have. In fact, the more criteria they can give you up front, the better, since it's imperative they feel the criteria are truly theirs, not merely a list of things you got them to agree with.

Here are two phrases you can use when introducing the buying criteria and asking for input:

- "We've talked about a lot of things on our call so far, so let's summarize. For anything to be the right solution for you, what are some of the main things that you'd want it to do?"

- "So that I can speak to what will provide the most value for your organization, for anything to be the right solution for your company, what are some of the main things you want it to accomplish?"

2. Provide Insights to Strengthen Their Buying Criteria

Rarely will buyers have considered everything they'll need in a solution. That's where you come in. Your job is to help them contemplate what that solution will look like. This is where you can make recommendations about criteria that encompass everything they need, and set yourself up to win their business. Here are a few examples of effective phrases you can use to introduce things for them to consider:

- "One thing a lot of other companies we work with have said is that . . . Is this also important to you?"

- "I wanted to get your feedback on . . . Is that something that you want in a solution as well?"

3. Confirm Their Buying Criteria

After your potential clients create their buying criteria, you'll want to make sure they feel ownership of it. Again, this is vital, since if they don't think it is really theirs, the endowment effect won't be activated, and they won't perceive as much value in it. To confirm they do, verbally repeat the criteria to them by saying something like "Just so I understand, for anything to be the right solution for you, you said you wanted it to [*list all of their criteria*]. Is that correct?" That also gives them a chance to consider it once more and add to it or omit anything that isn't of value to them.

Now that you have a basic understanding of the science behind the buying criteria and its key components, let's see what using it in the sale looks like. Here's an example of a buyer-seller interaction where the buying criteria is presented successfully.

SELLER: So that I can speak to what will provide the most value to you, for anything to be the right solution for your company, what are some of the main things you would want it to accomplish?

BUYER: Well, our current system is problematic because it's too complex, so people don't use it. And even when they do, we don't see much impact because it's outdated and doesn't connect with our other systems and software platforms.

SELLER: OK. I've jotted down those problems, and in a few minutes, I will share how we address ease of use and how our system will fully integrate with your other systems and software platforms. In addition to those, is there anything else that would be important for the right solution to include?

BUYER: No, I think those are the main things we've discovered so far.

SELLER: One thing a lot of other companies we work with have said is that the installation process was also very important to them. They tell us they want the installation of their new system not to disrupt their business. Is that also important to you?

BUYER: Actually, yes—I'm glad you brought that up. I've heard some horror stories about new-system installations. We can't have it disrupting our business.

SELLER: I'll make a note of that. One final thing I wanted to get your feedback on is what happens after the installation. Many companies in your situation have told us that if anything goes wrong with the system, they want to be sure that the provider will help them resolve the issue quickly, with minimal disruption to their business. How important is it to have high-quality service so that in the unlikely event that something does go wrong, you have someone who can help you fix the problem quickly?

BUYER: That's extremely important. We want a provider who will stand behind the system with strong service.

SELLER: Makes sense. OK, so I understand, for anything to be the right solution for you, first, you wanted to make sure that the new system is easy to use and connects with your other systems and software platforms. Second, you wanted to make sure the installation isn't disruptive to your business and doesn't cause any aggravations. And finally, you wanted whatever provider you choose to stand behind their system and provide exceptional service. Did I get everything?

BUYER: Yes, that's exactly what we are looking for.

SELLER: Excellent. Let's go over our system and what we offer, and I'll make sure I address each of those areas you told me were important to you.

BUYER: Sounds great.

Helping potential clients create and own their buying criteria enables you to position your company, product, or service in a way that will prepare them to perceive the high levels of value you will provide them. And it will serve your potential clients well by helping them feel confident they are making a buying decision that's in their best interest.

Let's put what you've just learned into practice. The first thing to do is identify the main benefits your solution offers that could be part of your potential client's buying criteria. Take a moment to list four of those below.

1. _____

2. _____

3. _____

4. _____

Now review the buyer-seller interaction I just shared and modify the words to reflect your selling situation. Practice using it until you can do so without notes. You'll find that when you deploy it in the sale, it will empower your buyers to perceive the value in what you offer, create certainty that yours is the right solution, and naturally guide them into a positive buying decision they can be confident about.

Throughout this chapter, we've covered some potent ways to take your sales to a whole new level. In the next chapter, I'll share three unusual—and surprisingly effective—strategies that will further boost your results.

CHAPTER 7

Three Outside-the-Box Strategies That Grow Sales

CAN YOU CONNECT THE DOTS TO SOLVE THE PUZZLE below?

Before you scoff at how easy it seems, there's a catch: You must draw no more than three straight, continuous lines that pass through each dot just once, while never lifting your pen from the page. Take a moment to see if you can figure it out.

Though seemingly straightforward, this puzzle is challenging for one specific reason: Our brains instinctively try to create order by imposing an imaginary box around the dots. The problem is that when you attempt to keep the three lines within the confines of this imaginary box, it makes the puzzle impossible to solve. It's only after you realize you must think outside the box (pun intended) that the solution becomes clear.

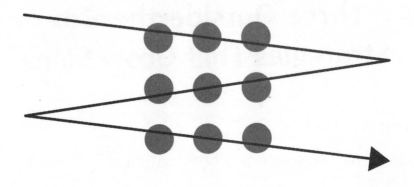

I share this classic puzzle (known as the nine-dot puzzle, which dates back to at least 1914) because it illustrates how we unconsciously impose limits on ourselves that impede our ability to get the results we want. This is especially true in selling. Often, salespeople fall back on outdated, conventional thinking when trying to solve today's complex selling challenges. To stay ahead of the curve, you need to implement innovative, evidence-based practices instead. In this chapter, I share three remarkable strategies that will help you sell outside the box. Like the nine-dot puzzle, some are more complex than they may seem at first glance. This means that once you've practiced and mastered them, you'll have an edge over your competition and a better chance of winning the sale. Let's get started by looking at how presenting something negative about your product or service can actually help you sell more.

Strategy #1: Use the Blemishing Effect to Increase Your Sales

Could sharing negative information about your product or service *increase* your sales? Before you dismiss this idea as preposterous, consider a study that found using the blemishing effect—which is when you present a small piece of unfavorable information in an otherwise positive description of a product or service—boosts feelings of trust and increases the likelihood of buying.[1] In one experiment, behavioral scientists Danit Ein-Gar, Baba Shiv, and Zakary Tormala presented a product to one group of shoppers and shared only positive information about it. To another group, they presented the same favorable information plus one unfavorable detail. The consumers in the latter group purchased it at a much higher rate than those who had received only positive information.

Though it may seem counterintuitive, when used correctly, the blemishing effect enhances feelings of trust in buyers. Your willingness to be open and candid about any less-than-perfect aspects of what you're selling communicates that you are honest and have their best interests in mind.[2] It also increases their comfort with a product or service because they feel that they have an accurate and complete understanding of it. Conversely, when salespeople share only the positive, it can cause buyers to grow suspicious that they aren't disclosing all the information, which increases the risk they feel, which makes them less likely to agree to a purchase.

Now, before you start arbitrarily presenting negative information about your product or service, there are a few things to be aware of. The blemishing effect works only if the shortcoming shared with buyers is not "central to their value proposition."[3] In other words, it's worth using this strategy only if the less-than-favorable information isn't something that matters much to your potential clients. Let's say a prospective client is looking for a virtual training solution their employees can access anytime. You could share how your training solution is provided virtually and can be utilized 24/7 but that help desks are open only during normal business hours, if you know the latter isn't important to your prospective client.

This leads to my next point: You should use the blemishing effect strategy only *after* you have a detailed understanding of what matters to your buyers and know that you can meet all their essential needs. It should be no surprise that sharing unfavorable information about your product or service that *is* essential to them will hurt your chances. After all, why would a buyer want to invest if you tell them that what you're offering doesn't have a feature they specifically need? (What's more, it is unproductive and unethical to sell something that you know will not meet their needs.) So don't try to implement the blemishing effect if you are still gaining an understanding of their requirements. Utilize it only later in the sales process once you have a full grasp of their needs and perspectives.

Another key to successfully using the blemishing effect is presenting the drawbacks immediately after you've delivered the relevant, positive information. That contrast makes the positive features of what you're selling stand out even more. As Ein-Gar, Shiv, and Tormala put it, "When individuals encounter weak negative information after already having received positive information, the weak negative information ironically highlights or increases the salience of the positive information. This makes the positive information seem more positive and ultimately fosters more positive evaluations."[4]

To employ the blemishing effect, ask yourself what's a minor, slightly unfavorable detail you could disclose after you've presented an important benefit of your product or service? Remember to tailor what you share to your potential client. Each buyer will have particular things that matter more to them. When implemented correctly, this tactic will help your prospective clients see more value in your product or service, and as a result, increase both their trust in you and the number of deals you close successfully with them.

Strategy #2: Focus on Your Nonverbal Delivery

Would it surprise you to learn that most of your communication is nonverbal? Two of the most celebrated studies ever conducted on communication identified that words accounted for just 7 percent of the message that comes across.[5] What made this research—which was published in 1967—legendary was that it revealed that nonverbal signals are an integral part of the communication process.[6] Since then, hundreds of studies have further established that what is communicated nonverbally heavily shapes how information is perceived.[7] In fact, our nonverbal communication accounts for around 90 percent of the emotions we convey.[8]

I first became aware of the impact of nonverbal behaviors on the communicative process when I was obtaining my master's degree. In fact, I was so convinced of its importance that it became the focus of my thesis. Since then, I've seen how effective nonverbal communication naturally improves salespeople's performance.

The main obstacle to effective nonverbal communication is that, unlike verbal communication, which is closely monitored and filtered, most people rarely scrutinize their nonverbal signals.[9] It's no different when it comes to selling. Indeed, most salespeople are unaware what their nonverbal behaviors are conveying to potential clients. Yet, when you're a sales professional, all your communication matters.[10] When salespeople exhibit unhelpful or off-putting nonverbal behavior, it hinders their effectiveness. This is why it's vital you become aware of and intentional about what you are conveying without words. Here's a look at four nonverbal actions you can put into practice right away to enhance your persuasive ability.

1. Use Strategic Pauses

Ed Tate is one of the top professional speakers and speech coaches in North America. I remember the first time I saw one of his award-winning talks—and one point in particular when he gained the attention of everyone in the room without uttering a sound. That's because Ed is a master at using strategic pauses to engage an audience and highlight a point.

Strategic pauses are a crucial tool to boost your effectiveness. The difference between a normal pause and a strategic one is whether you intentionally take a beat after you share a statement that you want your interlocutor to think through. That brief silence stops the flow of information and gives buyers the space to reflect on what you've just shared, which improves both their engagement and comprehension of your message.[11] As educational psychologist Raymond Wlodkowski explains, "Pauses can greatly enhance verbal instruction. You can use them to . . . capture attention by contrasting sound with silence, signal learners to listen, emphasize an important point, provide time for reflection, and create suspense or expectation."[12]

Here are three ways to pause like a pro:

- **Plan your pauses.** The biggest benefit of a well-timed pause during your presentations is it signals to buyers that what you just said was significant and encourages them to take that moment to mull it over, increasing the likelihood they'll consider what you've presented and be persuaded by it.[13] To use strategic pauses effectively, try planning them out. Identify when you should pause after an important point. Then practice it a few times. What you'll find is that after planning and practicing, pausing will become second nature. Your brain will begin inserting pauses after you present a key detail.

- **Keep your pauses concise.** A pause should be no more than four seconds, according to scientist Kristina Lundholm Fors, whose thought-provoking research identified that pausing any longer was distracting to listeners and took the focus off the message.[14] The most effective pauses, she discovered, were roughly half a second to three seconds, which improved listeners' comprehension and prompted them to reflect on what was shared.

- **Replace filler words with pauses.** Filler words such as "um," "ah," and "er" don't add value to a conversation and can even be distracting. Social psychologists have identified that they reduce the influence and credibility of speakers because they make them sound like they're not confident in what they are saying.[15]

Whenever you're trying to think of what you're going to say next, I recommend pausing briefly to collect your thoughts. This will help you avoid using "um" or "uh" or other expressions that make you sound uncertain, and will make your presentation more compelling and influential. If you're not sure how often you use filler words when selling (it's likely more than you think), try recording your next presentation and listening to it, counting the filler words. Or ask a colleague to observe your next sales call and write down any filler words you use and, if possible, when they noticed you say them. Being aware of how frequently you use them is the first step toward breaking the habit. Replacing them with pauses takes practice, since most of us use them every day. But once you develop the habit of pausing instead of filling the silence, you'll come across as much more persuasive.

2. Make Eye Contact

Eye contact is one of the most significant nonverbal behaviors.[16] Even more, a *lack* of eye contact is universally associated with dishonesty in cultures around the world. It's viewed as a signal that someone is hiding something, whether or not this is actually the case.[17] Strong eye contact, on the other hand, is associated with confidence and trustworthiness.[18] In one experiment that demonstrates this particularly well, social psychologists Gordon Hemsley and Anthony Doob created a courtroom simulation to analyze the impact of eye contact on how jurors perceived witnesses' testimonies.[19] Half of the jurors heard testimony from witnesses who each made regular eye contact with lawyers. The other half observed testimony from witnesses who averted their gaze downward when testifying. Witnesses who didn't make eye contact were perceived as unreliable, and the defendant for whom they testified was much more likely to be found guilty. This study reminds us that failing to make eye contact can cause anyone to doubt your message.

Not only that, when people make eye contact with those they are conversing with, they are thought to be more intelligent.[20] Research published in *Psychological Science* found when a speaker made eye contact during a conversation, participants were more engaged and attentive. When the speaker stopped making eye contact, participants became disengaged and shifted their attention away.[21] And a meta-analysis of forty-nine scientific studies evaluating the influence of nonverbal behaviors on compliance with a persuasive request concluded that certain nonverbal behaviors, like eye contact, are as important as (and in some cases even more impactful than) words when it comes to persuasion.[22]

Let's delve into how to leverage the power of eye contact in any situation.

- **Make eye contact with everyone.** When presenting to multiple buyers at once, it's easy to focus on the most vocal person or the highest-ranking executive. Great salespeople make eye contact with everyone they're talking to, which demonstrates they are attentive to the whole team and ensures that everyone feels valued.

- **Focus on buyers, not your notes or presentation slides.** Eye contact communicates your sincerity and conviction in what you're presenting. As a result, you should prepare adequately so that you can make eye contact with buyers and not feel the need to stare at your notes or presentation slides. Now, that doesn't mean that you shouldn't ever glance away, but if you are fixated on your notes, then you haven't prepared adequately. Your focus (and eye contact) should always be centered on those you are selling to.

- **If you are selling virtually, look into the camera.** When selling virtually (via a web-conferencing platform or video call), you'll instinctively want to look at the buyers' faces on your screen. However, if your camera is not located close to your line of sight, it will appear to them like you're gazing downward, upward, or off to the side. To avoid this, look directly into the camera as often as possible so that everyone on the other end feels like you are making eye contact. Though this may feel odd, you'll get comfortable with it after practice. More importantly, it will make it easier for you to engage with buyers and clearly demonstrate that you are truly focused on them.

- **Maintain eye contact when buyers are speaking as well.** One common mistake is not continuing to make eye contact when buyers are speaking or responding. Too many salespeople look at their notes or look away to prepare their response. This behavior causes buyers to feel that they aren't being listened to, which diminishes rapport—not to mention their confidence in moving forward with the sale.

- **Keep your verbal and nonverbal communication in sync.** When presenting to a group, how long should you hold eye contact? Strive for consistency between your verbal and nonverbal behaviors. I recommend maintaining eye contact with buyers while conveying a particular thought, which normally will be a sentence or two. Once you are done sharing the point, you can transition your gaze at the same time that you verbally shift to a new sentence or topic. This will keep your verbal and nonverbal signals in sync, which will inspire potential clients to see you as both competent and trustworthy.

3. Smile More, Sell More

The simple act of smiling has many benefits when it comes to selling. It makes you seem more attractive, establishes connection and camaraderie, and naturally improves your mood.[23] Smiling also prompts others to view you as more approachable and competent.[24] In fact, numerous studies have proven that smiling during job interviews creates a positive first impression and raises your chances of getting an offer.[25] Smiling also helps you establish rapport and convey positive emotions, which make you more persuasive.[26]

Smiling is also contagious: When we see others smiling, or even look at a picture of someone smiling, we're also likely to smile as well.[27] The reason is because our brains contain mirror neurons that cause us to imitate the behaviors we observe.[28] And smiling naturally puts both you and your buyers in a more receptive emotional state. So crack a grin, and when they smile back, it will not only improve your rapport; it will increase your chances of earning the sale.[29]

If smiling is so easy to do—and so beneficial—why don't salespeople smile more? Usually, it's a lack of awareness: They don't realize they aren't smiling. Here are some easy-to-execute ways to ensure you're reaping the advantages of a smile:

- **Get a small mirror and place it next to your phone or video camera.** Notice the facial expressions you make when on the phone or in a videoconference. Are you smiling? If not, intentionally focus on doing so. Even if someone can't see you on the other end, they can usually tell if you are smiling or not.

- **When entering any sales call or meeting, begin with a smile.** It doesn't matter if it's a face-to-face meeting, video call, or phone conversation. Unless the situation calls for a more somber mood—for example, when discussing the problem your buyer has that your service solves, or something sad or serious in nature—default to a smile.

- **If possible, take a video of yourself selling, and then watch the recording with the sound off, paying close attention to your facial expressions.** Are you smiling? Frowning? Contorting your face in a way that could be distracting? Once you've noted your default expressions, use that awareness to identify any changes you need to make, and then practice them.

4. Gesture to Make a Difference

Displaying confidence in what you sell is crucial.[30] And one of the best ways to communicate this confidence is through nonverbal behaviors. In fact, researchers have confirmed that when you express confidence nonverbally, it conveys your trustworthiness.[31] A study published in the *Proceedings of the National Academy of Sciences* also identified that when you nonverbally display confidence, it boosts rapport and makes you more interesting.[32]

One nonverbal behavior that will help you persuasively convey your confidence in what you are selling is gesturing with your hands. In fact, researchers have found that the very act of gesturing stimulates the brain, helping it process information and think more clearly.[33] In other words, your gestures can fuel your thoughts and help you present more effectively to buyers.

Your gestures can also influence whether or not you earn a sale. In one experiment, social scientists asked groups of experienced investors to watch an entrepreneur present a new technology product.[34] Each of the groups experienced the same presentation but with a different emphasis. Some of the investors witnessed the entrepreneur use figurative language, including metaphors, analogies, and anecdotes. Another group observed the entrepreneur display frequent gestures when conveying the information. Investors who witnessed the presentation with the gestures were 12 percent more likely to want to invest. One of the researchers described their findings this way: "Studies have certainly shown that gestures can convey excitement and make investors attribute more passion to entrepreneurs. But we found that gestures communicate more about the business ideas too. When we surveyed the investors who'd watched the pitches, we found that people who'd seen the gesturing version were more likely to say they had a good understanding of the new device."[35]

The following are three things you can do to harness the power of gestures:

- **Allow yourself to gesture.** We naturally move our hands when we talk to help communicate what we're saying. Yet when salespeople become nervous or tense, they often tend to restrict their gestures, keeping their arms stiffly at their sides or gripping their notes or a desk or lectern. Remember, gestures help you think clearly, convey your confidence, and make you more persuasive. So whenever you start to feel yourself tensing up, take a deep breath and give yourself the freedom to move your hands in a way that feels natural.[36]

- **Use gestures to enhance your presentation.** When salespeople gesture, it makes their presentation more interesting and engaging. In addition, gesturing with your hands can help you better convey your ideas. For example, if you are speaking about how a certain course of action will grow sales, you could move your hands away from one another to visually demonstrate that growth. When sharing a critical concept on a slide, you could motion toward the slide to signal that you're going to share something significant. Or if you want to bring up something one of your buyers stated in the past, you could gesture toward them with an open hand, palm up, to visually reinforce that you are sharing their idea and crediting them for it. Basic hand movements like these will help your audience absorb what you are presenting and increase the chances they'll be positively influenced by it.

- **Avoid using a gesture over and over again.** As influential as gestures are, if you overuse any particular one, it can become distracting and reduce the positive effect of what you are sharing. For example, when salespeople watch a video of themselves selling, they'll frequently notice they repeat the same hand movement, to the point that it becomes counterproductive. This is usually due to a lack of awareness. To make sure this doesn't happen to you, I suggest (as I recommended in the previous action on smiling) taking a video of yourself selling and watching it with the sound off. Notice your gestures and think about the impression they make. Do they communicate confidence and competence? Do you move your hands in a repetitive or distracting manner, or do you keep them stiffly by your sides? Can you identify any ways you could have used gestures to enhance your communication? Analyzing how you use hand movements will help you become aware of how you can motion in productive ways.

The four actions we've covered will help you enhance your delivery and, as a result, your overall communication. Now let's turn our attention to the final out-of-the-box strategy. It increases results as much as the others, but what sets it apart is that it will also boost your enjoyment of your life outside of work.

Strategy #3: Cultivate Optimism

Selling is hard. As I've noted before, there's the constant pressure to perform, close new business, and keep existing clients happy amid hypercompetitive and increasingly complex selling situations. That's why this last strategy focuses on navigating these challenges and improving your win rates by fostering optimism in your work.

Does optimism really positively influence sales outcomes? Yes! Consider a well-known study in which behavioral scientists Martin Seligman and Peter Schulman analyzed the performance of insurance salespeople.[37] They found that those who scored high in optimism achieved 37 percent more sales than their less optimistic colleagues. And salespeople who ranked in the top 10 percent for optimism sold 88 percent more than those who were in the top 10 percent for pessimism. What's more, when Seligman and Schulman compared those salespeople who scored in the top half for optimism to those in the bottom half, they found that the former group sold more and remained in the profession of sales for twice as long as the latter.

Other studies have come to similar conclusions: Optimists outsell pessimists on average by 20 to 40 percent.[38] As Schulman explains in his aptly titled article "Applying Learned Optimism to Increase Sales Productivity," published in the *Journal of Personal Selling and Sales Management*, "Optimism predicts sales productivity among salespeople in various industries and companies."[39] Optimistic people tend to take an active role in problem-solving, persist in the face of obstacles or rejection, and have greater task concentration and effort. All this is why optimism increases your probability of success.[40]

That said, if you're not feeling so optimistic about your ability to look on the bright side, don't worry. Optimism, like mindsets and grit, is something you can learn and improve on.[41] And regardless of how optimistic you are, with the constant barrage of challenges that we all face, couldn't you use a little more positivity in your life? Here are two science-backed ways to develop a more confident and upbeat outlook.

1. Reject Negative Thoughts

The world can be a scary and uncertain place, so it's no wonder it's hard to be optimistic. Now, you and I may not be able to change the state of the world, but we are in control of how we respond to it. For each of us, there are specific times when negativity creeps in. The key to reducing its influence is to identify when you are prone to it. Remember, you are not your thoughts. Your mind may produce ideas that you may not like or even agree with. You don't have to accept every idea that pops into your head. It's *your* mind and you can control what you think about.

As you start evaluating your thoughts, look for when they tend to turn pessimistic. As we discussed in chapter 1, negative beliefs that cause you to feel like you are a failure or like you can't achieve your goals are not accurate. But they can become self-fulfilling prophecies if you don't take steps to nip them in the bud. In reflecting on when you are most negative, ask yourself if it's in specific situations, around particular people, or after watching or listening to certain things. Ask yourself:

- What in your life (people, situations, or media you consume) prompts you to have pessimistic thoughts?

- What can you do to reduce the negative influence of those people, situations, or things?

- What in your life empowers you to embrace an optimistic mindset?

- What can you do to increase the positive influence those things have on you?

As a general rule, if you feed your mind negativity, you will find it difficult, if not impossible, to cultivate an optimistic mentality. So I challenge you to discard those things in your life that pull you down. They are damaging your career; after all, it's nearly impossible to be a creative problem-solver when you are in a negative state of mind. Likewise, I encourage you to actively pursue things that help you become the optimistic person you want to be. Making these changes isn't easy and takes time and practice, but it's worth it to achieve the success you're looking for. And I know you can do it.

2. Focus on Gratitude

To be candid, in the past, whenever I heard business or sales leaders talk about gratitude, I didn't pay much attention. It always seemed like something one should agree with in theory but that in practice would have little real impact. However, my views on this have radically changed. A few years ago, I was amazed to find that many scientific studies, stretching back almost a century, have proven that gratitude is a useful tool for reducing negative emotions and increasing positive ones.[42] What I also discovered is that it naturally puts you in an optimistic mindset.[43] In fact, it's nearly impossible to be pessimistic and also simultaneously be thankful or appreciative. Researchers have also discovered that being grateful increases well-being and positive emotions and reduces anxiety, resentment, hostility, and depression.[44] As Harvard Medical School reports, "Gratitude helps people feel more positive emotions, relish good experiences, improve their health, deal with adversity, and build strong relationships."[45]

If you're still skeptical about gratitude's effectiveness, consider a ten-week study that researchers Robert Emmons and Michael Mc-Cullough conducted in which they randomly assigned participants to three different groups.[46] They asked the first group to write down five things they were grateful for at the end of each week. Responses ranged from "waking up this morning" to "the generosity of friends" and even "the Rolling Stones." They asked the second group to reflect on and write down at the end of each week five hassles they had experienced that annoyed or bothered them. This group's responses included "hard to find parking," "doing a favor for a friend who didn't appreciate it," and the ever-frustrating "stupid people driving." The third group was told to write down five events or circumstances that affected them over the past week. This group recounted everything from "flew to Sacramento" and "learned CPR" to "cleaned out my shoe closet." The study's results revealed that those in the gratitude group had better health, were happier, and were far more confident and upbeat about each upcoming week than participants in the other two groups. That's the power of gratitude: A little can have a big impact.

Gratitude can have a dramatic effect on your career too. When you apply it on the job, it makes you more optimistic, enables you to feel and convey positive emotions, assists you in bouncing back quickly from rejection, and makes it easier to build rapport and trust with your buyers—all vital elements of successful selling.

One of the best ways to train your brain toward gratitude is to write down what you are thankful for. This is a great exercise to do at the beginning of each day. After a few weeks, you'll find it will help you live in a more grateful (and optimistic) mental state throughout the day and thrive overall.

Putting It All into Practice

We've been focusing on how you can take your sales to the next level. Before we go into the final part of the book, let's do a quick review of this section. In chapter 4, you learned how you can use the Six Whys® to align the way you sell with the way people form their buying decisions, as well as how asking the right questions will help your buyers think through and respond positively to the value you are offering. Then in chapter 5, I shared a method to help you reframe any challenging situation you encounter. Chapter 6 revealed how science can supercharge your sales process and your results. And in this chapter, you learned three outside-the-box strategies that will help you sell more effectively. Now let's explore how to take what you've learned so far and act on it in ways that will bring you lasting success, starting with how to ensure that you always sell with integrity.

PART 3

Achieving Lasting Sales Success

CHAPTER 8

Sell with Integrity

AS YOU KNOW BY NOW, ONE OF THE CORE PRINCIPLES OF my selling philosophy—and of this book—is that the most effective way to sell is to align your approach with how the brain is influenced and makes the decision to purchase. That said, this raises an important question: Does this science-backed approach give salespeople too much power that they could use to manipulate others? I've heard this question from students when I lecture at business schools, from salespeople during my trainings, and from media interviewers. I appreciate the question because it's prompted by a genuine, heartfelt concern that I share. And I believe the question is essential to address, as the answer reveals both the responsibility we all have to serve those we sell to and the safeguards each of us can adopt to ensure we never sell in ways that are unethical or manipulative.

Before we dive into what it means to sell ethically and with integrity—and how each of us can guarantee we always do so—I want to call your attention to two key points. First, the fact that people are even raising the question of whether this methodology can be used to manipulate others is a testament to how effective it really is. Throughout my career, I've witnessed countless sales trainings from many different instructors, and not once have I heard anyone wonder if their lessons were so impactful that they could be employed for unscrupulous purposes. That's because the majority of traditional sales trainings espouse techniques that are superficial, outdated, or downright ineffective, so attendees don't question whether what they are learning will give them the ability to easily manipulate others. To the contrary, they wonder if the simplistic ideas being presented will have any impact on their sales at all. I call your attention to this to highlight once again the vast difference between old-school sales training that relies on anecdotal examples and evidence-based sales training like what you've learned in this book.

Second and most important, the *only* way to be successful in selling (irrespective of what sales techniques you use) is to sell ethically. When you lie, exaggerate, withhold essential information, or otherwise compromise what you know to be right for a commission check, regardless of the circumstances, you've sold something that should never be for sale: your integrity. In fact, selling with a lack of integrity will destroy your career faster than almost anything else.

Fortunately, you don't need to lower your ethical standards in order to be effective in selling. Research published in the *Journal of Personal Selling and Sales Management* has confirmed that when salespeople sell with integrity, they experience increased job satisfaction and performance.[1] Numerous studies analyzing the impact of selling ethically on performance have found it consistently generates better results.[2] While salespeople who distort the truth may close a few deals in the short term to unsuspecting clients, they always underperform over time. That's especially true in today's transparent marketplace where information (and reports of bad behavior) spreads quickly.[3] After all, buyers swiftly lose trust in salespeople when they behave in ways that compromise their integrity—a major problem since trust is the binding force in any relationship.[4] So when it comes to how you sell, it literally pays to do the right thing.

Not only does behaving ethically pay off for salespeople; it pays off for their companies too. In another study in the *Journal of Personal Selling and Sales Management,* sales leaders put how to sell ethically on the list of essential topics their teams need training on.[5] And for good reason: When salespeople act dishonestly, they lose sales, and their companies pay a steep price. Surveys have found that 80 percent of buyers say the ethicality of a company's business practices has a direct effect on their decision to purchase from them.[6] When one employee acts unethically, people naturally assume others in the organization will behave in similar ways.[7] This is why after one bad experience, most buyers never give that company a second chance.[8] Simply put, in our modern, hypercompetitive business climate, it's usually one strike and you're out—for good!

Ethical Leadership Improves Sales Results

A 2019 research study found that sales leaders who act ethically inspire greater levels of trust from their salespeople and are more likely to have top performing teams.[9] *Harvard Business Review* editor-in-chief Adi Ignatius summarized the impact of ethical leadership in his article "The Thing About Integrity" when he wrote, "Leaders who prioritize integrity themselves tend to run organizations that discourage winning at any cost and, in the process, cultivate higher employee engagement and more-profitable growth."[10] Leading ethically is not just the right thing to do; it also makes the most business sense.

On top of this, when salespeople behave in ways that are unethical, they do a disservice to everyone in the profession. The *International Journal of Sales Transformation* reports that an alarming 31 percent of sales managers believe that "sales shame" negatively impacts their team's growth.[11] Sales shame is the negative feeling many salespeople have about their job. It often stems from the desire to distance oneself from the undesirable stereotype of a slick, pushy, dishonest huckster, an outdated perspective that still haunts the profession. A 2020 Gallup poll, for instance, asked people to "rate the honesty and ethics" of various occupational groups.[12] The three highest-ranked professions were nurses (89 percent), medical doctors (77 percent), and grade school teachers (75 percent). At the bottom sat business executives (17 percent), advertising practitioners (10 percent), car salespeople (8 percent), and members of Congress (8 percent). While the perception of the profession is slowly improving, many people still view it like Wendell Berry did when he wrote that selling is "the craft of persuading people to buy what they do not need, and do not want, for more than it is worth."[13] The fact is, that *isn't* selling. It's manipulation, which is reprehensible and something the vast majority of sales professionals (including myself!) are adamantly against. When salespeople engage in unscrupulous practices, they perpetuate negative stereotypes and do a disservice to buyers and sellers alike.

Over the past few decades, there has been a concerted effort to elevate the profession and help people recognize selling for what it truly is: a meaningful way to serve others. That said, many salespeople wonder what the difference is between influencing buyers and manipulating them. Let's dig into this key distinction, as well as investigate when influence can become manipulation and what salespeople can do to ensure they never fall into unethical behaviors.

The Difference Between
Influence and Manipulation

The discussion around influence versus manipulation is not new. In ancient Greece, the father of persuasion, Aristotle, clashed with a group of teachers known as the Sophists over this very issue. The Sophists became infamous for their teaching of rhetoric, and Aristotle protested that they did not care about truth but would promote any idea (right or wrong, good or bad) for a fee. He asserted the Sophists were engaging in manipulation because they intentionally deceived people and caused harm for their own financial gain.[14]

Today the debate rages on. To discern the difference, it's essential to understand the ethics that undergird influence. There are some who believe that it's "ethically neutral."[15] That is to say, it's neither good nor bad, but an impartial process. I've found that a more accurate, evidence-backed way of looking at influence is to adopt the Aristotelian viewpoint, which maintains that it is good because it is one of the primary means through which truth becomes known.[16] Through the process of persuasion, one person puts forth an idea with evidence, and others may freely choose to either accept or reject that appeal.[17]

It's also through the process of influence that positive change occurs.[18] As a matter of fact, it's so deeply engrained in human communication that at times it is almost invisible.[19] Influence (and its more direct form, persuasion) is the basis for our legal system, counseling, and democracy itself.[20] Communication scholars Robert Gass and John Seiter sum it up neatly:

Persuasion helps forge peace agreements between nations. Persuasion helps open up closed societies. Persuasion is crucial to the fund-raising efforts of charities and philanthropic organizations. Persuasion convinces motorists to buckle up when driving or to refrain from driving when they've had a few too many drinks. Persuasion is used to convince an alcoholic or drug-dependent family member to seek professional help . . . In short, persuasion is the cornerstone of a number of positive, prosocial endeavors. Very little of the good that we see in the world could be accomplished without persuasion.[21]

Ultimately, this is where the difference lies between influence and manipulation. Correctly applied, persuasion and influence are agents for positive change. When people use influence to help others (whether it's persuading them to stay safe, motivating and inspiring them to achieve their goals, or offering them a service that solves a problem), it's a good thing. However, when people pervert influence or persuasion and wield it unethically, as a means to get what they want, while not helping advance the position of others, that's when it becomes manipulation, which is destructive.[22] Here are three straightforward, reliable ways to detect manipulation and ensure you avoid it.

1. Intention

Intention is a primary factor in judging whether a request is manipulative. To put it simply, if a person attempts to convince others to embrace an idea or a behavior that is not in their best interest, that person is engaging in manipulation. Sadly, people frequently fall into the trap of abusing others in the pursuit of what they desire for themselves. One of the root causes of this Machiavellian mindset is not viewing others as equals. Anytime you put your needs ahead of a solution for everyone, it makes you susceptible to pursuing manipulative behaviors. The renowned philosopher Immanuel Kant wrote about this when he suggested that the foundational precept of morality is treating a person as a human being, not merely as a means to get what you want.[23]

All of us in the profession of selling must guard against viewing buyers or anyone else as merely a means to a sale. Our focus must continuously be on helping others. If the solution you can offer buyers will not adequately address and resolve their problem, you should inform them of this and voluntarily walk away from the sale. It may sound extreme, but it's not: Doing what's in the best interest of others is always the smart thing to do. After all, if you mislead someone once, why would they trust you with any future business? What's more, they're likely to tell everyone they know to steer clear as well. If you can't help a potential client solve their problem, then you should disqualify yourself and look for buyers that you can truly help.

2. Withholding or Distorting Truth

Another hallmark of manipulation is distorting or withholding the truth, crucial facts, or essential information. In sales, this can be seen in those who exaggerate the advantages of an idea, a product, or a service in order to get more people to buy it. It was this form of manipulation that prompted the rise of the popular warning *caveat emptor* (Latin for "let the buyer beware"), reminding potential purchasers to verify that the product's quality matches the seller's claims before money exchanges hands. Even today, most people have experienced the frustration of being told one thing about a product, only to realize after buying it that they've been misled by embellished or downright false claims. Once again, this is wrong, as anything other than honest representation is blatant manipulation.

3. Coercion

Coercion is the third and most obvious component of a manipulative appeal. It is the removal of free choice, and it's often presented as an ultimatum—do this or else. In contrast, persuasion involves influence but never pressure or force. As communication expert Dr. Richard Perloff writes, "A defining characteristic of persuasion is free choice. At some level the individual must be capable of accepting or rejecting the position that has been urged on him or her."[24] Therefore, an invitation that one is unable to say no to is not persuasive; it is coercive and thus manipulative.

By now, hopefully it's obvious there is a significant difference between influence and manipulation.[25] Influence is a prosocial endeavor that advances the positions of all involved. In contrast, a manipulative appeal is one that, if adopted, would negatively impact another. Manipulation is morally wrong and counterproductive to the interests of all involved.[26] In fact, if you work in sales, you are a professional influencer, so an accurate and robust understanding of both the appropriateness of influence and the three primary elements of manipulation is critical. Knowing these will help you work ethically and ensure that you never engage in manipulative behavior.

When Salespeople Are Most Likely to Engage in Unethical Behaviors

In spite of most salespeople's good intentions, some fall prey to acting in ways that compromise their integrity. Fortunately, numerous studies have identified the two sets of circumstances in which salespeople are most likely to fall into unethical practices, which I'll share with you now. Armed with this knowledge, you can stay vigilant, so you won't give in to the temptation to sell in ways that will hurt your buyers—and ultimately your career.

Situation #1: When Your Sales Are Low

As we saw in our discussion of optimism, in our profession—as in so many others—there is continuous pressure to perform. Social scientists have discovered that when salespeople are struggling, they are more likely, out of desperation, to resort to unethical behaviors.[27] And there is a particular time when salespeople are most susceptible to feeling this pressure: when they are just beginning their careers.[28] As researchers Willy Bolander, William Zahn, Terry Loe, and Melissa Clark explain, "Periods of performance failure appear to overwhelm new salespeople's normal moral decision making, and as failures accumulate, unethical behaviors increase."[29]

If you are struggling to meet your quota, be on guard against any impulse to embrace manipulative behaviors. These actions will never fix low performance; they only compound the problem, making it worse. The best way to correct poor sales is to focus on identifying what is holding you back (something we addressed in chapter 4) and then make the necessary changes. If you are new to the profession, realize that the likelihood you'll be tempted to use unethical tactics is higher now than it probably will be at any other time in your career. If you're feeling pressured to compromise your integrity for a short-term win, seek out a colleague or manager and ask for help. Take this seriously because otherwise it can end your career when you've only just begun. And you've worked too hard to let a poor choice jeopardize your future.

Situation #2: When You Experience High Levels of Stress

When we feel stressed at work for prolonged periods, it can make us more susceptible to doing something that compromises our integrity.[30] The reason is that when we experience high levels of stress, it reduces our mental abilities, increasing the likelihood of making an unethical choice we'll later regret.[31] As we become stressed, our bodies secrete cortisol, a powerful and long-lasting hormone that keeps you alert.[32] Cortisol is the reason why after a particularly nerve-racking day you have a hard time unwinding and going to sleep.[33] Human beings were made to experience stress for only a short period—think running from a tiger, not a tense work environment.[34] So when stress is sustained, the brain is adversely affected by the continued exposure to cortisol, which hinders the processing and recall of information, making it hard to perform cognitive tasks.[35] As social psychologist Daniel Goleman says, "Stress makes people stupid."[36]

Now, this doesn't let anyone off the hook. All of us are accountable for our choices, good or bad, regardless of whether we are tense or not. What the science provides is insight into when we're most likely to be enticed to act in ways that compromise our integrity. Knowing this will help you stay vigilant, even if you're feeling burnt out. If you feel your resolve weakening or particularly vulnerable to making a regrettable choice, don't hesitate to reach out to those you trust, explain your dilemma, and ask for support. No one becomes successful alone; we all need help from time to time to make the right choices. Be honest about the pressure you're under and the lure of compromising to get a quick win. Ask for suggestions of other ways to get out of the challenging situation. Doing so is often the difference between whether you are able to stand up to temptation or not.

How to Ensure You Don't Compromise Your Integrity

The key to resisting the temptation to engage in unethical practices is to be prepared for it. The following three principles will strengthen your resolve and help you maintain high levels of integrity for your entire career.

Principle #1: Always Put Your Buyers' Needs First

One science-backed way to avoid unethical sales behaviors is to concentrate on meeting the needs of your potential clients. In fact, numerous studies have confirmed that when salespeople maintain a buyer-centric focus they are far less likely to engage in manipulative tactics, even when they are stressed and underperforming.[37]

The positive impact of a buyer-centered way of selling was clearly demonstrated in a study published in the *Journal of Business Ethics* in which researchers had participants sell to a buyer via a webcam.[38] The salespeople were unable to see or hear the buyers but were informed the buyers could see and hear them. At the end of each presentation, they were told whether or not the buyer would purchase their product and then immediately put into another sales situation with a new buyer. What researchers uncovered was that when the salespeople struggled to close a few deals in a row, they were more likely to disregard buyers' needs and start to make false statements about their product, such as "This is the last one!" or "There is something uniquely special about this item," in order to force a sale. Another common manipulative behavior was to coerce buyers with desperate pleas like "Please help me out," and "It is up to you to help me do well."

Interestingly, one thing made a noticeable difference in keeping these salespeople from unethical behaviors: a reminder from researchers to keep their attention on how they could help the buyers. When the struggling salespeople periodically received a written message reminding them to "stay focused on the buyer's needs," they were significantly less likely to misrepresent their product or exhibit manipulative behaviors. Furthermore, many research studies have proved that a buyer-centered approach not only helps you sell better but also helps you sell more.[39] (For strategies on how to do this, refer back to chapter 4 of this book and chapters 2, 3, and 6 of *The Science of Selling*.)

Principle #2: Choose to Act with Integrity

Integrity isn't only a concept to endorse; it's something you must choose to live out. These three actions will help you sell with integrity.

1. **Realize Your Personal and Professional Integrity Are Linked:** The integrity you display in your personal life heavily influences and often determines how much integrity you have when selling. Don't believe me? Consider research published in the *Proceedings of the National Academy of Sciences* identifying that business executives who cheated on their spouse were more than twice as likely to engage in unethical business practices, compared with those who hadn't been unfaithful.[40] Another study also found a strong correlation between business leaders who broke the law in their personal lives and the likelihood they would perpetrate fraud on the job.[41] This research even drove editors at the *Harvard Business Review* to recommend publicly that boards

analyze executives' off-the-job behaviors, because things like DUIs and even traffic tickets are predictors of whether they would engage in work misconduct.[42]

If you lie, cheat, and manipulate in your personal life, you're far more likely to resort to those same behaviors in the professional world. On the flip side, if you are an ethical, honorable person, then the likelihood you'll be a businessperson or sales professional who consistently acts with integrity and treats others with respect is very high.

2. **Embrace Authenticity:** Being authentic is an important part of what it means to sell with integrity. If you mislead buyers into believing something about you or your product that isn't true, it will damage your credibility. What's more, if you are not authentic, people will instinctively pick up on it, and it will erode their trust in you, diminishing your persuasiveness in the process. Consider a study published in *Organizational Behavior and Human Decision Processes* about an experiment with job seekers.[43] Some were told to talk authentically about themselves, while others modified their responses to what they thought the interviewers wanted to hear. Those who were being genuine were 26 percent more likely to be hired than those who adapted to try to fit their perceptions of the interviewers' preferences. Here's how behavioral scientist Francesca Gino sums up the studies on authenticity: "Simply being yourself makes a better impression than catering to another person's interests and expectations. It not only feels better; it also improves the likelihood that you will achieve your goal."[44]

Being authentic will also help you sell more. I recall a person, whom we'll call Roger, that I coached many years ago when I first started my firm. Roger was an experienced salesperson who had taken a new position in an unfamiliar industry and was struggling. In our first meeting, Roger informed me he had begun using a new technique he hoped would improve his performance. He was copying the speech patterns of the top-performing salesperson in the office next to him. The colleague he was mimicking had lived in a rural area and naturally spoke in a slow, unassuming manner with many long pauses and a strong southern accent. I informed Roger that pretending to speak like someone else wouldn't increase his sales. Rather, buyers would sense he wasn't being genuine, which would decrease their confidence in him. To make my point, I asked Roger what he would do if he ran into one of his clients while at the grocery store with his family. Would he suddenly start talking in a southern accent in front of his wife and kids? Whatever he did, he'd look and feel foolish. Worse, he'd erode his credibility with both. As soon as I said this, Roger confessed that since he'd begun copying his colleague's way of speaking, his sales still hadn't budged. I recommended that he instead focus on being real and honest. Roger and I also identified that he wasn't obtaining an adequate understanding of his potential clients' needs, which limited his ability to compellingly present his product to them. After he corrected these problems, Roger's sales increased and eventually rivaled his successful colleague's, no southern accent required.

At its core, authenticity means being yourself and not trying to trick people into believing something false or inaccurate about you in order to get ahead. Anytime you engage in deception, it damages trust, influence, and sales.

3. **Act Honestly:** Four behavioral scientists conducted a series of experiments involving more than 1,500 participants to analyze the negative effects of dishonest behavior.[45] One of their conclusions was that engaging in dishonest behavior reduces empathic accuracy (i.e., sensing the thoughts and feelings of others). Given that effective selling is built on understanding buyers' points of view and responding to them, this means that when salespeople (or anyone, for that matter) are dishonest, they undermine their ability to connect with their clients and sell to them successfully.

Even more concerning is another finding of the research: "The link between dishonest behavior and empathic accuracy may create a vicious cycle, in which an individual who engages in dishonest acts becomes increasingly more socially isolated and unsupported, thus making it easier to rationalize future dehumanization and dishonest behavior."[46] In other words, every time you act dishonestly, it makes it easier and more likely you'll do so again in the future.

Engaging in deceitful behavior is counterproductive for many reasons. Once your unethical conduct is discovered, it will hurt your reputation and most likely ruin your career. It also destroys your chances of selling to that client in the future. What's more, the guilt of knowing you harmed another person will take a personal toll. Resolve to tell the truth, even if it costs you the sale.[47] As important as selling is, certain things are undeniably more valuable. Your reputation—not to mention your conscience—is one of them. Likewise, keeping your word, respecting others, and treating people with dignity and equality are always the right things to do, sale or no sale.

You probably can already tell if you're being honest or not. That said, if you're ever unsure or just need a reminder, here are some safeguards that will help you sell in an honorable way:

- Do what you say you will do, even when it's hard.

- If you make a mistake, take responsibility and do everything in your power to make it right.

- Don't misrepresent yourself or your company, product, or service.

- Never withhold relevant information that buyers need to know.

- Always answer buyers' questions truthfully.

Integrity is the bedrock of effective selling. Acting honestly, ethically, and in your buyers' best interests will ensure that you, your company, and those you sell to have better relationships and more success.

Principle #3: Live Out Your Integrity Statement

A precursor to acting with integrity is making a strong commitment to it. Let's use some of the science we've learned to ensure that you never compromise on what you know is right. We are going to create a nudge (which we learned about in chapter 6) by developing an integrity statement: a concise affirmation that establishes how you will respond when tempted to engage in manipulative behaviors.

Even if you're already committed to selling ethically, you can still get value from creating an integrity statement. Remember in chapter 3 when we covered how writing down your goals will strengthen your commitment to them and make it more likely you'll act on them? You'll receive the same benefits here.

Integrity Statements in Action: A Case Study

In 2009, a group of graduates from Harvard Business School created the MBA Oath, which is a formal commitment to create value responsibly and ethically.[48] Since then, each year the graduating MBAs have the option of taking the pledge. And Harvard isn't the only business school that does this: "Over 10,000 students representing more than 100 schools around the world have taken the MBA Oath."[49] The power of the MBA Oath is that it creates a strong commitment to integrity, which increases the likelihood that these MBAs will act responsibly throughout their careers.

As you think about designing an integrity statement you'll adhere to, one thing to consider is what management expert Peter Drucker called the mirror test, which involves asking yourself, "What kind of person do I want to see in the mirror in the morning?"[50] Will that person be a liar or manipulator, or will you be someone who does what is right, even when it's difficult? Your integrity statement should encapsulate those values you want to see every time you look in the mirror.

To help you think through and craft your own integrity statement, take a look at three examples of great ones:

- "I will do what is in the best interest of my clients, regardless of the financial costs."

- "I will never lie or mislead others, and I will always treat people how I would want to be treated."

- "I will present myself, my company, and my product accurately, and I will always be truthful, even if it costs me a sale."

Take a moment to jot down your own. It should be something you feel strongly about and can default to whenever you are faced with a tough or tempting situation, so take your time in considering it.

Integrity statement:

_____

_____

One final thought on integrity. Over the course of my career, I've received many accolades and awards, but one of my proudest moments came early on, before I became a sales trainer. At my second sales job, I was the number one performing off-site salesperson in the company. A few years after I left this position, I ran into one of my former colleagues, who was still a salesperson there. As we were catching up, he suddenly blurted out, "I never forgot what you told me." I couldn't recall for the life of me what he was talking about, so I asked him, "What did I tell you?" He smiled and declared, "You said I didn't have to lie to be a great salesperson. And you were right." I've never forgotten that conversation. And in my years of selling, training, and helping organizations improve their sales processes since, I've come to realize that what people remember about you—what really matters—isn't just how much you sold, but also *how* you sold. It's only through selling ethically that you'll experience true success.

We've covered a lot so far. In the next, and final, chapter, I'll give you a formula you can follow to create positive career change. So if you are ready to take your career to the next level, read on.

CHAPTER 9

Take Your Sales Career to the Next Level

MANY YEARS AGO I WAS IN A JOB THAT WASN'T RIGHT FOR me. The position wasn't aligned with who I wanted to be or what I wanted for my life. But I didn't know what to do; I felt stuck. Secretly, I hoped someone would "discover" me and put me on the path to accomplishing my dreams. Day after day I felt more and more trapped until it finally dawned on me that no one was coming to my rescue. My success wasn't anyone else's responsibility. If I wanted to change my career, then I would need to do it. It took a while, but eventually I realized I hadn't been looking at my situation the right way. I thought what needed to change was my job and other outside factors. However, the frustration I was experiencing was primarily a result of my mindsets, traits, and behaviors. I realized that I had control over them, and if I could improve each, my life and work would also improve. That awareness liberated me and helped me radically transform my career for the better.

If my experience resonates with you—if you too desire something more—then this chapter is for you. Your sales and career can drastically improve, but as I learned the hard way, it's ultimately up to you. For your career to change, you must change; no one else is going to fix it for you. And it starts with taking responsibility for your successes *and* your failures.

Think about it: When you work hard and surpass your goals, who should get the majority of the credit? If your company awards bonuses to high-performing employees, who should receive yours? It's safe to say that nearly everyone would have the same response to these questions: You should receive the credit and your name should be on the check. It would be unjust to give the credit or bonus to anyone else, since you earned it through your hard work.

Now here's another question: When you aren't successful, when you fall short of your goals, who is responsible? If you are finding this question more challenging to answer, you're not alone. We have a natural inclination to want the credit for our wins but not the blame for our losses.[1] In fact, this tendency is so well established that behavioral scientists have a name for it: self-attribution bias.[2] It occurs when people attribute their success to their abilities but—in an effort to protect their self-esteem—assign the cause of their failures to external factors they cannot control.[3]

Too often salespeople fall prey to self-attribution bias, and in doing so, they blame their poor performance on bad leads, a weak economy, prices being too high, or an incompetent manager. Though all these factors matter, they are likely only part of why the salespeople didn't achieve the outcomes they wanted. Instead of falling under the sway of the self-attribution bias, I invite you to adopt the mindset that the *primary* reason you aren't getting the results you want is because your approach is limiting you in some way. Embracing this way of thinking is empowering and inspires you to examine what's truly holding you back and then to make the necessary changes to overcome those obstacles and generate superior results.

Over my career training salespeople, I've witnessed firsthand how once they take ownership of their results, they naturally begin taking action to grow their abilities, which in turn improves their performance and their overall careers. So let me ask you, do you believe that your success and failure are your responsibility or someone else's? Give this some thought and document your answers below. Don't skip this exercise, because the implications of writing out your answer can be profound.

Who is responsible for your successes?

_____

Who is responsible for your failures?

_____

Owning both the positive and negative outcomes you generate is the first step to taking your career to the next level. Let's now look at the specific steps you can take to make the changes needed to enhance your sales and career.

How to Architect Change

To positively transform your career, you'll need a plan. That's why I'm going to share my formula for change, which consists of four proven strategies that together will provide you with a path forward. Much like we saw in chapter 3, where you learned seven goal-attainment strategies, using just one of these change-producing strategies will make a noticeable difference. However, using all four will create a compounding effect that will make it much more likely you'll experience the transformation you desire.

Strategy #1: Start with a Sprint

As we learned in chapter 4, one of the most significant barriers to change is the status quo bias—the strong tendency to keep things as they stand, even if you're unhappy.[4] If you've ever tried to make an adjustment in your life and struggled to get started, you've experienced the influence of the status quo bias.[5] The good news is that you can minimize its effect. First, you'll want to be clear on exactly what you want to achieve, why it matters to you, and the initial steps you need to take (for a refresher, take a look at chapters 2 and 3). Once you're ready to act, one of the best ways to break through the status quo bias is with a short burst of focused action. So instead of trying to slowly chip away at it, think of it as a wall that you can blast through with one big push.

Using a surge of activity to sprint toward career-enhancing change is something I've done many times, and I've helped clients utilize this approach to create rapid results. It generates the excitement and energy you'll need to build enough momentum to propel you forward.

One guideline when preparing for this sort of radical action: It should last for only a brief amount of time, usually a few hours to a few days. This is because you are going to temporarily remove all balance from your life. Your sole focus for this short period will be this extreme amount of activity that brings you closer to your desired career change. This type of intense concentration is not sustainable. It's only a launching pad. Keeping up this singular focus and strenuous pace for longer than a few days could negatively affect your life and relationships and even cause burnout, derailing the progress you've made.

You may be wondering what taking a massive step forward looks like. Here are three examples of how my clients have done it:

• I have clients who periodically have me conduct a few days of intense coaching with several of their salespeople. I have each of the salespeople meet with me for around two hours, during which they present part or all of their sales process as if I were a potential customer. Then I'll give them specific feedback on how they can improve. They spend the rest of the day working on implementing the changes I recommend. The following day we meet again and review the progress they've made. What's amazing is the vast improvement in performance between the first demonstration on day one and the second, after the full day of practice. Best of all, their hard work pays off: The average increase in win rates for the folks who complete these sales sprints is 31 percent.

• Two salespeople who sell for a large client of mine decided to team up and help each other improve a skill they both felt weak in: handling challenging objections from buyers. For three days in a row, they stayed at their office three hours late to work on this together, listing all the objections they encounter and then documenting, from the training they'd received, strong responses to each. After reviewing their notes, they took turns practicing, with one person acting like a client sharing an objection while the other responded. By the end of the three days, both of them felt much more confident handling objections. And their hard work also paid off: The following quarter was the best each had ever experienced at the company.

• Inspired by a workshop I led for her employer, one salesperson took a bold step toward her goal of becoming the top seller at her company. She devoted the entire weekend after the training to incorporating what she'd learned from it into her sales process. First, she recorded herself selling the way she typically would. After observing the recording, she made notes on what she could improve based on the strategies she'd learned, practiced making those improvements, and recorded herself again, repeating this until she was satisfied. Though she continued making minor tweaks to her sales process over the next few months, she credits the training and that weekend of practice as the reason for an upturn in sales that vaulted her to achieving the highest volume in her organization.

If these examples seem extreme, that's because they are—by design. A big burst of action is what's often needed to smash through the status quo bias and move you closer to the outcomes you want.

Let's put this into practice with a quick exercise to identify a big step you can take to break through the status quo bias and make major improvements in your career.

Change you desire to make:

_____

Your sprint:

_____

Preparations you need to make before taking the leap:

_____

_____

To set yourself up for success when embarking on a sprint, consider these two things:

1. While advancing swiftly toward the change you desire will yield some quick results, it may not be enough on its own. Significant transformation requires consistent effort over weeks, months, or even years (something we'll talk about in the next section). The power of the sprint is that it enables you to take a giant leap forward, increasing the likelihood you'll continue working toward your objective over the long haul.[6]

2. Because of the focused action and dedication this approach demands, you may need to talk with others (your family, friends, or employer) before you begin. For instance, you may need to get some feedback from your manager before starting your sprint or ask your family for support while you devote this short but intensely focused time to improving your sales outcomes.

Once you've been able to achieve some speedy progress, the next strategy we'll discuss is the best way to build on it and make lasting change in your performance and career.

Strategy #2: Make Small Incremental Improvements

Though taking a big step forward is a great way to make quick progress and build momentum, significant, lasting changes are usually created on a smaller scale over extended periods. Most of these come through small, consistent tweaks to your daily activities and behaviors that move you closer to your dreams. By focusing on improving a little every day, you can produce big achievements.[7]

This is exactly what the British Olympic cycling team found when they ended their seventy-six-year streak of not winning a gold medal. They broke down the elements of a bike race to the essentials needed to win and focused on enhancing each by a mere 1 percent. They used a wind tunnel to identify which racing suits were the most aerodynamic, painted the floor of the team truck white so they could spot dust that could hinder bike performance, and even had a surgeon teach them how to properly wash their hands to avoid illness so they could have as many healthy training days as possible.[8] Their hope was that these small upgrades would have a compounding effect and enhance their overall performance. And they were right. In the 2008 Beijing Olympics, they won an incredible seven out of ten gold medals.[9]

Don't Underestimate the Power of Small Incremental Changes

One of my favorite games is chess. The origin of the game is shrouded in mystery, but legend has it, the poor inventor showed chess to a king who was so delighted by the game that he offered the inventor anything he wanted. The inventor shrewdly asked that a grain of rice be placed on the first square of the chessboard. Then two grains on the second square, and four on the third, with the number of grains doubling on each of the subsequent squares. Believing this to be a small reward, the king agreed. However, his advisers informed him that he would be unable to grant the request.

Why? By the final, sixty-fourth square, the amount of rice would be eighteen quintillion grains, more than all the rice on the earth.[10] I share this legend to call your attention to its wisdom. Much like the king, we have the tendency to undervalue how much small incremental enhancements can generate remarkable outcomes.

This commitment to ongoing, incremental improvement isn't always easy or fun. But it is essential if you want to take your sales and/or career to the next level. When I was first learning how to apply science to selling, I kept a quote on the wall next to my desk that I would look at every day, attributed to motivational speaker Jim Rohn: "We must all suffer from one of two pains: the pain of discipline or the pain of regret. The difference is discipline weighs ounces while regret weighs tons." Those words inspired me when I felt like quitting or just taking it easy for a day. There isn't anything glamorous about the daily grind. It just works better than anything else.

The good news is that this approach also requires less willpower over time, since small acts of regular self-discipline increase willpower strength.[11] As behavioral scientist Heidi Grant Halvorson explains, "Self-control is learned and developed and made stronger (or weaker) over time . . . You can get more self-control the same way you get bigger muscles—you've got to give it regular workouts."[12] For example, in one study, researchers observed participants who followed an exercise program for two months—a feat that required them to exert a high amount of discipline.[13] Before beginning the workouts, participants performed a series of laboratory tasks designed to measure their self-control. Then after completing the two months of exercise, they took the self-control assessment again, showing significant improvement on it. Even more intriguing was that the participants reported enhanced impulse control in other parts of their lives as well. They drank less alcohol, smoked fewer cigarettes, curbed impulsive spending, ate healthier foods, and even did more chores around the house. Overall, the boost in self-control they got from regularly working out benefited many areas of their lives. Similarly, as you begin pushing yourself to continually focus on making incremental improvements, you'll find that it requires less willpower over time.[14] So expect it to be challenging when you start, but know that you'll reap the benefits and find it will take less self-control to continue on.

Before we move on to Strategy #3, let's pause to go through an exercise to make sure you're set up for success. Think of the career-enhancing change you desire to make. Now, what are a few specific actions you can take on a regular basis to move in that direction? Perhaps it's meeting with a colleague or your sales manager every week for an hour to work on growing your sales abilities, or reading at least one book on selling or business every two weeks, or investing twenty minutes a day learning and practicing new skills. Whatever it is, write it down so that you'll be ready to act on it.

Change you desire to make:

_____

Small incremental improvements:

_____

_____

_____

Strategy #3: Invest in Yourself

Meaningful career change always requires significant investment in yourself, whether that's time or money or both. In fact, one major reason why many salespeople are low performers is because they underinvest in themselves and their careers, relying on the companies they work for to provide them with the training they need. As I've mentioned, you are responsible for your success. If you are able to get your employer to pay for the training you need, that's great, but if not, you'll need to work it out on your own. Elite salespeople know that the sacrifices they make to improve their abilities are the best investments they could ever make. As I shared in chapter 2, there is always a price for success, but it's worth it. Those short-term sacrifices pay serious dividends in the long run. As the philosopher and poet James Allen famously wrote, people "are anxious to improve their circumstances, but are unwilling to improve themselves; they therefore remain bound."[15] There are many places in your life where it's admirable to be frugal; investing in your future isn't one of them.

Stop for a moment to identify one change you would like to make regarding your career. Maybe it's to drastically improve your sales skills so that you can double your income, to be the top salesperson at your company, or to become a sales manager. Below is an exercise in which you can write down the transformation you want, what you anticipate you'll need to achieve it, and whether or not you are willing to do so. That will help you identify whether the change is worth pursuing and also mentally prepare you for what it will take to achieve what you want.

Change you desire to make:

_____

Investments you may need to make the change happen:

_____

**If required, are you willing to make these investments?
Yes No**

If you circled "No" or hesitated to circle "Yes," pause for a moment to reflect on why. Perhaps this isn't the right change for you, or maybe the payoff simply isn't worth the investment. It's good to identify this early on, because it's never wise to pursue something that you are not willing to pay the price to obtain.

At this point, you know you want to make a big change, you know the power of an intense sprint, and you recognize that you'll need to keep making incremental shifts over time to create lasting progress. Most of all, you (hopefully) appreciate the value that comes from investing in yourself. The final strategy I'll leave you with is a powerful ally you can turn to anytime to make change easier.

Strategy #4: Adapt Your Environment to Foster Success

If there's one thing that science has proved over and over again, it's that human beings are heavily influenced by their environment.[16] This notion goes all the way back to the first half of the twentieth century when Kurt Lewin, considered to be the father of social psychology, stated his famous equation B = f (P, E), which asserts that behavior (B) is a function (f) of a person (P) and the environment (E) that person is in.[17] Lewin's insight has been validated in thousands of experiments since then, including many I've shared throughout this book.[18]

Even minor modifications in our environment can sway how

we behave.[19] For instance, one fascinating study discovered that when diners were primed with menus that included indulgent descriptors of a restaurant's vegetable dishes (twisted citrus-glazed carrots, sweet sizzling green beans, and tangy lime-seasoned beets), they were much more likely to choose the veggies and rate them as tasty than were diners who had been shown only basic or healthy descriptors of those dishes.[20]

The research on how environment triggers behavior reveals a critical concept that you can utilize too: If you alter your surroundings, you can predictably prompt certain behaviors in yourself. Here are two powerful ways you can leverage your surroundings to inspire actions that will launch you to the outcome you desire.

1. Link a Specific Setting with Certain Behaviors

As we explored in chapter 3, scheduling when you will do something increases the odds you'll actually do it. Another effective way to make certain behaviors—like those that improve your career—easier to do is to link them with a specific setting or cue. A good example of this is a behavioral treatment for insomnia known as stimulus control therapy, which involves using your bed only for sleep (no reading, watching TV, etc.).[21] That means you get into bed only once you are ready to sleep, and if you can't fall asleep, you get out of bed and don't go back until you feel sleepy.[22] Your brain learns to associate your bed exclusively with sleeping, which increases the chance that you'll fall asleep quickly there.

There are many ways that you can apply this same concept to prompt you to work on improving your sales expertise. Here are two examples:

• Take advantage of your commute to expand your sales knowledge by listening only to sales-related audiobooks or podcasts. This will help you link your commute with learning, which will make it more likely that you will learn as you go.

- Designate a specific space for your sales development. For example, choose a chair in your home that you sit in only when you are practicing your skills. Just as associating your bed with sleep helps fight insomnia, within a short time merely sitting in that chair will put you in the right mindset to work on growing those abilities.

2. Reduce Friction by Eliminating Distractions

To make a major change, you'll need to keep your focus on the activities that will make it happen. You'll have to remove distractions that hinder you from focusing on what you desire to accomplish. One amusing example of this comes from a well-known social science experiment that occurred in an extremely unusual place: the men's bathroom at Amsterdam's Schiphol Airport. In an effort to increase cleanliness, behavioral economist Aad Kieboom convinced airport authorities to etch an image of a black housefly on the bottom of the urinals. The hypothesis was that giving men something to focus on and aim at would increase their accuracy and reduce mess around the urinals. And it worked! Kieboom's assistants found (I won't go into how) that spillage decreased by 80 percent, resulting in an 8 percent reduction in cleaning costs.[23]

Eliminating distractions and creating prompts that enhance focus aren't just a way to improve bathroom hygiene; they're also something you can use to eliminate friction and make your own environment more conducive to supporting whatever you're pursuing. As social scientists Kristen Berman and Evelyn Gosnell explain, "Behavioral science has shown that people can be deterred from taking action by even minor amounts of choice, added steps, time, effort, and decision-making. These types of behavioral 'frictions' (perceived or real) generally decrease the probability that a given behavior takes place."[24]

Being successful is hard, and the friction of distraction makes it even harder. This is why you'll want to be relentless in identifying any distractions that make it difficult for you to keep your focus on what matters most. Some salespeople free up time to pursue their goals by reducing the number of movies or TV shows they watch or how long they spend on social media. Others remove distractions that keep them from performing at their best by eliminating alcohol or making sure they get at least eight hours of sleep every night. Still others will give up a negative habit that steals their time and money, or they'll reduce the influence of a pessimistic person who drags them down. So ask yourself, What distractions are hindering your success? Then decide which are more valuable, the distractions or your goals, and act accordingly.

Your Next Steps

Throughout this book, I've sought to communicate one overarching idea: Science provides real, actionable insights that will help you take your sales—and your career—to new heights. A science-backed way of selling also offers a more accurate way of thinking about your approach that will give you an edge in today's hyper-competitive marketplace. On top of that, it will provide you clarity as to why you or someone on your team is underperforming and the mindsets, traits, and behaviors that can boost your or their effectiveness.

Yet the reason I am most passionate about selling is because it is a meaningful way to serve others. Through it, you can help people solve their most challenging problems, accomplish their personal and professional goals, and improve their lives. Sales generate the revenue that provides jobs and spurs economic growth. In fact, it plays a vital role in our careers, our communities, and the world. That's why I strongly believe that selling—and the way we sell—is simply too important to be based on anything other than proven science.

My hope is that you'll use the ideas in this book to take your sales and career to the next level. I've given you the road map; the rest is up to you. So what are you waiting for? Get out there and sell something.

Five Ways You Can Supercharge Your Sales with Science

1. **Book David to speak to your group.** He'll weave humor, stories, and science together in a way that will engage your audience and provide them with proven strategies they can implement immediately.

2. **Have David deliver a training workshop or seminar.** His science-backed training will guide you in developing the knowledge and skills you need to take your organization's sales to the next level.

3. **Get David's science-based virtual sales training.** This includes 20 different courses, 165 quizzes and tests, and nearly 80 simulations that allow you to practice what you've learned and receive instant feedback. The result is a learning experience that rapidly boosts sales effectiveness and results.

4. **Utilize David's sales coaching to boost your sales production.** He's an expert at helping companies improve how they coach their salespeople, and he also provides no-nonsense, highly customized sales coaching that will empower you to attain extraordinary sales results.

5. **Read this book.** Apply its lessons in your organization and your selling environment.

Don't lose sales that should be yours. Contact David today about his proven, science-based selling strategies:

www.HoffeldGroup.com

info@HoffeldGroup.com

Acknowledgments

To me, this book is more than a book on selling. It reveals how each of us can leverage science-backed insights to improve not only our careers but also our lives. As a result, I am beholden to the many scientists whose research is the foundation of this book. Their work has both enriched the profession of sales and our world.

I begin the book with a quote from one of my sales heroes, Robert N. McMurry. Early in my career, I stumbled on McMurry's vision that a scientific understanding of human psychology was the missing link that could elevate selling. His work motivated me to apply science to the act of selling and keep at it even when it became challenging and took much longer than expected. I only hope that my work will inspire others the way his did me.

Throughout the writing process I was fortunate to have the amazing Stephanie Bowen assisting me. Her support and passion for the book was inspiring and her brilliant insights elevated every page. She was also masterful in helping me improve the structure of the book and refine the ideas contained within it. At this point, I can't imagine writing a book without her.

Special thanks to Nina Shield, executive editor at TarcherPerigee Books, a division of Penguin Random House. Her recommendations and edits took the book to the next level. In fact, the entire team at TarcherPerigee was wonderful to work with, as everyone who touched the book improved it in some way.

I am indebted to my literary agent, Leila Campoli, who, early in the process, helped me cultivate the direction for this book and has been my trustworthy guide throughout the publishing process. Also, thanks to Andy Krahn for creating the illustrations and his commitment to excellence.

Researching and writing a book is a time-consuming endeavor— at least the way I do it. That's why I'm so thankful for the support of my wife, Sarah. She read my early drafts and enabled me to devote large blocks of time to writing. Additionally, I am especially grateful that years before my first book, she listened to my dream of how science could positively transform sales and allowed me to invest significant amounts of time and money to make that dream a reality.

I am blessed to be the father of three wonderful children, Jolene, David, and Joseph, who willingly endured their dad writing yet another book. My hope is that this book will help each on their journey to become who they were created to be.

I am grateful to NoEl Hoffeld for her edits on each chapter. Her insights prompted me to clarify my thinking throughout each stage of the writing process. And special thanks to Norman Hoffeld, who showed me at a young age how one can influence people ethically and still be effective.

It has been said that the best book to write is the one you want to read. This is certainly true in this case. For those sales professionals who, like me, want science-based strategies that are proven to work, this book is for you. And now that you have it, use it and you'll experience how you will Sell More with Science.

Notes

INTRODUCTION: USE SCIENCE TO SELL MORE

1. Noah J. Goldstein, Steve J. Martin, and Robert B. Cialdini, *Yes! 50 Scientifically Proven Ways to Be Persuasive* (New York: Free Press, 2008), 2.

2. Carl Sagan, interview with Charlie Rose, May 27, 1996, https://www .youtube.com/watch?v=U8HEwO-2L4w&feature=emb_logo.

CHAPTER 1: HOW YOU THINK DETERMINES THE RESULTS YOU PRODUCE

1. David Myers, *Social Psychology*, 9th international ed. (New York: McGraw-Hill, 2008), 6.

2. Kurt Lewin, *Principles of Topological Psychology* (New York: McGraw-Hill, 1936).

3. Christina Draganich and Kristi Erdal, "Placebo Sleep Affects Cognitive Functioning," *Journal of Experimental Psychology: Learning, Memory, and Cognition* 40, no. 3 (2014): 857–64.

4. Peter Schulman, "Applying Learned Optimism to Increase Sales Productivity," *Journal of Personal Selling and Sales Management* 19, no. 1 (1999): 31.

5. C. C. Benight and A. Bandura, "Social Cognitive Theory of Posttraumatic Recovery: The Role of Perceived Self-Efficacy," *Behavior Research and Therapy* 42, no. 10 (2005): 1129–48; Albert Bandura, *Self-Efficacy: The Exercise of Control* (New York: Freeman, 1997); Richard M. Ryan and Arlen C. Moller, "Competence as Central, but Not Sufficient, for High-Quality Motivation," in *Handbook of Competence and Motivation*, 2nd ed., eds. Andrew J. Elliot, Carol S. Dweck, and David S. Yeager (New York: Gilford Press, 2017), 218.

6. A. Stajkovic and F. Luthans, "Self-Efficacy and Work-Related Performance: A Meta-Analysis," *Psychological Bulletin* 123 (1998): 240–61.

7. "Victor Serebriakoff; Built Mensa into 100,000-Member Organization," *Los Angeles Times*, January 7, 2000, www.latimes.com /archives/la-xpm-2000-jan-07-mn-51649-story.html.

8. Douglas Martin, "Victor Serebriakoff, 87, Dies; Oversaw the Growth of Mensa," *New York Times*, January 10, 2000, 7.

9. *Mensa International*, www.mensa.org; Mark Dettinger, "The History of Mensa," *Mensa Switzerland*, July 6, 2012, members.mensa.ch/ history.

10. M. Blittner, J. Goldberg, and M. Merbaum, "Cognitive Self-Control Factors in the Reduction of Smoking Behavior," *Behavior Therapy* 9, no. 4 (1978): 553–61.

11. Saul Kassin, Steven Fein, and Hazel Rose Markus, *Social Psychology*, 7th ed. (Belmont, CA: Wadsworth, 2008), 120.

12. R. Rosenthal and L. Jacobson, *Pygmalion in the Classroom* (New York: Crown, 1992).

13. Bill Taylor, "What Breaking the 4-Minute Mile Taught Us About the Limits of Conventional Thinking," *Harvard Business Review*, March 9, 2018, https://hbr.org/2018/03/what-breaking-the-4-minute-mile -taught-us-about-the-limits-of-conventional-thinking.

14. Yoram (Jerry) Wind and Colin Crook, *The Power of Impossible Thinking* (Upper Saddle River, NJ: Wharton School Publishing, 2005), 22.

15. Taylor, "What Breaking the 4-Minute Mile Taught Us."

16. Wind and Crook, *The Power of Impossible Thinking*, 22.

17. K. B. Carey and M. P. Carey, "Changes in Self-Efficacy Resulting from Unaided Attempts to Quit Smoking," *Psychology of Addictive Behaviors* 7, no. 4 (1993): 219–24.

18. Daniel Goleman, "New Scales of Intelligence Rank Talent for Living," *New York Times*, April 5, 1988.

19. E. Winner, "Exceptionally High Intelligence and Schooling," *American Psychologist* 52, no. 10 (October 1997); Daniel Goleman, *Emotional Intelligence* (New York: Bantam, 2006), 47; Robert Sternberg, "Intelligence, Competence, and Expertise," in *The Handbook of Competence and Motivation*, eds. Andrew Elliot and Carol S. Dweck (New York: Guilford Press, 2005); K. Anders Ericsson, Roy W. Roring, and Kiruthiga Nandagopal, "Giftedness and Evidence for Reproducibly

Superior Performance: An Account Based on the Expert Performance Framework," *High Ability Studies* 18, no. 1 (2007): 3–56.

20. Faye Flam, "If You're So Smart, Why Aren't You Rich?," Bloomberg .com, December 22, 2016, accessed February 21, 2020, www .bloomberg.com/opinion/articles/2016-12-22/if-you-re-so-smart -why-aren-t-you-rich.

21. Elaine Hatfield, John T. Cacioppo, and Richard L. Rapson, *Emotional Contagion* (Cambridge, UK: Cambridge University Press, 1994), 79; Daniel Goleman, *Social Intelligence* (New York: Bantam Books, 2006), 13; Peter Totterdell, Steve Kellett, Katja Teuchmann, and Rob B. Briner, "Evidence of Mood Linkage in Work Groups," *Journal of Personality and Social Psychology* 74, no. 6 (1998): 1504–15.

22. Peter Aldhous, "Humans Prefer Cockiness to Expertise," *New Scientist*, June 3, 2009, retrieved March 16, 2016, www.newscientist.com/ article/mg20227115.500-humans-prefer-cockiness-to-expertise/.

23. Joseph J. Martocchio, "Effects of Conceptions of Ability on Anxiety, Self-Efficacy, and Learning in Training," *Journal of Applied Social Psychology* 79, no. 6 (1994): 819–25; Carol Dweck, *Mindset: The New Psychology of Success* (New York: Ballantine Books, 2016), 111; Robert Wood and Albert Bandura, "Impact of Conceptions of Ability on Self-Regulatory Mechanisms and Complex Decision Making," *Journal of Personality and Social Psychology* 56, no. 3 (1989): 407–15; Bandura, *Self-Efficacy*.

24. Myers, *Social Psychology*, 56.

25. Edwin A. Locke and Gary P. Latham, "Building a Practically Useful Theory of a Goal Setting and Task Motivation: A 35-Year Odyssey," *American Psychologist* 57, no. 9 (2002): 708.

26. A. Koriat, S. Lichtenstein, and B. Fischhoff, "Reasons for Confidence," *Journal of Experimental Psychology: Human Learning and Memory* 6, no. 2 (1980): 107–18.

27. S. White and E. Locke, "Problems with the Pygmalion Effect and Some Proposed Solutions," *Leadership Quarterly* 11, no. 3 (2000): 389–415; Bandura, *Self-Efficacy*.

28. Chris P. Neck and Charles C. Manz, "Thought Self-Leadership: The Influence of Self-Talk and Mental Imagery on Performance," *Journal of Organizational Behavior* 13, no. 7 (1992): 681–99.

29. Erika Andersen, "Learning to Learn," *Harvard Business Review*, March 2016.

30. Craig Valentine, *Secrets of the Champions: Simple Steps to Speaking Success* (CD), 2004.

31. David Hoffeld, *The Science of Selling: Proven Strategies to Make Your Pitch, Influence Decisions, and Close the Deal* (New York: TarcherPerigee, 2016), 17.

32. Dweck, *Mindset*, 213.

33. Carol S. Dweck, Chi-yue Chiu, and Ying-yi Hong, "Implicit Theories and Their Role in Judgements and Reactions: A World from Two Perspectives," *Psychological Inquiry* 6, no. 4 (1995): 268.

34. Hans S. Schroder, Megan E. Fisher, Yanli Lin, Sharon L. Lo, Judith H. Danovitch, and Jason S. Moser, "Neural Evidence for Enhanced Attention to Mistakes Among School-Aged Children with a Growth Mindset," *Developmental Cognitive Neuroscience* 24 (2017): 42–50.

35. Carol S. Dweck, *Self-Theories: Their Role in Motivation, Personality, and Development* (Philadelphia: Taylor and Francis/Psychology Press); C. H. Uthman, "Performance Effects of Motivational State: A Meta-Analysis," *Personality and Social Psychology Review* 1 (1997): 170–82.

36. J. A. Mangels, B. Butterfield, J. Lamb, C. Good, and C. S. Dweck, "Why Do Beliefs About Intelligence Influence Learning Success? A Social Cognitive Neuroscience Model," *Social Cognitive and Affective Neuroscience* 1, no. 2 (2006): 75–86.

37. Christopher G. Myers, Bradley R. Staats, and Francesca Gino, "'My Bad!': How Internal Attribution and Ambiguity of Responsibility Affect Learning from Failure," Harvard Business School NOM Unit Working Paper No. 14-104 (April 2014).

38. Francesca Gino and Bradley Staats, "Why Organizations Don't Learn," *Harvard Business Review*, November 2015.

39. Hoffeld, *The Science of Selling*, 17.

40. Dweck, *Mindset*, 50.

41. David S. Yeager and Carol Dweck, "Mindsets That Promote Resilience: When Students Believe That Personal Characteristics Can Be Developed," *Educational Psychologist* 47, no. 4 (2012): 302–14.

42. Chris Argyris, "Teaching Smart People How to Learn," *Harvard Business Review*, special issue (Winter 2019).

43. Jason S. Moser, Hans S. Schroder, Carrie Heeter, Tim P. Morgan, and Yu-Hao Lee, "Mind Your Errors: Evidence for Neural Mechanism Linking Growth Mind-Set to Adaptive Posterior Adjustments," *Psychological Science* 22 (2011): 1484–89.

44. Moser, Schroder, Heeter, Morgan, and Lee, "Mind Your Errors," 1484.

45. Wood and Bandura, "Impact of Conceptions of Ability on Self-Regulatory Mechanisms and Complex Decision Making," 408.

46. Laura Kray and Michael Haselhuhn, "Implicit Theories of Negotiation Ability and Performance: Longitudinal and Experimental Evidence," *Journal of Personality and Social Psychology* 93 (2007): 49–64.

47. Martocchio, "Effects of Conceptions of Ability on Anxiety, Self-Efficacy, and Learning in Training," 819–25; Richard Robins and Jennifer Pals, "Implicit Self-Theories in the Academic Domain: Implications for Goals Orientation, Attributions, Affects, and Self-Esteem Change," *Self and Identity* 1, no. 4 (2002): 313–36.

48. Peter Heslin, Gary Latham, and Don VandeWalle, "The Effect of Implicit Person Theory on Performance Appraisals," *Journal of Applied Psychology* 90, no. 5 (2005): 842–56; Peter Heslin, Don VandeWalle, and Gary Latham, "Keen to Help? Managers' IPT and Their Subsequent Employee Coaching," *Personnel Psychology* 59, no. 4 (2006): 871–902; Gino and Staats, "Why Organizations Don't Learn."

49. Rasmus Hougaard, Jacqueline Carter, and Kathleen Hogan, "How Satya Nadella Is Reinventing Microsoft's Culture," *Harvard Business Review* (July–August 2019), 82.

50. Herminia Ibarra and Anetta Rattan, "Microsoft: Instilling a Growth Mindset," July 9, 2019, https://herminiaibarra.com/microsoft -instilling-a-growth-mindset/.

51. Carol Dweck, "What Having a 'Growth Mindset' Actually Means," *Harvard Business Review*, special issue (Winter 2019).

52. Dweck, "What Having a 'Growth Mindset' Actually Means."

53. Neck and Manz, "Thought Self-Leadership."

54. Varda Liberman, Steven M. Samuels, and Lee Ross, "The Name of the Game: Predictive Power of Reputations Versus Situational Labels in Determining Prisoner's Dilemma Game Moves," *Personality and Social Psychology Bulletin* 30, no. 9 (2004): 1175–85; R. E. Kraut, "The Effects of Social Labeling on Giving to Charity," *Journal of Experimental Social Psychology* 9, no. 6 (1973): 551–62; J. K. Beggan and S. T. Allison, "More There Than Meets the Eyes: Support for the Mere-Ownership Effect," *Journal of Consumer Psychology* 6 (1997): 285–97; A. M. Tybout and R. F. Yalch, "The Effect of Experience: A Matter of Salience?," *Journal of Consumer Research* 6, no. 4 (1980):

406–12; Robert B. Cialdini, Nancy Eisenberg, Beth L. Green, Kelton Rhoads, and Renee Bator, "Undermining the Undermining Effect of Reward on Sustained Interest," *Journal of Applied Social Psychology* 28, no. 3 (1998): 253–67.

55. Carol S. Dweck, "The Power of Yet," TEDx Norrköping, YouTube, September 12, 2014, retrieved February 13, 2020, https://www.youtube.com/watch?v=J-swZaKN2Ic.

56. Daryl J. Bem, "Self-Perception Theory," in *Advances in Experimental Social Psychology*, vol. 6, ed. L. Berkowitz (New York: Academic Press, 1972), 2; Daryl J. Bem, "Self-Perception: An Alternative Interpretation of Cognitive Dissonance Phenomena," *Psychological Review* 74, no. 3 (1967): 183–200; R. H. Fazio, "Self-Perception Theory: A Current Perspective," in *Ontario Symposium on Personality and Social Psychology*, eds. M. P. Zanna, J. Olson, and C. Herman (Hillsdale, NJ: Erlbaum, 1978), 129–50; Barry R. Schlenker and James V. Trudeau, "Impact of Self-Presentations on Private Self-Beliefs: Effects of Prior Self-Beliefs and Misattribution," *Journal of Personality and Social Psychology* 58, no. 1 (1990): 22–32; A. E. Kelly and R. R. Rodriguez, "Publicly Committing Oneself to an Identity," *Basic and Applied Social Psychology* 28, no. 2 (2006): 185–91.

57. Kristi Hedges, "Make Sure Everyone on Your Team Sees Learning as Part of Their Job," *Harvard Business Review*, September 12, 2018, https://hbr.org/2018/09/make-sure-everyone-on-your-team-sees-learning-as-part-of-their-job.

CHAPTER 2: THE #1 TRAIT YOU NEED TO SUCCEED

1. "How to Predict Turnover on Your Sales Team," *Harvard Business Review*, July–August 2017, 22–24.

2. Bradford D. Smart and Greg Alexander, *Topgrading for Sales* (New York: Portfolio/Penguin, 2008), 5; Scott Fuhr, "Good Hiring Makes Good Cents," *Selling Power* (July/August/September 2012), 20; Joe Light, "More Workers Start to Quit," *Wall Street Journal*, May 25, 2010.

3. Lauren Eskreis-Winkler, Elizabeth Shulman, Scott Beal, and Angela Duckworth, "The Grit Effect: Predicting Retention in the Military, the Workplace, School and Marriage," *Frontiers in Psychology* 5, no. 36 (2014): 1–12.

4. Eskreis-Winkler, Shulman, Beal, and Duckworth, "The Grit Effect," 1.

5. Francis Galton, *Hereditary Genius: An Inquiry into Its Laws and Consequences* (London: Macmillan, 1892), 33.

6. Angela Duckworth, Christopher Peterson, Michael Matthews, and Dennis R. Kelly, "Grit: Perseverance and Passion for Long-Term Goals," *Journal of Personality and Social Psychology* 92, no. 6 (2007): 1087–101.

7. Angela Lee Duckworth, Teri A. Kirby, Eli Tsukayama, Heather Berstein, and K. Anders Ericsson, "Deliberate Practice Spells Success: Why Grittier Competitors Triumph at the National Spelling Bee," *Social Psychological and Personality Science* 2, no. 2 (2011): 174–81.

8. Eskreis-Winkler, Shulman, Beal, and Duckworth, "The Grit Effect."

9. A. L. Duckworth, P. D. Quinn, and M. E. P. Seligman, "Positive Predictors of Teacher Effectiveness," *Journal of Positive Psychology* 4, no. 6 (2009): 540–47.

10. Riley Dugan, Bryan Hochstein, Maria Rouziou, and Benjamin Britton, "Gritting Their Teeth to Close the Sale: The Positive Effect of Salesperson Grit on Job Satisfaction and Performance," *Journal of Personal Selling and Sales Management* 39, no. 2 (2018): 1–21.

11. Angela Duckworth, *Grit: The Power of Passion and Perseverance* (New York: Simon and Schuster, 2016), xv, 20.

12. Duckworth, *Grit*, 42.

13. Angela L. Duckworth and Patrick D. Quinn, "Development and Validation of the Short Grit Scale (Grit-S)," *Journal of Personality Assessment* 91, no. 2 (2009): 166–74.

14. Walter Mischel, Ebbe B. Ebbesen, and Antonette Raskoff, "Cognitive and Attentional Mechanisms in Delay of Gratification," *Journal of Personality and Social Psychology* 21, no. 2 (February 1972): 204–18; Walter Mischel and Ebbe B. Ebbesen, "Attention in Delay Gratification," *Journal of Personality and Social Psychology* 16, no. 2 (1970): 329–37; Walter Mischel, Yuichi Shoda, and Monica L. Rodriguez, "Delay of Gratification in Children," *Science* 244, no. 4907 (1989): 933–38.

15. Walter Mischel, *The Marshmallow Test* (New York: Little, Brown, 2014), 5.

16. W. Mischel, Y. Shoda, and M. L. Rodriguez, "Delay of Gratification in Children," *Science* 244, no. 4907 (1989): 933–38.

17. J.-C. Chebat and P. Kollias, "The Impact of Empowerment on Customer Contact Employees' Roles in Service Organizations," *Journal of Service Research* 3, no. 1 (2000): 66–81; M. D. Hartline and O. C. Ferrell, "The

Management of Customer-Contact Service Employees: An Empirical Investigation," *Journal of Marketing* 60, no. 4 (1996): 52–70.

18. W. Verbeke, B. Dietz, and E. Verwaal, "Drivers of Sales Performance: A Contemporary Meta-Analysis; Have Salespeople Become Knowledge Brokers?," *Journal of the Academy of Marketing Science* 39, no. 3 (2011): 407–28.

19. James C. Naylor, Robert D. Pritchard, and Daniel R. Ilgen, *A Theory of Behavior in Organizations* (New York: Academic Press, 1980); Orville C. Walker Jr., Gilbert A. Churchill Jr., and Neil M. Ford, "Organizational Determinants of the Industrial Salesmen's Role Conflict and Ambiguity," *Journal of Marketing* 39 (January 1975): 32–39; B. C. Krishnan, R. G. Netemeyer, and J. S. Boles, "Self-Efficacy, Competitiveness, and Effort as Antecedents of Salesperson Performance," *Journal of Personal Selling and Sales Management* 22, no. 4 (2002): 285–95; Dugan, Hochstein, Rouziou, and Benjamin, "Gritting Their Teeth to Close the Sale."

20. C. Cherniss, D. Goleman, R. Emmerling, K. Cowan, and M. Adler, *Bringing Emotional Intelligence to the Workplace* (New Brunswick, NJ: Consortium for Research on Emotional Intelligence in Organizations, Rutgers University, 1998).

21. C.-C. Chen and F. Jaramillo, "The Double-Edged Effects of Emotional Intelligence on the Adaptive Selling–Salesperson-Owned Loyalty Relationship," *Journal of Personal Selling and Sales Management* 34, no. 1 (2014): 33–50; D. L. Joseph and D. A. Newman, "Emotional Intelligence: An Integrative Meta-Analysis and Cascading Model," *Journal of Applied Psychology* 95, no. 1 (2010): 54–78.

22. M. K. McCuddy and B. L. Peery, "Selected Individual Differences and Collegians' Ethical Beliefs," *Journal of Business Ethics* 15, no. 3 (1996): 261–72.

23. N. Ntoumanis, L. C. Healy, C. Sedikides, J. Duda, B. Stewart, A. Smith, and J. Bond, "When the Going Gets Tough: The 'Why' of Goal Striving Matters," *Journal of Personality* 82, no. 3 (2014): 225–36.

24. Jim Collins, *Good to Great* (New York: HarperCollins, 2001), 1.

25. Sylvester Stallone, Story of Rocky (MGM Home Video, 2000), accessed February 21, 2020, https://www.youtube.com/watch?v=jOaI8T69Fog.

26. "The 49th Academy Awards, 1977," timeline, Academy of Motion Picture Arts and Sciences, Oscars.org, accessed February 21, 2020, https://www.oscars.org/oscars/ceremonies/1977.

27. G. H. Seijts and G. P. Latham, "The Construct of Goal Commitment: Measurement and Relationships with Task Performance," in *Problems and Solutions in Human Assessment*, eds. R. Goffin and E. Helmes (Dordrecht, Netherlands: Kluwer Academic, 2000), 315–32.

28. Stallone, Story of Rocky.

29. Daniel Goleman, *Working with Emotional Intelligence* (New York: Bantam Dell, 1998), 106; V. C. Plaut and H. R. Markus, "The 'Inside' Story: A Cultural-Historical Analysis of Being Smart and Motivated, American Style," in *Handbook of Competence and Motivation*, eds. Andrew Elliot and Carol Dweck (New York: Guilford, 2005); M. Uguroglu and H. Walberg, "Motivation and Achievement: A Quantitative Synthesis," *American Educational Research Journal* 16, no. 4 (1979): 375–89; Mihaly Csikszentmihalyi, *Good Business* (New York: Penguin, 2003), 38.

30. C. Fred Miao, Kenneth R. Evans, and Zou Shaoming, "The Role of Salesperson Motivation in Sales Control Systems—Intrinsic and Extrinsic Motivation Revisited," *Journal of Business Research* 60, no. 5 (2007): 417–25.

31. Christopher D. Nye, Rong Su, James Rounds, and Fritz Drasgow, "Vocational Interests and Performance: A Quantitative Summary of Over 60 Years of Research," *Perspective on Psychological Science* 7, no. 4 (2012): 384–403.

32. Verbeke, Dietz, and Verwaal, "Drivers of Sales Performance."

33. W. H. Macey, B. Schneider, K. M. Barbera, and S. A. Young, *Employee Engagement: Tools for Analysis, Practice, and Competitive Advantage* (Malden, MA: Wiley, 2009).

34. Mihaly Csikszentmihalyi, *Flow: The Psychology of Optimal Experience* (New York: HarperCollins, 2008), 4.

35. Mihaly Csikszentmihalyi, *Beyond Boredom and Anxiety* (San Francisco: Jossey-Bass, 1975).

36. Csikszentmihalyi, *Flow*.

37. Daniel Goleman, *Emotional Intelligence* (New York: Bantam Dell, 2006), 93.

38. S. Engeser and F. Rheinberg, "Flow, Performance and Moderators of Challenge-Skill Balance," *Motivation and Emotion* 32, no. 3 (2008): 158–72; E. Demerouti, "Job Characteristics, Flow, and Performance: The Moderating Role of Conscientiousness," *Journal of Occupational Health Psychology* 11, no. 3 (2006): 266–80; Robert Eisenberger, Jason

Jones, Florence Stinglhamber, Linda Shanock, and Amanda Randall, "Flow Experiences at Work: For High Need Achievers Alone?," *Journal of Organizational Behavior* 26, no. 7 (2005): 755–75.

39. A. Medhurst and S. Albrecht, "Salesperson Work Engagement and Flow: A Qualitative Exploration of Their Antecedents and Relationship," *Qualitative Research in Organizations and Management* 11, no. 1 (2016): 22–45.

40. Jeanne Nakamura and Mihaly Csikszentmihalyi, "Flow Theory and Research," in *Oxford Handbook of Positive Psychology*, eds. Shane J. Lopez and C. R. Snyder (Oxford, UK: Oxford University Press, 2009).

41. M. Csikszentmihalyi and J. LeFevre, "Optimal Experience in Work and Leisure," *Journal of Personality and Social Psychology* 56, no. 5 (1989): 815–22.

42. S. A. Jackson and M. Csikszentmihalyi, *Flow in Sports: The Keys to Optimal Experience and Performances* (Champaign, IL: Human Kinetics, 1999), 16; Csikszentmihalyi, *Good Business*, 44.

43. A. B. Bakker, "Flow Among Musical Teachers and Their Students: The Crossover of Peak Experiences," *Journal of Vocational Behavior* 66, no. 1 (2005): 26–44.

44. Alia Crum and Thomas Crum, "Stress Can Be a Good Thing If You Know How to Use It," in *On Mental Toughness* (Boston: Harvard Business Review Press, 2018), 72.

45. Alison Wood Brooks, "Get Excited: Reappraising Pre-Performance Anxiety as Excitement," *Journal of Experimental Psychology: General* 143, no. 3 (June 2014): 1144–58.

46. Csikszentmihalyi, *Good Business*, 38.

CHAPTER 3: THE SCIENCE OF ATTAINING YOUR SALES GOALS

1. E. A. Locke, K. N. Shaw, L. M. Saari, and G. P. Latham, "Goal Setting and Task Performance: 1969–1980," *Psychological Bulletin* 90, no. 1 (1981): 125–52; G. P. Latham and E. A. Locke, "Self-Regulation Through Goal Setting," *Organizational Behavior and Human Decision Processes* 50, no. 2 (1991): 212–47; G. P. Latham, "The Reciprocal Effects of Science and Practice: Insights from the Practice and Science of Goal Setting," *Canadian Psychology* 42, no. 1 (2001): 1–11; D. C. Zetik and A. F. Stuhlmacher, "Goal Setting and Negotiation Performance: A Meta-Analysis," *Group Processes and Intergroup Relations* 5, no. 1 (2002): 35.

2. Gary P. Latham, *Work Motivation: History, Theory, Research, and Practice* (Thousand Oaks, CA: Sage, 2011), 194.

3. Franki Y. H. Kung and Abigail A. Scholer, "Moving Beyond Two Goals: An Integrative Review and Framework for the Study of Multiple Goals," *Personality and Social Psychology Review* 25, no. 2 (2021): 130–52.

4. G. P. Latham, "The Motivational Benefits of Goal Setting," *Academy of Management Executive* 18, no. 4 (2004): 126–29; L. J. Rawsthorne and A. J. Elliot, "Achievement Goals and Intrinsic Motivation: A Meta-Analytic Review," *Personality and Social Psychology Review* 3, no. 4 (1999): 326–44; C. H. Utman, "Performance Effects of Motivational State: A Meta-Analysis," *Personality and Social Psychology Review* 1, no. 2 (1997): 170–82; M. J. Middleton and C. Midgely, "Avoiding the Demonstration of Lack of Ability: An Underexplored Aspect of Goal Theory," *Journal of Educational Psychology,* 89, no. 4 (1997): 710–18; J. M. Harackiewicz, K. E. Barron, S. M. Carter, A. T. Lehto, and A. J. Elliot, "Predictors and Consequences of Achievement Goals in the College Classroom: Maintaining Interest and Making the Grade," *Journal of Personality and Social Psychology* 73, no. 6 (1997): 1284–95; A. Kaplan and M. L. Maehr, "Achievement Goals and Student Well-Being," *Contemporary Educational Psychology* 24, no. 4 (1999): 330–58; P. R. Pintrich, "An Achievement Goal Theory Perspective on Issues in Motivation Terminology, Theory, and Research," *Contemporary Educational Psychology* 25, no. 1 (2000): 92–104; T. R. Mitchell and D. Daniels, "Motivation," in *Comprehensive Handbook of Psychology: Industrial Organizational Psychology* 12, eds. W. C. Borman, D. R. Ilgen, and R. J. Klimosk (New York: Wiley, 2003), 225–54.

5. H. Sujan, B. A. Weitz, and N. Kumar, "Learning Orientation, Working Smart, and Effective Selling," *Journal of Marketing* 58, no. 3 (1994): 39–52; Eric Fang, Kenneth R. Evans, and Shaoming Zou, "The Moderating Effect of Goal-Setting Characteristics on the Sales Control Systems–Job Performance Relationship," *Journal of Business Research* 58, no. 9 (2005): 1214–22.

6. W. Verbeke, B. Dietz, and E. Verwaal, "Drivers of Sales Performance: A Contemporary Meta-Analysis; Have Salespeople Become Knowledge Brokers?," *Journal of the Academy of Marketing Science* 39, no. 3 (2011): 407–28.

7. D. C. Zetik, and A. F. Stuhlmacher, "Goal Setting and Negotiation Performance: A Meta-Analysis," *Group Processes and Intergroup Relations* 5, no. 1 (2002): 35.

8. Mark Roberge, *The Sales Acceleration Formula* (New York: Wiley, 2015), 179.

9. Edwin Locke and Gary Latham, "Building a Practically Useful Theory of Goal Setting and Task Motivation: A 35-Year Odyssey," *American Psychologist* 57, no. 9 (2002): 706; Gary Latham and Edwin Locke, "New Developments in and Directions for Goal-Setting Research," *European Psychologist* 12, no. 4 (2007): 290–300; J. R. Baum and Edwin A. Locke, "The Relationship of Entrepreneurial Traits, Skill, and Motivation to Subsequent Venture," *Journal of Applied Psychology* 89, no. 4 (2004): 587–98.

10. John Ratey, *A User's Guide to the Brain: Perception, Attention, and the Four Theaters of the Brain* (New York: Random House, 2001), 247.

11. Locke and Latham, "Building a Practically Useful Theory of Goal Setting and Task Motivation," 706.

12. Locke and Latham. "Building a Practically Useful Theory of Goal Setting and Task Motivation," 706.

13. Heidi Grant and Carol Dweck, "Clarifying Achievement Goals and Their Impact," *Journal of Personality and Social Psychology* 85, no. 3 (2003): 541–53; E. S. Elliott and C. S. Dweck, "Goals: An Approach to Motivation and Achievement," *Journal of Personality and Social Psychology* 54, no. 1 (1988): 5–12; C. S. Dweck and E. L. Leggett, "A Social-Cognitive Approach to Motivation and Personality," *Psychological Review* 95, no. 2 (1988): 256–73.

14. A. Drach-Zahavy and M. Erez, "Challenge Versus Threat Effects on the Goal-Performance Relationship," *Organizational Behavior and Human Decision Processes* 88, no. 2 (2002): 667–82.

15. Don VandeWalle, Steven Brown, and William Cron, "The Influence of Goal Orientation and Self-Regulation Tactics on Sales Performance: A Longitudinal Field Test," *Journal of Applied Psychology* 84, no. 2 (1999): 249–59.

16. Harish Sujan, Barton A. Weitz, and Nirmalya Kumar, "Learning Orientation, Working Smart, and Effective Selling," *Journal of Marketing* 58, no. 3 (1994): 39–52.

17. Latham and Locke, "New Developments in and Directions for Goal-Setting Research," 295.

18. C. S. Carver and M. F. Scheier, *On the Self-Regulation of Behavior* (New York: Cambridge University Press, 1998); E. T. Higgins, "Self-Discrepancy: A Theory Relating Self and Affect," *Psychological Review*

94, no. 3 (1987): 319–40; E. A. Locke and G. P. Latham, *A Theory of Goal Setting and Task Performance* (Upper Saddle River, NJ: Prentice Hall, 1990).

19. M. J. Louro, R. Pieters, and M. Zeelenberg, "Dynamics of Multiple Goal Pursuit," *Journal of Personality and Social Psychology* 93, no. 2 (2007): 174–93.

20. A. Fishbach, R. Dhar, and Y. Zhang, "Subgoals as Substitutes or Complements: The Role of Goal Accessibility," *Journal of Personality and Social Psychology* 91, no. 2 (2006): 232–42.

21. M. Erez and I. Zidon, "Effects of Goal Acceptance on the Relationship of Goal Setting and Task Performance," *Journal of Applied Psychology* 69, no. 1 (1984): 69–78; Locke and Latham, "Building a Practically Useful Theory of Goal Setting and Task Motivation," 705–17; Latham and Locke, "New Developments in and Directions for Goal-Setting Research," 290–300.

22. H. Klein, M. Wesson, J. Hollenbeck, and B. Alge, "Goal Commitment and the Goal-Setting Process: Conceptual Clarification and Empirical Synthesis," *Journal of Applied Psychology* 84, no. 6 (1999): 885–96.

23. Locke and Latham, "Building a Practically Useful Theory of Goal Setting and Task Motivation," 705–17.

24. Murray R. Barrick, Michael K. Mount, and Judy P. Strauss, "Conscientiousness and Performance of Sales Representatives: Test of the Mediating Effects of Goal Setting," *Journal of Applied Psychology* 78, no. 5 (1993): 715–22.

25. Peter Heslin, Jay Carson, and Don VandeWalle, "Practical Applications of Goal Setting Theory to Performance Management," in *Performance Management: Putting Research into Action*, eds. James Smithers and Manuel London (San Francisco: Wiley, 2009), 89–107; Latham, *Work Motivation*, 195.

26. Latham and Locke, "New Developments in and Directions for Goal-Setting Research."

27. J. Hollenbeck, C. Williams, and H. Klein, "An Empirical Examination of the Antecedents of Commitment to Difficult Goals," *Journal of Applied Psychology* 74, no. 1 (1989): 18–23.

28. Locke and Latham, "Building a Practically Useful Theory of Goal Setting and Task Motivation," 707.

29. Howard Klein, Robert Lount Jr., Hee Man Park, and Bryce Lindford, "When Goals Are Known: The Effects of Audience Relative Status on

Goal Commitment and Performance," *Journal of Applied Psychology* 105, no. 4 (2020): 372–89.

30. David A. Kolb and Richard Boyatzis, "Goal-Setting and Self-Directed Behavior Change," *Human Relations* 23, no. 5 (1970): 439–57.

31. Olga Stavrova, Tila Pronk, and Michail Kokkoris, "Choosing Goals That Express the True Self: A Novel Mechanism of the Effect of Self-Control on Goal Attainment," *European Journal of Social Psychology* 49 (2019): 1329–36.

32. David Mayer and Herbert Greenberg, "What Makes a Good Salesman," *Harvard Business Review*, July–August 2006.

33. Gabriele Oettingen, Doris Mayer, A. Timur Sevincer, Elizabeth J. Stephens, Hyeon-ju Pak, and Meike Hagenah, "Mental Contrasting and Goal Commitment: The Mediating Role of Energization," *Personality and Social Psychology Bulletin* 35, no. 5 (2009): 608–22; Gabriele Oettingen, "Future Thought and Behaviour Change," *European Review of Social Psychology* 23, no. 1 (2012): 1–63; S. E. Taylor, L. B. Pham, I. D. Rivkin, and D. A. Armor, "Harnessing the Imagination: Mental Simulation, Self-Regulation, and Coping," *American Psychologist* 53, no. 4 (1998): 429–39.

34. Angela Duckworth, Teri Kirby, Gabriele Oettingen, and Anton Gollwitzer, "From Fantasy to Action: Mental Contrasting with Implementation Intentions (MCII) Improves Academic Performance in Children," *Social Psychological and Personality Science* 4, no. 6 (2013): 2.

35. Oettingen, Mayer, Timur Sevincer, Stephens, Pak, and Hagenah, "Mental Contrasting and Goal Commitment."

36. K. B. Johannessen, G. Oettingen, and D. Mayer, "Mental Contrasting of a Dieting Wish Improves Self-Reported Health Behaviour," *Psychology and Health* 27, no. 2 (2012): 43–58; P. Sheeran, P. Harris, J. Vaughan, G. Oettingen, and P. M. Gollwitzer, "Gone Exercising: Mental Contrasting Promotes Physical Activity Among Overweight, Middle-Aged, Low-SES Fishermen," *Health Psychology* 32, no. 7 (2013): 802–9; G. Oettingen, D. Mayer, and J. Thorpe, "Self-Regulation of Commitment to Reduce Cigarette Consumption: Mental Contrasting of Future with Reality," *Psychology and Health* 25, no. 8 (2010): 961–77; A. Gollwitzer, G. Oettingen, T. Kirby, and A. L. Duckworth, "Mental Contrasting Facilitates Academic Performance in School Children," *Motivation and Emotion* 35, no. 4 (2011): 403–12; Heidi Grant Halvorson, *Succeed: How We Can Reach Our Goals* (New York: Penguin, 2011); Gabriele Oettingen, "Stop Being So Positive," *Harvard Business Review*, October

27, 2014, https://hbr.org/2014/10/stop-being-so-positive; G. Oettingen and E. Stephens, "Mental Contrasting Future and Reality: A Motivationally Intelligent Self-Regulatory Strategy," in *The Psychology of Goals*, eds. G. Moskowitz and H. Grant (New York: Guilford, 2009).

37. G. Oettingen, "Expectancy Effects on Behavior Depend on Self-Regulatory Thought," *Social Cognition* 18, no. 2 (2000): 101–29; G. Oettingen, D. Mayer, J. S. Thorpe, H. Janetzke, and S. Lorenz, "Turning Fantasies About Positive and Negative Futures into Self-Improvement Goals," *Motivation and Emotion* 29, no. 4 (2005): 237–67; Oettingen, Mayer, and Thorpe, "Self-Regulation of Commitment to Reduce Cigarette Consumption"; G. Oettingen, E. J. Stephens, D. Mayer, and B. Brinkmann, "Mental Contrasting and the Self-Regulation of Helping Relations," *Social Cognition* 28, no. 4 (2010): 490–508; G. Oettingen, H. J. Pak, and K. Schnetter, "Self-Regulation of Goal-Setting: Turning Free Fantasies About the Future into Binding Goals," *Journal of Personality and Social Psychology* 80, no. 5 (2001): 736–53; G. Oettingen, M. K. Marquardt, and P. M. Gollwitzer, "Mental Contrasting Turns Positive Feedback on Creative Potential into Successful Performance," *Journal of Experimental Social Psychology* 48, no. 5 (2012): 990–96; Oettingen, Mayer, Timur Sevincer, Stephens, Pak, and Hagenah, "Mental Contrasting and Goal Commitment," 608–22.

38. G. Oettingen and A. Kappes, "Mental Contrasting of the Future and Reality to Master Negative Feedback," in *Handbook of Imagination and Mental Simulation*, eds. K. D. Markman, W. M. P. Klein, and J. A. Suhr (New York: Psychology Press, 2009), 395–412; Oettingen, Mayer, Timur Sevincer, Stephens, Pak, and Hagenah, "Mental Contrasting and Goal Commitment"; Kappes, Oettingen, and Pak, "Mental Contrasting and the Self-Regulation of Helping Relations."

39. Andreas Kappes, Henrik, Signmann, and Gabriele Oettingen, "Mental Contrasting Instigates Goal Pursuit by Linking Obstacles of Reality with Instrumental Behavior," *Journal of Experimental Social Psychology* 48, no. 4 (2012): 811–18.

40. Oettingen, "Stop Being So Positive."

41. Oettingen, Pak, and Schnetter, "Self-Regulation of Goal-Setting."

42. G. Oettingen and P. M. Gollwitzer, "Strategies of Setting and Implementing Goals: Mental Contrasting and Implementation Intentions," in *Social Psychological Foundations of Clinical Psychology*, eds. J. E. Maddux and J. P. Tangney (New York: Guilford Press, 2010), 114–35.

43. Steven Yantis, "The Neural Basis of Selective Attention: Cortical Sources and Targets of Attentional Modulation," *Current Directions in Psychological Science* 17, no. 2 (2008): 86–90.

44. Nelson Cowan, "The Magical Number 4 in Short-Term Memory: A Reconsideration of Mental Storage Capacity," *Behavioral and Brain Sciences* 24, no. 1 (2001): 87–114; George A. Miller, "The Magical Number Seven, Plus or Minus Two: Some Limits of Our Capacity for Processing Information," *Psychological Review* 63 (1956): 81–97.

45. Daniel J. Levitin, *The Organized Mind* (New York: Dutton, 2016), 16.

46. Daniel Kahneman, *Thinking, Fast and Slow* (New York: Farrar, Straus and Giroux, 2011), 23.

47. Dina Amso and Gaia Scerif, "The Attentive Brain: Insights from Developmental Cognitive Neuroscience," *Nature Reviews: Neuroscience* 16, no. 10 (2015): 606–19; John Medina, *Brain Rules* (Seattle: Pear Press, 2008), 71.

48. John Haugeland, *Having Thought: Essays in the Metaphysical of Mind* (Cambridge, MA: Harvard University Press, 1998), 159–60; Medina, *Brain Rules*, 79; Herbert A. Simon, *Administrative Behavior*, 4th ed. (New York: Simon and Schuster, 1997), 90.

49. J. Fan, B. D. McCandliss, T. Sommer, A. Raz, and M. I. Posner, "Testing the Efficiency and Independence of Attentional Networks," *Journal of Cognitive Neuroscience* 14, no. 3 (2002): 340–47; S. E. Petersen and M. I. Posner, "The Attention System of the Human Brain: 20 Years After," *Annual Review of Neuroscience* 35 (2012): 73–89; M. I. Posner and S. E. Petersen, "The Attention System of the Human Brain," *Annual Review of Neuroscience* 13 (1990): 25–42; R. Desimone and J. Duncan, "Neural Mechanisms of Selective Visual Attention," *Annual Review of Neuroscience* 18 (1995): 193–222.

50. James Driskell, Carolyn Copper, and Aidan Moran, "Does Mental Practice Enhance Performance?," *Journal of Applied Psychology* 79, no. 4 (1994): 481–92; John Arden, *Rewire Your Brain* (Hoboken, NJ: John Wiley and Sons, 2010), 9; Eleanor A. Maguire, David G. Gadian, Ingrid S. Johnsrude, Catriona D. Good, John Ashburner, Richard S. Frackowiak, and Christopher D. Firth, "Navigation-Related Structural Change in the Hippocampi of Taxi Drivers," *Proceedings of the National Academy of Sciences* 97, no. 8 (2000): 4398–403.

51. Robert B. Cialdini, "Harnessing the Science of Persuasion," *Harvard Business Review*, October 2001.

52. Pierce J. Howard, *The Owner's Manual for the Brain* (Austin: Bard Press, 2006), 797.

53. Kalina Christoff, "Thinking," in *The Oxford Handbook of Cognitive Neuroscience, Volume 2: The Cutting Edges*, eds. Kevin Ochsner and Stephen Kosslyn (Oxford, UK: Oxford University Press, 2014), 318–33.

54. A. S. Chulef, S. J. Read, and D. A. Walsh, "A Hierarchical Taxonomy of Human Goals," *Motivation and Emotion* 25, no. 3 (2001): 192–232.

55. Karl Weick, "Small Wins: Redefining the Sale of Social Problems," *American Psychologist* 39, no. 1 (1984): 40–49.

56. Locke and Latham, "Building a Practically Useful Theory of Goal Setting and Task Motivation," 708.

57. R. Bagozzi and S. Kimmel, "A Comparison of Leading Theories for the Prediction of Goal-Directed Behaviors," *British Journal of Social Psychology* 34, no. 4 (December 1995): 437–61.

58. Jonathan Haidt, *The Happiness Hypothesis* (New York: Perseus Books, 2006), 3–4.

59. Heidi Grant, "Get Your Team to Do What It Says It's Going to Do," *Harvard Business Review*, May 2014.

60. Peter Gollwitzer, "Implementation Intentions: Strong Effects of Simple Plans," *American Psychologist* 54, no. 7 (1999): 495.

61. Peter Gollwitzer and Paschal Sheeran, "Implementation Intentions and Goal Achievement: A Meta-Analysis of Effects and Processes," *Advances in Experimental Social Psychology* 38, no. 6 (2006): 69–119; Peter Gollwitzer, "Goal Achievement: The Role of Intentions," *European Review of Social Psychology* 4, no. 1 (1993): 141–85; Gollwitzer, "Implementation Intentions," 493–503; Peter Gollwitzer and Veronika Brandstätter, "Implementation Intentions and Effective Goal Pursuit," *Journal of Personality and Social Psychology* 73, no. 1 (1997): 186–99.

62. Gollwitzer and Sheeran, "Implementation Intentions and Goal Achievement."

63. Sarah Milne, Sheina Orbell, and Paschal Sheeran, "Combining Motivational and Volitional Interventions to Promote Exercise Participation: Protection Motivation Theory and Implementation Intentions," *British Journal of Health Psychology* 7, no. 2 (2002): 163–65.

64. Gollwitzer and Brandstätter, "Implementation Intentions and Effective Goal Pursuit"; Christopher J. Armitage, "Efficacy of a Brief Worksite Intervention to Reduce Smoking: The Roles of Behavioral

and Implementation Intentions," *Journal of Occupational Health Psychology* 12, no. 4 (2007): 376–90.

65. Veronika Brandstätter, Angelika Lengfelder, and Peter Gollwitzer, "Implementation Intentions and Efficient Action Initiation," *Journal of Personality and Social Psychology* 81, no. 5 (2001): 946–60; Paschal Sheeran and Sheina Orbell, "Implementation Intentions and Repeated Behavior: Augmenting the Predictive Validity of the Theory of Planned Behavior," *European Journal of Social Psychology* 29 (1999): 349–69; Peter Gollwitzer, Sarah Milne, Paschal Sheeran, and Thomas Webb, "Implementation Intentions and Health Behaviors," in *Predicting Health Behavior,* 1st ed., ed. M. Conner (New York: Open University Press, 2005), 276–323; Katherine L. Milkman, John Beshears, James J. Choi, David Laibson, and Brigitte C. Madrian, "Using Implementation Intentions Prompts to Enhance Influenza Vaccination Rates," *Proceedings of the National Academy of Sciences* 108, no. 26 (June 2011): 10415–20; Katherine Milkman, John Beshears, James Choi, David Laibson, and Brigitte Madrian, "Planning Prompts as a Means of Increasing Preventive Screening Rates," *Preventive Medicine* 56, no. 1 (2012): 92–93; David Nickerson and Todd Rogers, "Do You Have a Voting Plan? Implementation Intentions, Voter Turnout, and Organic Plan Making," *Psychological Science* 21, no. 2 (2010): 194–99.

66. Gollwitzer and Sheeran, "Implementation Intentions and Goal Achievement."

67. Grant, "Get Your Team to Do What It Says It's Going to Do."

68. Heidi Grant, "Nine Things Successful People Do Differently," *Harvard Business Review OnPoint,* Summer 2018, 12–13.

69. Richard Thaler, "Some Empirical Evidence on Dynamic Inconsistency," *Economic Letters* 8, no. 3 (1981): 201–7.

70. W. K. Bickel, A. L. Odum, and G. J. Madden, "Impulsivity and Cigarette Smoking: Delay Discounting in Current, Never, and Ex-Smokers," *Psychopharmacology* 146, no. 4 (1999): 447–54; N. M. Petry, "Pathological Gamblers, with and Without Substance Use Disorders, Discount Delayed Rewards at High Rates," *Journal of Abnormal Psychology* 110, no. 3 (2001): 482–87; C. E. Sheffer, J. Mackillop, A. Fernandez, D. Christensen, W. K. Bickel, M. W. Johnson, L. Panissidi, J. Pittman, C. T. Franck, J. Williams, and M. Mathew, "Initial Examination of Priming Tasks to Decrease Delay Discounting," *Behavioural Processes* 128 (2016): 144–52.

71. L. Green, J. Myerson, D. Lichtman, S. Rosen, and A. Fry, "Temporal Discounting in Choice Between Delayed Rewards: The Role of Age and Income," *Psychology and Aging* 11, no. 1 (1996): 79–84; J. L. Jaroni, S. M. Wright, C. Lerman, and L. H. Epstein, "Relationship Between Education and Delay Discounting in Smokers," *Addictive Behaviors* 29, no. 6 (2004): 1171–75; Gergana Nenkov, J. Inman, and John Hulland, "Considering the Future: The Conceptualization and Measurement of Elaboration on Potential Outcomes," *Journal of Consumer Research* 35, no. 1 (2008): 126–41.

72. H. E. Hershfield, D. G. Goldstein, W. F. Sharpe, J. Fox, L. Yeykelis, L. L. Carstensen, and J. N. Bailenson, "Increasing Saving Behavior Through Age-Progressed Renderings of the Future Self," *Journal of Marketing Research* 48 (2011): S23–37.

73. George Ainslie, "Specious Reward: Behavioral Theory of Impulsiveness and Impulse Control," *Psychological Bulletin* 82, no. 4 (1975): 463–96; Jon Elster, "Ulysses and Sirens: A Theory of Imperfect Rationality," *Social Science Information* 16, no. 5 (1977): 469–526; R. Thaler and Hersh M. Shefrin, "An Economic Theory of Self-Control," *Journal of Political Economy* 89, no. 2 (1981): 392–406.

74. Nenkov, Inman, and Hulland, "Considering the Future: The Conceptualization and Measurement of Elaboration on Potential Outcomes," 126–41.

75. Hershfield, Goldstein, Sharpe, Fox, Yeykelis, Carstensen, and Bailenson, "Increase Savings Behavior Through Age-Progressed Renderings of the Future Self."

CHAPTER 4: HELP POTENTIAL CLIENTS FORM BUYING DECISIONS

1. Brent Adamson, "New B2B Buying Journey & It's Implications for Sales," Gartner, accessed June 10, 2020, www.gartner.com/en/sales /insights/b2b-buying-journey.

2. Brent Adamson, "Gartner Keynote: The Key to B2B Sales Is Customer Self-Confidence," *Smarter with Gartner*, September 17, 2019, www .gartner.com/smarterwithgartner/gartner-keynote-key -b2b-sales-customer-self-confidence.

3. CSO Insights, *Selling in the Age of Ceaseless Change: The 2018–2019 Sales Performance Report*, 5.

4. CSO Insights, *Selling in the Age of Ceaseless Change*, 8.

5. Herbert A. Simon, *Administration Behavior*, 4th ed. (New York: Free Press, 1997), 88.

6. J. Dillard, J. Hunter, and M. Burgoon, "Sequential-Request Persuasive Strategies: Meta-Analysis of Foot-in-the-Door and Door-in-the-Face," *Human Communication Research* 10, no. 4 (1984): 461–88; E. Fern, K. Monroe, and R. Avila, "Effectiveness of Multiple Request Strategies: A Synthesis of Research Results," *Journal of Marketing Research* 23, no. 2 (1986): 144–52; J. Burger, "The Foot-in-the-Door Compliance Procedure: A Multiple-Process Analysis and Review," *Personality and Social Psychology Review* 3, no. 4 (1999): 303–25; M. Goldman, C. Creason, and C. McCall, "Compliance Employing a Two-Feet-in-the-Door Procedure," *Journal of Social Psychology* 114, no. 2 (1981): 259–65; E. Schein, "The Chinese Indoctrination Program for Prisoners of War: A Study of Attempted 'Brainwashing,'" *Psychiatry* 19, no. 2 (1956): 149–72; J. P. Dillard, "The Current Status of Research on the Sequential-Request Compliance Techniques," *Personality and Social Psychology Bulletin* 17 (1991): 283–88; N. Gueguen and C. Jacob, "Fundraising on the Web: The Effect of an Electronic Foot-in-the-Door on Donation," *CyberPsychology and Behavior* 6, no. 2 (2001): 705–9.

7. S. J. Sherman, "On the Self-Erasing Nature of Errors of Prediction," *Journal of Personality and Social Psychology* 39, no. 2 (1980): 211–21; J. L. Freedman and S. C. Fraser, "Compliance Without Pressure: The Foot-in-the-Door Technique," *Journal of Personality and Social Psychology* 4, no. 2 (1966): 195–202.

8. R. V. Joule, "Tobacco Deprivation: The Foot-in-the-Door Technique Versus the Low-Ball Technique," *European Journal of Social Psychology* 17, no. 3 (1987): 361–65.

9. Richard Thaler, *Misbehaving: The Making of Behavioral Economics* (New York: W. W. Norton, 2015), 154; William Samuelson and Richard Zeckhauser, "Status Quo Bias in Decision Making," *Journal of Risk and Uncertainty* 1, no. 1 (1988): 7–59.

10. Praveen Aggarwal, Stephen B. Castleberry, Rick Ridnour, and C. David Shepherd, "Salesperson Empathy and Listening: Impact on Relationship Outcomes," *Journal of Marketing Theory and Practice* 13, no. 3 (2005): 16–31; Lucette B. Comer and Tanya Drollinger, "Active Empathetic Listening and Selling Success: A Conceptual Framework," *Journal of Personal Selling and Sales Management* 19, no. 1 (1999): 15–29.

11. Nassim Nicholas Taleb, *Antifragile: Things That Gain from Disorder* (New York: Random House, 2014).

12. Taleb, *Antifragile*, 3.

13. Frank V. Cespedes, *Aligning Strategy and Sales* (Boston: Harvard Business Review Press, 2014), 149.

14. Mark Lindwall, Norbert Kriebel, Scott Santucci, Bradford J. Holmes, and Michael Shrum, *How Prepared Do Sales Reps Think They Are* (Forrester, 2014), https://www.forrester.com/report/How+Prepared+Do+Sales+Reps+Think+They+Are/-/E-RES104705.

15. Mike Schultz, "Sales Leaders' Top 10 Wish List," *International Journal of Sales Transformation*, June 1, 2020, https://www.journalofsalestransformation.com/sales-leaders-top-10-wish-list/.

16. K. P. Bauman and G. Geher, "We Think You Agree: The Detrimental Impact of the False Consensus Effect on Behavior," *Current Psychology* 21, no. 4 (2002): 293–318; J. Krueger and J. S. Zeiger, "Social Categorization and the Truly False Consensus Effect," *Journal of Personality and Social Psychology* 65, no. 4 (1993): 670–80; G. Marks and N. Miller, "Ten Years of Research on the False-Consensus Effect: An Empirical and Theoretical Review," *Psychological Bulletin* 102, no. 1 (1987): 72–90.

17. Richard Thaler, "Mental Accounting and Consumer Choice," *Marketing Science* 4, no. 3 (1985): 199–214.

18. Neil Rackham and John DeVincentis, *Rethinking the Sales Force* (New York: McGraw-Hill, 1998), 10–11.

19. Kevin Blankenship and Traci Craig, "Language and Persuasion," *Journal of Experimental Social Psychology* 43, no. 1 (2007): 112–18; L. A. Hosman and S. A. Siltanen, "Hedges, Tag Questions, Message Processing, and Persuasion," *Journal of Language and Social Psychology* 30, no. 3 (2011): 341–49.

20. Diana I. Tamir and Jason P. Mitchell, "Disclosing Information About the Self Is Intrinsically Rewarding," *Proceedings of the National Academy of Sciences* 109, no. 21 (2012): 8038–43.

CHAPTER 5: HOW TO REFRAME ANY SALES SITUATION

1. I. P. Levin and G. J. Gaeth, "Framing of Attribute Information Before and After Consuming the Product," *Journal of Consumer Research* 15, no. 3 (1988): 374–78.

2. Barbara McNeil, Stephen G. Pauker, Harold C. Sox Jr., and Amos Tversky, "On the Elicitation of Preference for Alternative Therapies," *New England Journal of Medicine* 306, no. 21 (1982): 1259–62.

3. K. J. Dunegan, "Framing, Cognitive Modes, and Image Theory: Toward an Understanding of a Glass Half Full," *Journal of Applied Psychology* 78, no. 3 (1993): 491–503.

4. W. J. Qualls and C. P. Puto, "Organizational Climate and Decision Framing: An Integrated Approach to Analyzing Industrial Buying Decisions," *Journal of Marketing Research* 26, no. 2 (1989): 179–92.

5. Amos Tversky and Daniel Kahneman, "The Framing of Decisions and the Psychology of Choice," *Science* 211, no. 4481 (January 30, 1981): 453–58.

6. Daniel Kahneman, *Thinking, Fast and Slow* (New York: Farrar, Straus and Giroux, 2011), 367.

7. A. Alter, J. Aronson, J. Darley, C. Rodriguez, and D. Ruble, "Rising to the Threat: Reducing Stereotype Threat by Reframing the Threat as a Challenge," *Journal of Experimental Social Psychology* 46, no. 1 (2010): 166–71; F. Autin and J. Croizet, "Improving Working Memory Efficiency by Reframing Metacognitive Interpretation of Task Difficulty," *Journal of Experimental Psychology: General* 141, no. 4 (March 5, 2012): 610–18.

8. F. D. Schoorman, R. C. Mayer, C. A. Douglas, and C. T. Hetrick, "Escalation of Commitment and the Framing Effect: An Empirical Investigation," *Journal of Applied Social Psychology* 24, no. 6 (1994): 509–28; P. H. Schurr, "Effects of Gain and Loss Decision Frames on Risky Purchase Negotiations," *Journal of Applied Psychology* 72, no. 3 (1987): 351–58; T. M. Marteau, "Framing of Information: Its Influence upon Decisions of Doctors and Patients," *British Journal of Social Psychology* 28, no. 1 (1989): 89–94; K. J. Dunegan, "Fines, Frames and Images: Examining Formulation Effects on Punishment Decisions," *Organizational Behavior and Human Decision Processes* 68, no. 1 (1996): 58–67; R. M. Kramer, "Windows of Vulnerability or Cognitive Illusions? Cognitive Processes and the Nuclear Arms Race," *Journal of Experimental Social Psychology* 25, no. 1 (1989): 79–100; I. P. Levin, "Associative Effects of Information Framing," *Bulletin of the Psychonomic Society* 25, no. 2 (1987): 85–86; I. P. Levin, R. D. Johnson, C. P. Russo, and P. J. Deldin, "Framing Effects in Judgment Tasks with Varying Amounts of Information," *Organizational Behavior and Human Decision Processes* 36, no. 3 (1985): 362–77; Richard Thaler, "Mental Accounting and Consumer Choice," *Marketing Science* 4, no. 3 (1985): 199–214; Amos Tversky and Daniel Kahneman, "The Framing of Decisions and the Psychology of Choice," *Science* 211,

no. 4481 (1981): 453–58; Amos Tversky and Daniel Kahneman, "Advances in Prospect Theory: Cumulative Representation of Uncertainty," *Journal of Risk and Uncertainty* 5, no. 4 (1992): 297–323; David Clark and Aaron Beck, *Cognitive Therapy for Anxiety Disorders* (New York: Guilford Press, 2011); Albert Ellis, *Overcoming Destructive Beliefs, Feelings, and Behaviors* (New York: Prometheus Books, 2001).

9. This picture is based on the work of psychologist Joseph Jastrow, who in 1899 used a similar picture to analyze how perception can be swayed. Chloe Farand, "Duck or Rabbit? The Image That Tells You How Creative You Are," February 16, 2016, *Independent*, https://www.independent.co.uk/news/science/duck-and-rabbit-illusion-b1821663.html.

10. Irwin Levin, Sandra Schneider, and Gary Gaeth, "All Frames Are Not Created Equal: A Typology and Critical Analysis of Framing Effects," *Organizational Behavior and Human Decision Processes* 76, no. 2 (1998): 149–88.

11. Vladas Griskevicius, Robert Cialdini, and Noah Goldstein, "Applying (and Resisting) Peer Influence," *MIT Sloan Management Review*, January 1, 2008, sloanreview.mit.edu/article/applying-and-resisting-peer-influence/.

12. Steve Martin, "98% of *HBR* Readers Love This Article," *Harvard Business Review*, Idea Watch, October 2012.

13. Stanley Milgram, Leonard Bickman, and Lawrence Berkowitz, "Note on the Drawing Power of Crowds of Different Size," *Journal of Personality and Social Psychology* 13, no. 2 (1969): 79–82.

14. R. Bond and P. Smith, "Culture and Conformity: A Meta-Analysis of Studies Using Asch's (1952b, 1956) Line Judgment Task," *Psychological Bulletin* 119, no. 1 (1996): 111–37.

15. "The Importance of Social Proof as a Trust Signal," Wharton Online, August 13, 2019, online.wharton.upenn.edu/blog/the-importance-of-social-proof-as-a-trust-signal/; Wharton Business School, *Digital Marketing Guide for Non-Digital Marketers*, 2020, 8.

16. E. A. Greenleaf and D. R. Lehmann, "A Typology of Reasons for Substantial Delay in Consumer Decision Making," *Journal of Consumer Research* 22, no. 2 (1995): 186–99; J. P. Simmons and L. D. Nelson, "Intuitive Confidence: Choosing Between Intuitive and Nonintuitive Alternatives," *Journal of Experimental Psychology: General* 135, no. 3 (2006): 409–48; M. Thomas and G. Menon, "When

Internal Reference Prices and Price Expectations Diverge: The Role of Confidence," *Journal of Marketing Research* 44, no. 3 (2007): 401–9.

17. R. Hamilton, J. Hong, and A. Chernev, "Perceptual Focus Effects in Choice," *Journal of Consumer Research* 34, no. 2 (2007): 187–99.

18. Jerry M. Burger, "Increasing Compliance by Improving the Deal: The That's-Not-All Technique," *Journal of Personality and Social Psychology* 51, no. 2 (2008): 277–83.

19. Adam Grant and David Hofmann, "It's Not All About Me: Motivating Hand Hygiene Among Health Care Professionals by Focusing on Patients," *Psychological Science* 22, no. 12 (2011): 1494–99.

20. M. Whitby, C. L. Pessoa-Silva, M. L. McLaws, B. Allegranzi, H. Sax, E. Larson, W. H. Seto, L. Donaldson, and D. Pittet, "Behavioural Considerations for Hand Hygiene Practices: The Basic Building Blocks," *Journal of Hospital Infection* 65, no. 1 (2007): 1–8; A. Gawande, "Notes of a Surgeon: On Washing Hands," *New England Journal of Medicine* 350, no. 13 (2004): 1283–86.

21. R. Klitzman, "Post-Residency Disease and the Medical Self: Identity, Work, and Health Care Among Doctors Who Become Patients," *Perspectives in Biology and Medicine* 49, no. 4 (2006): 542–52.

22. Forrester Research, *Q4 2013 North America and Europe Executive Buyer Insight Online Survey.*

23. Clayton M. Christensen, Scott Cook, and Taddy Hall, "What Customers Want from Your Products," Working Knowledge, *Harvard Business Review*, January 16, 2006, hbswk.hbs.edu/item/what -customers-want-from-your-products.

24. Kahneman, *Thinking, Fast and Slow*, 283.

25. S. Gächter, H. Orzen, E. Renner, and C. Starmer, "Are Experimental Economists Prone to Framing Effects? A Natural Field Experiment," *Journal of Economic Behavior and Organization* 70, no. 3 (2009): 443–46; Levin, Schneider, and Gaeth, "All Frames Are Not Created Equal."

26. Christopher Trepel, Craig R. Fox, and Russell A. Poldrack, "Buyer Theory on the Brain? Toward a Cognitive Neuroscience of Decision Under Risk," *Cognitive Brain Research* 23 (2005): 39.

27. Melanie B. Tannenbaum, Justin Helper, Rick S. Zimmerman, Lindsey Saul, Samantha Jacobs, Kristina Wilson, and Dolores Albarracín, "Appealing to Fear: A Meta-Analysis of Fear Appeal Effectiveness and Theories," *Psychological Bulletin* 141, no. 6 (2015): 1178–204.

28. Marti Gonzales, Elliot Aronson, and Mark Costanzo, "Using Social

Cognition and Persuasion to Promote Energy Conservation: A Quasi-Experiment," *Journal of Applied Social Psychology* 18, no. 12 (1988): 1049–66.

29. Daniel Kahneman and Amos Tversky, "Buyer Theory: An Analysis of Decision Under Risk," *Econometrica* 47, no. 2 (1979): 273.

30. Matthew Feinberg and Robb Willer, "From Gulf to Bridge: When Do Moral Arguments Facilitate Political Influence," *Personality and Social Psychology Bulletin* 40, no. 12 (2015): 1665–81.

31. Robb Willer and Matthew Feinberg, "The Key to Political Persuasion," *New York Times*, November 15, 2015.

CHAPTER 6: SUPERCHARGE YOUR SALES PROCESS WITH SCIENCE

1. Lee Ross, "The Intuitive Psychologist and His Shortcomings: Distortions in the Attribution Process," in *Advances in Experimental Social Psychology*, vol. 10, ed. L. Berkowitz (New York: Academic Press, 1977); Edward Jones and Victor Harris, "The Attribution of Attitudes," *Journal of Experimental Social Psychology* 3, no. 1 (1967): 2–24.

2. Gordon Moskowitz and Michael Gill, "Person Perception," in *The Oxford Handbook of Cognitive Psychology*, ed. Daniel Reisberg (Oxford, UK: Oxford University Press, 2014); Douglas Krull, Michelle Hui-Min Loy, Jennifer Lin, Ching-Fu Wang, Suhong Chen, and Xudong Zhao, "The Fundamental Attribution Error: Correspondence Bias in Individualist and Collectivist Cultures," *Personality and Social Psychology Bulletin* 25, no. 10 (1999): 1208–19; Darren Lagdridge and Trevor Butt, "The Fundamental Attribution Error: A Phenomenological Critique," *British Journal of Social Psychology* 43, no. 3 (2010): 357–69.

3. Jonathan K. Frenzen and Harry L. Davis, "Purchasing Behavior in Embedded Markets," *Journal of Consumer Research* 17, no. 1 (1990): 1–12.

4. Christoph H. Loch and Yaozhong Wu, "Social Preferences and Supply Chain Performance: An Experimental Study," *Management Science* 54, no. 11 (2008): 1835–49.

5. Robert H. Gass and John S. Seiter, *Persuasion, Social Influence, and Compliance Gaining*, 4th ed. (New York: Allyn and Bacon, 2011); Jerry M. Burger, Shelley Soroka, Katrina Gonzago, Emily Murphy, and Emily Somervell, "The Effect of Fleeting Attraction on Compliance to Requests," *Personality and Social Psychology Bulletin* 27, no. 12 (2001): 1578–86.

6. Amy J. C. Cuddy, Matthew Kohut, and John Neffinger, "Connect Then Lead," *Harvard Business Review*, July–August 2013, 56.

7. Dariusz Dolinski, Magdalena Nawrat, and Rudak Iza, "Dialogue Involvement as a Social Influence Technique," *Personality and Social Psychology Bulletin* 27, no. 12 (2001): 1395–406.

8. M. Morris, J. Nadler, T. Kurtzberg, and L. Thompson, "Schmooze or Lose: Social Friction and Lubrication in Email Negotiations," *Group Dynamics* 6, no. 1 (2002): 89–100.

9. Deborah Small, George Loewenstein, and Paul Slovic, "Sympathy and Callousness: The Impact of Deliberative Thought on Donations to Identifiable and Statistical Victims," *Organizational Behavior and Human Decision Processes* 102, no. 2 (2007): 143–55.

10. Chip Heath and Dan Heath, *Made to Stick* (New York: Random House, 2008), 242–43.

11. L. Cozolino and S. Sprokay, "Neuroscience and Adult Learning," in *The Neuroscience of Adult Learning*, New Directions for Adult and Continuing Education, no. 110, eds. Sandra Johnson and Kathleen Taylor (San Francisco: Jossey-Bass, 2006); Greg J. Stephens, Lauren J. Silbert, and Uri Hasson, "Speaker-Listener Neural Coupling Underlies Successful Communication," *Proceedings of the National Academy of Science* 107, no. 32 (2010): 14425–30.

12. Melinda Krakow, Robert Yale, Jakob Jensen, Nick Carcioppolo, and Chelsea Ratcliff, "Comparing Mediational Pathways for Narrative- and Argument-Based Messages: Believability, Counterarguing, and Emotional Reaction," *Human Communication Research* 44, no. 3 (2018): 299–321; Emily Moyer-Guse and Robin Nabi, "Explaining the Effects of Narrative in an Entertainment Television Program: Overcoming Resistance to Persuasion," *Human Communication Research* 36, no. 1 (2009): 26–52.

13. Melanie Green and Timothy Brock, "The Role of Transportation in the Persuasiveness of Public Narrative," *Journal of Personality and Social Psychology* 79, no. 5 (2000): 701–21; Jay A. Conger, "The Necessary Art of Persuasion," *Harvard Business Review OnPoint*, Fall 2010, 54.

14. Rebecca Krause and Derek Rucker, "Strategic Storytelling: When Narratives Help Versus Hurt the Persuasive Power of Facts," *Personality and Social Psychology Bulletin* 46, no. 2 (2019): 217.

15. Mark Lindwall, "Why Don't Buyers Want to Meet with Your Salespeople," Forrester Research blog, September 29, 2014, https://

go.forrester.com/blogs/14-09-29-why_dont_buyers_want_to_meet
_with_your_salespeople/.

16. San Bolkan and Peter Andersen, "Image Induction and Social
Influence: Explication and Initial Tests; Basic and Applied Social
Psychology," *Basic and Applied Social Psychology* 31, no. 4 (2009):
317–24.

17. Richard H. Thaler and Cass R. Sunstein, *Nudge* (New York: Penguin
Books, 2009), 6; Richard Thaler, *Misbehaving: The Makings of
Behavioral Economics* (New York: W. W. Norton, 2015), 325.

18. Alan Samson, ed. *The Behavioral Economics Guide 2016*, https://www
.behavioraleconomics.com; Richard Thaler, "Nobel Lecture: Richard
Thaler, the Sveriges Riksbank Prize in Economic Sciences," YouTube,
February 19, 2013, retrieved May 16, 2020, https://www.youtube
.com/watch?v=ej6cygeB2X0.

19. David Eagleman, *The Brain: The Story of You* (New York: Pantheon,
2015), 87.

20. Eric J. Johnson and Daniel Goldstein, "Do Defaults Save Lives?,"
Science 302, no. 5649 (2003): 1338–39; Brigitte C. Madrian and Dennis
F. Shea, "The Power of Suggestion: Inertia in 401(k) Participation and
Savings Behavior," *Quarterly Journal of Economics* 116, no. 4 (2001):
1149–87.

21. Richard H. Thaler and Shlomo Benartzi, "Save More Tomorrow:
Using Behavioral Economics to Increase Employee Saving," *Journal of
Political Economy* 112, no. 1 (2004): S164–87.

22. Daniel Kahneman, Jack L. Knetsch, and Richard H. Thaler,
"Experimental Tests of the Endowment Effect and the Coase
Theorem," *Journal of Political Economy* 98, no. 6 (1990): 1325–48.

23. Ziv Carmon and Dan Ariely, "Focusing on the Forgone: How Value
Can Appear So Different to Buyers and Sellers," *Journal of Consumer
Research* 27, no. 3 (2000): 360–70.

24. K. M. M. Ericson and A. Fuster, "The Endowment Effect," *Annual
Review of Economics* 6, no. 1 (2014): 555–79; D. Kahneman, J. L.
Knetsch, and R. H. Thaler, "Anomalies: The Endowment Effect, Loss
Aversion, and Status Quo Bias," *Journal of Economic Perspectives* 5,
no. 1 (1991): 193–206.

25. Richard Thaler, "Toward a Positive Theory of Consumer Choice,"
Journal of Economic Behavior and Organization 1, no. 1 (1980): 39–60.

26. Michael Norton, Daniel Mochon, and Dan Ariely, "The IKEA Effect:

When Labor Leads to Love," *Journal of Consumer Psychology* 22, no. 3 (2012): 453–60.

27. Norton, Mochon, and Ariely, "The IKEA Effect."

CHAPTER 7: THREE OUTSIDE-THE-BOX STRATEGIES THAT GROW SALES

1. Danit Ein-Gar, Bab Shiv, and Zakary L. Tormala, "When Blemishing Leads to Blossoming: The Positive Effect of Negative Information," *Journal of Consumer Research* 38, no. 5 (2012): 846–59.

2. K. D. Williams, M. Bourgeois, and R. T. Croyle, "The Effects of Stealing Thunder in Criminal and Civil Trials," *Law and Human Behavior* 17, no. 6 (1993): 597–609; Elaine Walster (Hatfield) and L. Festinger, "The Effectiveness of 'Overheard' Persuasive Communications," *Journal of Abnormal and Social Psychology* 65, no. 6 (1962): 395–402.

3. Ein-Gar, Shiv, and Tormala, "When Blemishing Leads to Blossoming," 847.

4. Ein-Gar, Shiv, and Tormala, "When Blemishing Leads to Blossoming," 847.

5. Albert Mehrabian and Susan R. Ferris, "Inference of Attitudes from Nonverbal Communication in Two Channels," *Journal of Consulting Psychology* 31, no. 3 (1967): 248–52; Albert Mehrabian and Morton Wiener, "Decoding of Inconsistent Communications," *Journal of Personality and Social Psychology* 6, no. 1 (1967): 109–14.

6. Albert Mehrabian, *Silent Messages* (Stamford, CT: Wadsworth, 1980).

7. J. K. Burgoon, "Nonverbal Signals," in *Handbook of Interpersonal Communication*, eds. M. L. Knapp and G. R. Miller (Beverly Hills: Sage, 1985), 344–90; D. Archer and R. M. Akert, "Words and Everything Else: Verbal and Nonverbal Cues in Social Interpretation," *Journal of Personality and Social Psychology* 35, no. 6 (1977): 443–49; M. Argyle, *Social Interaction* (New York: Atherton Press, 1970); B. M. DePaulo and H. S. Friedman, "Nonverbal Communication," in *The Handbook of Social Psychology*, vol. 2, ed. D. T. Gilbert, S. T. Fiske, and G. Lindsey, 4th ed. (New York: McGraw-Hill, 1998), 3–40.

8. Daniel Goleman, *Emotional Intelligence* (New York: Random House, 2006), 97.

9. Ellen Langer, "Rethinking the Role of Thought in Social Interaction," in *New Directions in Attribution Research*, vol. 2, eds. J. H. Harvey, W. J. Ickles, and R. F. Kidd (New York: Wiley, 1978), 35–58; Ellen Langer,

"Minding Matters," in *Advances in Experimental Social Psychology*, vol. 22, ed. L. Berkowitz (New York: Addison-Wesley, 1989), 137–73.

10. P. Anderson, "Influential Actions: Nonverbal Communication and Persuasion," in *Readings in Persuasion, Social Influence, and Compliance Gaining*, eds. Robert H. Gass and John S. Seiter (Boston: Allyn and Bacon, 2004), 165–80.

11. Nathaniel Gage and David Berliner, *Educational Psychology*, 6th ed. (Boston: Houghton Mifflin, 1998).

12. Raymond Wlodkowski, *Enhancing Adult Motivation to Learn*, 3rd ed. (San Francisco: Wiley and Sons, 2008), 243.

13. Michael B. McCaskey, "The Hidden Messages Managers Send," *Harvard Business Review*, November–December 1979.

14. Kristina Lundholm Fors, "Production and Perception of Pauses in Speech" (doctoral dissertation in linguistics, University of Gothenburg, August 17, 2015).

15. Bonnie Erickson, E. Lind, Bruce Johnson, and William O'Barr, "Speech Style and Impression Formation in a Court Setting: The Effects of 'Powerful' and 'Powerless' Speech," *Journal of Experimental Social Psychology* 14, no. 3 (1978): 266–79.

16. Saul Kassin, Steven Fein, and Hazel Rose Markus, *Social Psychology*, 7th ed. (Belmont, CA: Wadsworth, 2008).

17. Robert H. Gass and John S. Seiter, *Persuasion, Social Influence, and Compliance Gaining*, 4th ed. (Boston: Allyn and Bacon, 2011), 248.

18. C. L. Kleinke, "Gaze and Eye Contact: A Research Review," *Psychological Bulletin* 100, no. 1 (1986): 78–100; J. Kellerman, J. Lewis, and J. D. Laird, "Looking and Loving: The Effects of Mutual Gaze on Feelings of Romantic Love," *Journal of Research in Personality* 23, no. 2 (1989): 145–61; Sarah-Jayne Blakemore and Uta Firth, "How Does the Brain Deal with the Social World," *NeuroReport* 15, no. 1 (2004): 119–28.

19. Gordon D. Hemsley and Anthony N. Doob, "The Effect of Looking Behavior on Perceptions of a Communicator's Credibility," *Journal of Applied Social Psychology* 8, no. 2 (1978): 136–44.

20. Nora Murphy, "Appearing Smart: The Impression Management of Intelligence, Personal Perception Accuracy, and Behavior in Social Interaction," *Personality and Social Psychology Bulletin* 33, no. 3 (2007): 325–39.

21. Malia Mason, Elizabeth Tatkow, and C. Neil Macrae, "The Look of

Love: Gaze Shifts and Person Perception," *Psychological Science* 16, no. 3 (2005): 236–39.

22. Chris Segrin, "The Effects of Nonverbal Behavior on Outcomes of Compliance Gaining Attempts," *Communication Studies* 44, nos. 3–4 (1993): 169–87.

23. Simone Schnall and James Laird, "Keep Smiling: Enduring Effects of Facial Expressions and Postures on Emotional Experience," *Cognition and Emotion* 17, no. 5 (2003): 787–97; Emma Otta, Beatriz Barcellos Pereira Lira, Nadia Maria Delevati, Otávio Pimentel Cesar, and Carla Salati Guirello Pires, "The Effect of Smiling and of Head Tilting on Person Perception," *Journal of Psychology* 128, no. 3 (1994): 323–31; Earnest Able and Michael Kruger, "Smile Intensity in Photographs Predicts Longevity," *Psychological Science* 21, no. 4 (2010): 542–44; Fritz Strack, Leonard Martin, and Sabine Stepper, "Inhibiting and Facilitating Conditions of the Human Smile: A Nonobtrusive Test of the Facial Feedback Hypothesis," *Journal of Personality and Social Psychology* 54, no. 5 (1988): 768–77.

24. D. Leathers, *Successful Nonverbal Communication*, 3rd ed. (Boston: Allyn and Bacon, 1997).

25. Ray Forbes and Paul Jackson, "Non-verbal Behavior and the Outcome of Selection Interviews," *Journal of Occupational Psychology* 53 (1980): 65–72; Paul Washburn and Milton Hakel, "Visual Cues and Verbal Content as Influences on Impressions Formed After Simulated Employment Interviews," *Journal of Applied Psychology* 58, no. 1 (1973): 137–41.

26. Nicolas Guéguen and Jacques Fischer-Lokou, "Hitchhiker's Smiles and Receipt of Help," *Psychology Reports* 94, no. 3 (2004): 756–60.

27. Ulf Dimberg and Monika Thunberg, "Rapid Facial Reactions to Emotional Facial Expression," *Scandinavian Journal of Psychology* 39, no. 1 (2000): 39–46.

28. Michael S. Gazzaniga, Richard B. Ivry, and George R. Mangun, *Cognitive Neuroscience*, 3rd ed. (New York: W. W. Norton, 2009), 618–20; J. L. Lakin and T. L. Chartrand, "Using Nonconscious Behavioral Mimicry to Create Affiliation and Rapport," *Psychological Science* 14, no. 4 (2003): 334–39; R. B. van Baaren, R. W. Holland, K. Kawakami, and A. van Knippenberg, "Mimicry and Prosocial Behavior," *Psychological Science* 15, no. 1 (2004): 71–74; Jerry M. Burger, Nicole Messian, Shebani Patel, Alicia del Prado, and Carmen Anderson, "What a Coincidence! The Effects of Incidental Similarity on

Compliance," *Personality and Social Psychology Bulletin* 30, no. 1 (January 2004): 35–43; Randy Garner, "What's in a Name? Persuasion Perhaps," *Journal of Consumer Psychology* 15, no. 2 (2005): 108–16.

29. Robin J. Tanner, Rosellina Ferraro, Tanya L. Chartrand, James R. Bettman, and Rick van Baaren, "Of Chameleons and Consumption: The Impact of Mimicry on Choice and Preferences," *Journal of Consumer Research* 34 (2007): 754–66.

30. Elaine Hatfield, John T. Cacioppo, and Richard L. Rapson, *Emotional Contagion* (Cambridge, UK: Cambridge University Press, 1994); W. D. Hutchinson, K. D. Davis, A. M. Lozano, and J. O. Dostrovsky, "Pain-Related Neurons in the Human Cingulate Cortex," *Nature-Neuroscience* 2, no. 5 (1999): 403–5; C. K. Hsee, E. Hatfield, J. G. Carlson, and C. Chemtob, "The Effect of Power on Susceptibility to Emotional Cognition," *Cognition and Emotion* 4 (1990): 327–40; Daniel Goleman, Richard Boyatzis, and Annie McKee, "The Emotional Reality of Teams," *Journal of Organization Excellence* 21, no. 2 (Spring 2002): 55–65.

31. Elizabeth Tenney, Nathan Meikle, David Hunsaker, Don Moore, and Cameron Anderson, "Is Overconfidence a Social Liability? The Effect of Verbal Versus Nonverbal Expressions of Confidence," *Journal of Personality and Social Psychology* 116, no. 3 (2019): 396–415.

32. Tanya Vacharkulksemsuk, Emily Reit, Poruz Khambatta, Paul Eastwick, Eli Finkel, and Dana Carney, "Dominant, Open Nonverbal Displays Are Attractive at Zero-Acquaintance," *Proceedings of the National Academy of Sciences* 113, no. 15 (2016).

33. Carolyn Gergoire, "The Fascinating Science Behind 'Talking' with Your Hands," *HuffPost*, retrieved October 11, 2020, https://www.huffpost.com/entry/talking-with-hands-gestures_n_56afcfaae4b0b8d7c230414e; David McNeill, *Gesture and Thought* (Chicago: University of Chicago Press, 2005).

34. Jean Clarke, Joep Cornelissen, and Mark Healey, "Actions Speak Louder Than Words: How Figurative Language and Gesturing in Entrepreneurial Pitches Influences Investment Judgments," *Academy of Management Journal* 62, no. 2 (2018).

35. Nicole Torres, "When You Pitch an Idea, Gestures Matter More Than Words," *Harvard Business Review*, May–June 2019.

36. David A. Frank, *Creative Speaking*, 2nd ed. (Lincolnwood, IL: National Textbook Company, 1995), 24–25.

37. Martin Seligman and Peter Schulman, "Explanatory Style as a Predictor of Productivity and Quitting Among Life Insurance Sales Agents," *Journal of Personality and Social Psychology* 50, no. 4 (1986): 832–38.

38. Deirdre Coleman, "Happy Salespeople Are Better Performers," *International Journal of Sales Transformation*, December 13, 2019, https://www.journalofsalestransformation.com/the-gift-of -professional-burnout/; Peter Schulman, "Applying Learned Optimism to Increase Sales Productivity," *Journal of Personal Selling and Sales Management* 19, no. 1 (1999): 31–37.

39. Schulman, "Applying Learned Optimism to Increase Sales Productivity," 33–34.

40. S. Eronen, J.-E. Nurmi, and K. Salmela-Aro, "Optimistic, Defensive-Pessimistic, Impulsive and Self-Handicapping Strategies in University Environments," *Learning and Instruction* 8, no. 2 (1998): 159–77; L. S. Nes and S. C. Segerstrom, "Dispositional Optimism and Copying: A Meta-Analytic Review," *Personality and Social Psychology Review* 10, no. 3 (2006): 235–51.

41. Martin Seligman, *Learned Optimism: How to Change Your Mind and Your Life* (New York: Vintage, 2006); Schulman, "Applying Learned Optimism to Increase Sales Productivity."

42. Edmund Bergler, "Debts of Gratitude Paid in 'Guilt Denomination,'" *Journal of Clinical Psychopathology* 11 (1950): 57–62; F. Heider, *The Psychology of Interpersonal Relations* (New York: Wiley, 1958); M. E. McCullough, R. A. Emmons, and J. Tsang, "The Grateful Disposition: A Conceptual and Empirical Topography," *Journal of Personality and Social Psychology* 82, no. 1 (2002): 112–27.

43. Martin Seligman, *Flourish: A Visionary New Understanding of Happiness and Well-Being* (New York: Free Press, 2011), 30.

44. M. E. Young and T. S. Hutchinson, "The Rediscovery of Gratitude: Implications for Counseling Practice," *Journal of Humanistic Counseling* 51, no. 1 (2012): 99–113; Giacomo Bono, Robert Emmons, and Michael McCullough, "Gratitude in Practice and the Practice of Gratitude," *Positive Psychology in Practice*, eds. P. Alex Linley and Stephen Joseph (New York: Wiley, 2012), 559–76.

45. Harvard Medical School, "Giving Thanks Can Make You Happier," retrieved August 5, 2020, https://www.health.harvard.edu /healthbeat/giving-thanks-can-make-you-happier.

46. Robert Emmons and Michael McCullough, "Counting Blessings Versus Burdens: An Experimental Investigation of Gratitude and Subjective Well-Being in Daily Life," *Journal of Personality and Social Psychology* 84, no. 2 (2003): 377–89.

CHAPTER 8: SELL WITH INTEGRITY

1. Douglas Amyx, Shahid Bhuian, Dheeraj Sharma, and Katherine Loveland, "Salesperson Corporate Ethical Values (SCEV) Scale: Development and Assessment Among Salespeople," *Journal of Personal Selling and Sales Management* 28, no. 4 (2008): 387–402.

2. C. H. Schwepker and T. N. Ingram, "Improving Sales Performance Through Ethics: The Relationship Between Salesperson Moral Judgment and Job Performance," *Journal of Business Ethics* 15, no. 11 (1996): 1151–60; Sean Valentin, Philip Varca, Lynn Godkin, and Tim Barnett, "Positive Job Response and Ethical Job Performance," *Journal of Business Ethics* 91, no. 2 (2010): 195–206; E. D. Honeycutt, J. A. Siguaw, and T. G. Hunt, "Business Ethics and Job-Related Constructs: A Cross-Cultural Comparison of Automotive Salespeople," *Journal of Business Ethics* 14, no. 3 (1995): 235–48.

3. Jon Hawes, Kenneth Mast, and John Swan, "Trust Earning Perceptions of Sellers and Buyers," *Journal of Personal Selling and Sales Management* 9, no. 1 (1989): 1–8.

4. J. R. Priester and R. E. Petty, "Source Attributions and Persuasion: Perceived Honesty as a Determinant of Message Scrutiny," *Personality and Social Psychology Bulletin* 21, no. 6 (1995): 637–54.

5. Charles Schwepker and David Good, "Sales Management's Influence on Employment and Training in Developing an Ethical Sales Force," *Journal of Personal Selling and Sales Management* 27, no. 4 (2007): 325–39.

6. D. E. Lewis, "Corporate Trust a Matter of Opinion," *Boston Globe*, November 23, 2003.

7. David Trafimow, "The Effects of Trait Type and Situation Type on the Generalization of Trait Expectancies Across Situations," *Personality and Social Psychology Bulletin* 27, no. 11 (2001): 1463–68.

8. Myron Rothbart and Bernadette Park, "On the Confirmability and Disconfirmability of Trait Concepts," *Journal of Personality and Social Psychology* 50, no. 1 (1986): 131–42.

9. Charles Schwepker Jr., "Using Ethical Leadership to Improve Business-to-Business Salesperson Performance: The Mediating Roles of Trust in Manager and Ethical Ambiguity," *Journal of Business-to-Business Marketing* 26, no. 2 (2019).

10. Adi Ignatius, "The Thing About Integrity," *Harvard Business Review*, July–August 2019, 12.

11. Shaun Thompson, "Addressing the UK's Sales Shame," *International Journal of Sales Transformation* 5, no. 1 (2019).

12. Lydia Saad, "U.S. Ethics Ratings Rise for Medical Workers and Teachers," Gallup, December 22, 2020, retrieved May 31, 2021, https://news.gallup.com/poll/328136/ethics-ratings-rise-medical-workers-teachers.aspx.

13. Wendell Berry, *The Art of the Commonplace: The Agrarian Essays of Wendell Berry* (Berkeley, CA: Counterpoint Press, 2002), 43.

14. Aristotle, *Rhetoric*, trans. W. Rhys Roberts (Mineola, NY: Dover, 2004).

15. James McCroskey, *An Introduction to Rhetorical Communication* (Englewood Cliffs, NJ: Prentice Hall, 1972), 269.

16. Aristotle, *Rhetoric*, 1355a20.

17. Jay Conger, "The Necessary Art of Persuasion," *Harvard Business Review OnPoint*, Fall 2010, 46.

18. R. Evans, R. Rozelle, M. Mittelmark, W. Hansen, A. Bane, and J. Havis, "Deterring the Onset of Smoking in Children: Knowledge of Immediate Physiological Effects and Coping with Peer Pressure, Media Pressure, and Parent Modeling," *Journal of Applied Social Psychology* 8, no. 2 (1977): 126–35; A. Lipsitz, K. Kallmeyer, M. Ferguson, and A. Abas, "Counting on Blood Donors: Increasing the Impact of Social Reminder Calls," *Journal of Applied Social Psychology* 19 (1989): 1057–67; G. Breen and J. Matusitz, "Preventing Youths from Joining Gangs: How to Apply Inoculation Theory," *Journal of Applied Security Research* 4, no. 1 (2009): 109–28.

19. Herbert Simons, *Persuasion: Understanding, Practice, and Analysis*, 2nd ed. (New York: McGraw-Hill, 1986), 4.

20. Raymond S. Ross, *Understanding Persuasion*, 4th ed. (Englewood Cliffs, NJ: Simon and Schuster, 1994), 2.

21. Robert H. Gass and John S. Seiter, *Persuasion, Social Influence, and Compliance Gaining*, 4th ed. (New York: Allyn and Bacon, 2011), 3–4.

22. Aristotle, *Rhetoric*, 1355b5.

23. Immanuel Kant, *Groundwork of the Metaphysics of Morals*, trans. and

ed. Mary Gregor (Cambridge, UK: Cambridge University Press, 1998), 38.

24. Richard M. Perloff, *The Dynamics of Persuasion* (Hillsdale, NJ: Erlbaum, 1993), 16.

25. Cass R. Sunstein, *The Ethics of Influence* (New York: Cambridge University Press, 2016), 80.

26. Robert Cialdini, "Of Tricks and Tumors: Some Little Recognized Costs of Dishonest Use of Effective Social Influence," *Psychology and Marketing* 16, no. 2 (1999): 91–98.

27. R. McDevitt, C. Giapponi, and C. Tromley, "A Model of Ethical Decision Making: The Integration of Process and Content," *Journal of Business Ethics* 73, no. 2 (2007): 219–29; C. H. Schwepker and D. J. Good, "Exploring Sales Manager Quota Failure from an Ethical Perspective," *Marketing Management Journal* 17, no. 2 (2007): 156–68; S. D. Hunt and A. Z. Vasquez-Parraga, "Organizational Consequences, Marketing Ethics, and Salesforce Supervision," *Journal of Marketing Research* 30, no. 1 (1993): 78–90.

28. Willy Bolander, William Zahn, Terry Loe, and Melissa Clark, "Managing New Salespeople's Ethical Behaviors During Repetitive Failures: When Trying to Help Actually Hurts," *Journal of Business Ethics* 144, no. 3 (2017): 519–32.

29. Bolander, Zahn, Loe, and Clark, "Managing New Salespeople's Ethical Behaviors During Repetitive Failures," 522.

30. M. Selart and S. Johansen, "Ethical Decision Making in Organizations: The Role of Leadership Stress," *Journal of Business Ethics* 99, no. 2 (2011): 129–43; Bolander, Zahn, Loe, and Clark, "Managing New Salespeople's Ethical Behaviors During Repetitive Failures."

31. G. Gigerenzer and D. G. Goldstein, "Reasoning the Fast and Frugal Way: Models of Bounded Rationality," *Psychological Review* 103, no. 4 (1996): 650–69.

32. John Medina, *Brain Rules* (Seattle: Pear Press, 2008), 174.

33. Dolf Zillman, "Mental Control of Angry Aggression," in *Handbook of Mental Control*, eds. Daniel Wegner and James S. Pennebaker (Englewood Cliffs, NJ: Prentice Hall, 1993); Daniel Goleman, Richard Boyatzis, and Annie McKee, *Primal Leadership: Realizing the Power of Emotional Intelligence* (Boston: Harvard Business Press, 2002), 163.

34. O. M. Wolkowitz, V. Reus, H. Weingartner, K. Thompson, A. Breier, A. Doran, D. Rubinow, and D. Pickar, "Cognitive Effects of

Corticosteroids," *American Journal of Psychiatry* 147, no. 10 (1990): 1297–303; James Zull, *The Art of Changing a Brain: Helping People Learn by Understanding How the Brain Works* (Sterling, VA: Stylus, 2002); Bruce McEwen and R. M. Sapolsky, "Stress and Cognitive Function," *Current Opinions in Neurobiology* 5, no. 2 (1995); Pierce J. Howard, *The Owner's Manual for the Brain* (Austin: Bard Press, 2006), 816; Jacqueline Wood, Andrew Matthews, and Tim Dalglieish, "Anxiety and Cognitive Inhibition," *Emotion* 1, no. 2 (2001): 166–81.

35. Jeffrey B. Henriques and Richard J. Davidson, "Brain Electrical Asymmetries During Cognitive Task in Performance in Depressed and Nondepressed Subjects," *Biological Psychiatry* 42, no. 11 (1997): 1039–50; Medina, *Brain Rules*, 178.

36. Daniel Goleman, *Emotional Intelligence* (New York: Random House, 2006), 149.

37. N. Li and W. H. Murphy, "A Three-Country Study of Unethical Sales Behaviors," *Journal of Business Ethics* 111, no. 2 (2012): 219–35; Bolander, Zahn, Loe, and Clark, "Managing New Salespeople's Ethical Behaviors During Repetitive Failures"; V. Howe, K. Douglas Hoffman, and D. W. Hardigree, "The Relationship Between Ethical and Customer-Oriented Service Provider Behaviors," *Journal of Business Ethics* 13, no. 7 (1994): 497–506.

38. Bolander, Zahn, Loe, and Clark, "Managing New Salespeople's Ethical Behaviors During Repetitive Failures."

39. M. Rodriguez, H. Ajjan, and R. M. Peterson, "CRM/Social Media Technology: Impact on Customer Orientation Process and Organizational Sales Performance," *Journal of Marketing Development and Competitiveness* 8, no. 1 (2014): 85–97; C. Yilmaz, L. Alpkan, and E. Ergun, "Cultural Determinants of Customer- and Learning-Oriented Value Systems and Their Joint Effects on Firm Performance," *Journal of Business Research* 58, no. 10 (2005): 1340–52; Bolander, Zahn, Loe, and Clark, "Managing New Salespeople's Ethical Behaviors During Repetitive Failures"; B. J. Gray, S. Matear, and P. K. Matheson, "Improving Service Firm Performance," *Journal of Services Marketing* 16, no. 3 (2002): 186–200.

40. John Griffin, Samuel Kruger, and Gonzalo Maturana, "Personal Infidelity and Professional Conduct in 4 Settings," *Proceedings of the National Academy of Sciences* 116, no. 33 (2019).

41. Robert Davidson, Aiyesha Dey, and Abbie Smith, "Executives' 'Off-

the-Job' Behavior, Corporate Culture and Financial Reporting Risk," *Journal of Financial Economics* 117, no. 1 (2015): 5–28.

42. Idea Watch, "Why Boards Should Worry About Executives' Off-the-Job Behavior," *Harvard Business Review*, January–February 2020.

43. Francesca Gino, Ovul Sezer, and Laura Huang, "To Be or Not to Be Your Authentic Self? Catering to Others' Preferences Hinders Performance," *Organizational Behavior and Human Decision Processes* 158, no. 12 (2020): 83–100.

44. Francesca Gino, "Research: It Pays to Be Yourself," *Harvard Business Review*, February 13, 2020, https://hbr.org/2020/02/research-it-pays-to-be-yourself.

45. Julia Lee Cunningham, Ashley Hardin, Bidhan Parmar, and Francesca Gino, "The Interpersonal Costs of Dishonesty: How Dishonest Behavior Reduces Individuals' Ability to Read Others' Emotions," *Journal of Experimental Psychology: General* 148, no. 9 (2019).

46. Idea Watch, "Small Lies, Large Costs," *Harvard Business Review*, May–June 2020, 26.

47. Immanuel Kant, "On a Supposed Right to Lie from Altruistic Motives," in *Critique of Practical Reason and Other Writings in Moral Philosophy*, trans. and ed. Lewis White Beck (Chicago: University of Chicago Press, 1964), 346.

48. Max Anderson, "Why We Created the MBA Oath," *Harvard Business Review*, June 8, 2009, retrieved September 1, 2020, https://hbr.org/2009/06/why-we-created-the-mba-oath.

49. "About the Oath," MBA Oath, retrieved December 1, 2020, https://mbaoath.org/history-new/.

50. Peter Drucker, "Managing Oneself," *Harvard Business Review OnPoint*, March–April 1999.

CHAPTER 9: TAKE YOUR SALES CAREER TO THE NEXT LEVEL

1. Edward Jones and Steven Burglas, "Drug Choice as a Self-Handicapping Strategy in Response to Noncontingent Success," *Journal of Personality and Social Psychology* 36, no. 4 (1978): 405–17; Roy Baumeister and Steven Scher, "Self-Defeating Behavior Patterns Among Normal Individuals: Review and Analysis of Common Self-Destructive Tendencies," *Psychological Bulletin* 104, no. 1 (1988): 3–22; Dianne Tice, "Esteem Protection or Enhancement? Self-Handicapping

Motives and Attributions Differ by Trait Self-Esteem," *Journal of Personality and Social Psychology* 60, no. 5 (1991): 711–25.

2. Amy Mezulis, Lyn Abramson, Janet Hyde, and Benjamin Hankin, "Is There a Universal Positivity Bias in Attributions? A Meta-Analytic Review of Individual, Developmental, and Cultural Differences in the Self-Serving Attributional Bias," *Psychological Bulletin* 130, no. 5 (2004): 711–14.

3. Arvid Hoffmann and Thomas Post, "Self-Attribution Bias in Consumer Financial Decision-Making: How Investment Returns Affect Individuals' Belief in Skill," *Journal of Behavioral and Experimental Economics* 52 (2014): 23–28; James Shepperd, Wendi Malone, and Kate Sweeny, "Exploring Causes of the Self-Serving Bias," *Social and Personality Psychology Compass* 2, no. 2 (2008): 895–908; W. Keith Campbell and Constantine Sedikides, "Self-Threat Magnified the Self-Serving Bias: A Meta-Analytic Integration," *Review of General Psychology* 3 (1999): 23–43; Joris Lammers and Pascal Burgmer, "Power Increases the Self-Serving Bias in the Attribution of Collective Successes and Failures," *European Journal of Social Psychology* 49, no. 5 (2018): 1087–95.

4. William Samuelson and Richard Zeckhauser, "Status Quo Bias in Decision Making," *Journal of Risk and Uncertainty* 1, no. 1 (1988): 7–59.

5. Richard Thaler, *Misbehaving: The Making of Behavioral Economics* (New York: W. W. Norton, 2015), 154.

6. Hal Arkes and Catherine Blumer, "The Psychology of Sunk Cost," *Organizational Behavior and Human Decision Processes* 35, no. 1 (1985): 124–40; Howard Garland and Stephanie Newport, "Effects of Absolute and Relative Sunk Costs on the Decision to Persist with a Course of Action," *Organization Behavior and Human Decision Processes* 48, no. 1 (1991): 55–69.

7. A. S. Chulef, S. J. Read, and D. A. Walsh, "A Hierarchical Taxonomy of Human Goals," *Motivation and Emotion* 25, no. 3 (2001): 192–232.

8. Kevin Clark, "How a Cycling Team Turned the Falcons into NFC Champions," *The Ringer*, September 12, 2017, https://www.theringer.com/nfl/2017/9/12/16293216/atlanta-falcons-thomas-dimitroff-cycling-team-sky.

9. Eben Harrell, "How 1% Performance Improvement Led to Olympic Gold," *Harvard Business Review*, October 30, 2015, https://hbr.org/2015/10/how-1-performance-improvements-led-to-olympic-gold.

10. Alex Knapp, "The Seduction of the Exponential Curve," *Forbes*, November 17, 2011, https://www.forbes.com/sites/alexknapp/2011/11/17/the-seduction-of-the-exponential-curve.

11. Angela Duckworth, Heidi Grant, Benjamin Loew, Gabriele Oettingen, and Peter Gollwitzer, "Self-Regulation Strategies Improve Self-Discipline in Adolescents: Benefits of Mental Contrasting and Implementation Intentions," *Educational Psychology* 31, no. 1 (2011): 17–26; Mark Muraven and R. F. Baumeister, "Self-Regulation and Depletion of Limited Resources: Does Self-Control Resemble a Muscle?," *Psychological Bulletin* 126, no. 2 (2000): 247–59; Mark Muraven, "Practicing Self-Control Lowers the Risk of Smoking Lapse," *Psychology of Addictive Behaviors* 24, no. 3 (2010): 446–52.

12. Heidi Grant Halvorson, *Succeed* (New York: Penguin, 2011), xxi.

13. Megan Oaten and Ken Cheng, "Longitudinal Gains in Self-Regulation from Physical Exercise," *British Journal of Health Psychology* 11, no. 4 (2006): 717–33.

14. Mark Muraven, "Building Self-Control Strength: Practicing Self-Control Leads to Improved Self-Control Performance," *Journal of Experimental Social Psychology* 46, no. 2 (2010): 465–68; Mark Muraven, R. F. Baumeister, and D. M. Tice, "Longitudinal Improvement of Self-Regulation Through Practice: Building Self-Control Strength Through Repeated Exercise," *Journal of Social Psychology* 139, no. 4 (1999): 446–57.

15. James Allen, *As a Man Thinketh* (Lexington, KY: Best Success Books, 2008), 16.

16. T. L. Chartrand, J. Huber, B. Shiv, and R. Tanner, "Nonconscious Goals and Consumer Choice," *Journal of Consumer Research* 35, no. 2 (2008): 189–201; J. M. Burger, "Increasing Compliance by Improving the Deal: The That's-Not-All Technique," *Journal of Personality and Social Psychology* 51, no. 2 (1986): 277–83; Howard Kelley, "The Warm-Cold Variable in First Impressions of Persons," *Journal of Personality* 18, no. 4 (1950); W. Widmeyer and J. Loy, "When You're Hot, You're Hot! Warm-Cold Effects in First Impression of Persons and Teaching Effectiveness," *Journal of Educational Psychology* 80, no. 1 (1988): 118–21.

17. Yuichi Shoda, "Individual Differences in Social Psychology: Understanding Situations to Understand People, Understanding People to Understand Situations," in *The Sage Handbook of Methods in*

Social Psychology, eds. Carol Sansone, Carolyn Morf, and A. T. Panter (Thousand Oaks, CA: Sage Publications, 2004), 119.

18. Eric J. Johnson, John Hershey, Jacqueline Meszaros, and Howard Kunreuther, "Framing, Probability Distortions, and Insurance Decisions," in *Choices, Values, and Frames,* eds. Daniel Kahneman and Amos Tversky (New York: Cambridge University Press, 2000); Dan Ariely, *Predictably Irrational* (New York: HarperCollins, 2008); Richard E. Petty and John T. Cacioppo, *Communication and Persuasion: Central and Peripheral Routes to Attitude Change* (New York: Springer-Verlag, 1986); Richard E. Petty and John T. Cacioppo, "The Elaboration Likelihood Model of Persuasion," in *Advances in Experimental Social Psychology,* vol. 19, ed. L. Berkowitz (San Diego: Academic Press, 1986), 123–205.

19. Rajagopal Raghunathan, Rebecca Walker Naylor, and Wayne D. Hoyer, "The Unhealthy = Tasty Intuition and Its Effects on Taste Inferences, Enjoyment, and Choice of Food Products," *Journal of Marketing* 70, no. 4 (2006): 170–84.

20. Bradley Turnwald, Danielle Boles, and Alia Crum, "Association Between Indulgent Descriptions and Vegetable Consumption: Twisted Carrots and Dynamite Beets," *JAMA Internal Medicine* 177, no. 8 (2017): 1216–18.

21. Charles Morin, Richard Bootzin, Daniel J. Buysse, Jack Edinger, Colin Espie, and Kenneth L. Lichstein, "Psychological and Behavioral Treatment of Insomnia: Update of the Recent Evidence (1998–2004)," *Sleep* 29, no. 11 (2006): 1398–414.

22. Richard Bootzin, Dana Epstein, and James Wood, "Stimulus Control Instructions," in *Case Studies in Insomnia,* ed. Peter Hauri (Boston: Springer, 1991).

23. Kim Vincent, *The Human Factor: Revolutionizing the Way People Live with Technology* (New York: Routledge, 2006); Christopher Ingraham, "What's a Urinal Fly, and What Does It Have to with Winning a Nobel Prize?," *Washington Post,* October 9, 2017, https://www.washington post.com/news/wonk/wp/2017/10/09/whats-a-urinal-fly-and-what -does-it-have-to-with-winning-a-nobel-prize/; Richard H. Thaler and Cass R. Sunstein, *Nudge* (New York: Penguin Books, 2009), 4.

24. Kristen Berman and Evelyn Gosnell, "What Academics Can Learn from Industry," in *The Behavioral Economics Guide 2019,* ed. Alain Samson, 135. Retrieved from https://www. behavioraleconomics .com.

Index

Page numbers in *italic* refer to illustrations.

About the Author

DAVID HOFFELD is considered the number one authority on applying science to the process of selling. He is the author of the best-selling book *The Science of Selling* and the CEO and chief sales trainer at Hoffeld Group, one of the nation's top research-based sales and consulting firms. A popular and engaging speaker and sales trainer, he pioneered a revolutionary sales approach based on research in neuroscience, social psychology, and behavioral economics that's been proved to radically increase sales.

Because of the results his insights generate, David works with many of the most successful companies in the world, helping them improve their sales results. He's also lectured at Harvard Business School and has been featured in *Fortune, U.S. News & World Report, The Wall Street Journal, Fast Company, Harvard Business Review, Investor's Business Daily, Inc., Forbes,* CBS Radio, Fox News Radio, and other media. To learn more about his science-backed sales strategies, visit www.HoffeldGroup.com.